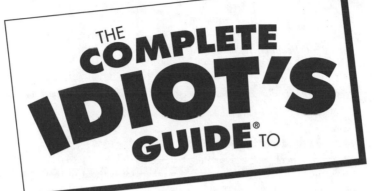

THE COMPLETE IDIOT'S GUIDE® TO

Criminal Investigation

by Alan Axelrod and Guy Antinozzi

ALPHA

A Pearson Education Company

To Anita and Ian
—AA
To Jennifer, Joshua, Salvatore, Vincent, Vito,
Dominic, and Rudy
—GA
And to the officers and the families of officers who gave all they had on September 11, 2001
—AA and GA

International Standard Book Number: 0-02-864346-1
Library of Congress Catalog Card Number: 2002108495

05 04 03   8 7 6 5 4 3 2 1

Interpretation of the printing code: The rightmost number of the first series of numbers is the year of the book's printing; the rightmost number of the second series of numbers is the number of the book's printing. For example, a printing code of 03-1 shows that the first printing occurred in 2003.

Printed in the United States of America

For marketing and publicity, please call: 317-581-3722

The publisher offers discounts on this book when ordered in quantity for bulk purchases and special sales.

For sales within the United States, please contact: Corporate and Government Sales, 1-800-382-3419 or corpsales@pearsontechgroup.com

Outside the United States, please contact: International Sales, 317-581-3793 or international@pearsontechgroup.com

Publisher: *Marie Butler-Knight*
Product Manager: *Phil Kitchel*
Managing Editor: *Jennifer Chisholm*
Acquisitions Editor: *Randy Ladenheim-Gil*
Development Editor: *Lynn Northrup*
Production Editor: *Katherin Bidwell*
Copy Editor: *Susan Aufheimer*
Illustrator: *Chris Eliopoulos*
Cover/Book Designer: *Trina Wurst*
Indexer: *Brad Herriman*
Layout/Proofreading: *Angela Calvert, Mary Hunt, Jodie Stafford, Kimberly Tucker*

Contents at a Glance

Contents

Foreword

No other profession in the world is more interesting, more intensively examined, more rigorously criticized, or more ponderously puzzled over than law enforcement. Everyone has questions, and everyone has an opinion—or two, or more. Whether it's the motorist who has been stopped for a traffic violation, the hardened criminal sitting in his cell, the appellate court judge considering a case on appeal, or the couch potato watching a hot pursuit on live TV, everyone thinks they know *something* about what it means to do the job of a police officer.

I suspect that the current reality-based TV fad started with the *Cops* show, which premiered on March 11, 1989, and gave civilians their first unsweetened taste of life on the job: what cops *really* do and what they *really* face, every day, every night. Ever since that first telecast, the popular interest has grown to tremendous proportions, so that whenever some citizens hear sirens or see flashing blue lights, they come running, camcorders in hand and ready to roll.

Americans have always had a love-hate relationship with the police, which, in a democracy, isn't all that unhealthy. Since the events of September 11, 2001, however, many of us in the law-enforcement community have been experiencing more of the love than the hate. We've felt an outpouring of appreciation for the job we do, along with a concern for our safety. The fact is that the courage and willingness to sacrifice manifested by the officers in New York on that day is exhibited every day by law enforcement professionals everywhere.

There has always been a combination of public fascination and public suspicion about police work. Today, after 9/11, the suspicion has increasingly yielded to the fascination, and people want more than ever to understand what law enforcement professionals do day-to-day—how they do it, and why they do it. Up to now, it hasn't been easy for the interested civilian to find a correct, factual, convenient one-stop source of information about criminology theory and criminal investigation practice. *The Complete Idiot's Guide to Criminal Investigation* is that source. It provides a comprehensive understanding of the whys and wherefores of police work, in a simple format and an easy-to-follow text, which makes for quick and highly absorbing reading.

As a 25-year law enforcement veteran with degrees in education and law, I am amazed at the amount of information contained here and the things *I* learned. Intended mainly for the interested lay person, this book should also be required reading for anyone entering the law enforcement profession or planning to enter it. And for the long-timer, like me, it provides a fresh look and a new perspective. As for the citizens we serve and protect, this book lays out in crisp detail the practices and operations that are standard for us, but often bewildering to the uninitiated. In addition to outlining current procedures, it gives the historical context in which those procedures developed, highlights landmark court cases, and explains the major theories that drive and impact the way police officers do their jobs.

You hold in your hands a solid and entertaining introduction to the separate, sometimes conflicting, but always overlapping domains of criminology, criminal investigation, and criminal justice. Alan Axelrod and Guy Antinozzi convey what it is like to work professionally with human behavior at its most selfish, vicious, and chaotic in an effort to protect life and property and to enable justice—human behavior at its most noble and compassionate.

—Bobby Tribble

Lead Firearms Instructor/Staff Instructor, Northeast Georgia Police Academy, Bogart, Georgia

Introduction

Good and evil. At any time, in any place, among any people of any culture, could anything be more basic than these eternally present, perpetually warring opposites?

The closest most of us get to evil is crime. We fear it. It consistently tops the list of concerns people express in public opinion polls— and with very good reason. About 13 million people, some 5 percent of the U.S. population, become victims of crime *each year*. Of this number, 1.5 million are victims of violent crime, *each year*.

But it's not just fear that motivates our interest in this evil called crime. Most of us have, it seems, a natural need for justice. A wrong, we feel, must not remain uncorrected or, at least, unpunished. That's why crime is such a compelling subject for novels, TV shows, films, and "true crime" narratives. A crime is committed, it throws the world off balance, and we cannot rest—we'll keep turning the pages, we'll stay glued to the TV, we won't leave the theater seat to get a tub of popcorn—until the crime is solved and the balance set right again.

Crime and punishment, like good and evil, are very basic to us all, summoning up our animal instincts for survival, arousing in us a primitive hunger for vengeance, yet also calling on our noblest aspirations for justice, for healing, and for making things right again.

Basic, yes, but hardly simple. Since time immemorial, societies have searched for the cause of crime. They have sought ways to prevent crime as well as ways to cure it. Each answer offered has shown promise, but also flaws. Absolute government and dictatorship surely stamp out some kinds of crime, but they do so by holding *everyone* prisoner. Democracy brings opportunity and freedom, but that includes the opportunity and freedom to commit crimes.

Driven by the most basic of human forces, rooted in the most basic human needs, desires, and perceptions, crime and the social response to crime are nevertheless highly complex subjects. We become outraged after seeing a TV news report of some terrible crime. We fume. We demand justice *now*. But then we learn more about the background of the suspect, a life of poverty, abuse, and victimization. Or we hear that the state's evidence against him is circumstantial—a suggestive case, perhaps, but hardly airtight. Or we learn that the prosecution's main witness is himself a felon, who has "cut a deal" in return for spilling his guts in testimony to convict the chief suspect. Or we listen to the prosecution's expert forensic witness interpret the evidence 100 percent one way, then listen further as the defense forensic expert reaches the opposite conclusion. And on and on it goes, the question of guilt or innocence spiraling farther and farther from what seemed the compelling core issues of simple good versus simple evil.

Most of us have strong feelings about crime, punishment, and justice. Yet, in our free society, these basic, urgent issues become so complex that we are pulled and pushed in a variety of directions and often find it almost impossible to take a stand. This book is intended to help us all sort things out.

The Complete Idiot's Guide to Criminal Investigation actually has two major subjects. Criminology is the disciplined inquiry into the causes and nature of crime, with the object of developing theories to understand and explain crime. Criminal investigation is an inquiry into a particular crime. It is the practical, rather than theoretical, process of discovering, collecting, analyzing, and presenting evidence to prove the truth or falsity of particular criminal issues in law. The two subjects, criminology and criminal investigation, are almost never treated in the same book—and yet they are both central to how society, especially a free society, deals with crime. Understanding crime, punishment, and justice, and taking a stand on these intimately bound issues, requires knowledge of criminological theory as well as the fascinating nitty-gritty of practical criminal investigation. Hence the double-pronged approach of this book.

Part 1, "Overview and Long View," surveys the scope and goals of criminology and the major historical schools of criminological thought, beginning, in fact, with prehistory and pushing on through the Enlightenment, the hard-nosed nineteenth century, and the first half of the twentieth.

Part 2, "In Theory," brings criminology up to date, inventorying and explaining the most important current thought on crime, its causes, its course, and its cure.

Part 3, "The Usual Suspects," begins to shift the focus of the book from criminology to criminal investigation. Here are chapters on how crimes are classified (and why it is necessary to classify them) and how modern cops attempt to profile criminals in order to understand, identify, and apprehend them.

Part 4, "On the Scene (and in the Lab)," begins with the police arrival at a crime scene and discusses how investigators size up the scene and interrogate suspects, witnesses, and victims. Chapters in this part explain just what evidence the cops look for, and how they find it, gather it, and analyze it, as well as the tools they use and the techniques they call upon.

Part 5, "The Body in Question," looks at what is often the single most compelling object at a crime scene: the body of the victim. Chapters in this part explain what investigators do at the scene and in the medical examiner's office. A special chapter is devoted to DNA evidence.

Part 6, "The Long Arm," begins with the origin and history of the professional police force in Europe and America, then explores police operations as they are today, including police organization, police communications and intelligence gathering, the science of lie detection, and certain "extreme" investigative methods: the use of truth serum, hypnosis, and psychics.

Part 7, "Crime in a Crystal Ball," looks forward to the future of crime—with emphasis on the burgeoning area of information and computer crime, as well as identity theft—and the future of police work.

The Complete Idiot's Guide to Criminal Investigation concludes with appendixes covering who's who in criminology and criminal investigation, milestones in crime and crime fighting, the police "Ten Code" communication system, and suggestions for further reading.

Extras

In addition to the main narrative of *The Complete Idiot's Guide to Criminal Investigation*, you'll find other types of useful information, including the following special features:

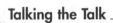

Talking the Talk

In these boxes you'll find definitions of the technical terms, jargon, and slang used by cops, criminologists, and criminals.

Sworn Statement

This feature offers quotations and quick facts concerning crime, criminology, and crime fighting.

By the Numbers

Here are the most revealing crime and crime-fighting statistics.

Case in Point
These boxes present important facts from real-life cases.

Acknowledgments

My thanks and respect to my co-author, Guy Antinozzi, who serves and protects.

I am also grateful for the fine work and support of the folks at Alpha, especially acquisitions editor Randy Ladenheim-Gil, development editor Lynn Northrup, production editor Katherin Bidwell, and copy editor Susan Aufheimer.

—Alan Axelrod

I would like to thank my father, Rudy Antinozzi, the only person more excited about this book than I am. The continued support of Bobby Tribble, Murrell Tyson, Andy Garrison, and Frank Broadrick, of the Northeast Georgia Police Academy, has been beyond measure. I will always be proud of my time with the Norcross (Georgia) Police Department, which was a great place to learn to be a police officer in a dynamic and challenging environment. I will forever be indebted to Detective David Aguilar and Corporal George Marchbanks for keeping me safe when I knew so little. Detective Dallas Stidd remains an example I can only hope to follow.

Tom Sturgis and Jed George, of GEICO, gave me an opportunity that few would have given up. Chief Rus Drew and Captain Travis Bryan, of the Agnes Scott College Police Department, renewed my idealism in the profession. Detective J. P. Hughes, of the DeKalb County Police Department, and Lieutenant Dave Hipple, of the Decatur Police Department, convinced me to be a police officer, and they are invaluable friends, especially when I try to take myself too seriously. Lieutenant Mike Booker, of the Decatur Police Department, Lieutenant Johnny Childs and Sergeant David Aderhold, of the DeKalb County Sheriff's Office, have never refused my many requests for assistance.

My professional good fortune continues with the daily support of the Honorable Gwen Keyes, Solicitor General of DeKalb County, Georgia, in whose department I am a Special Investigator. Along with her top staff, Qader Baig, Jill Peterson, and Rob Mikell, she maintains a level of excellence in the pursuit of justice and service to victims and the community.

I also wish to recognize Chris DePree, Ph.D., neighbor, astronomer, and author. He thought of me when this book came to his attention. And thanks as well to my co-author, Alan Axelrod, for his patience and guidance.

My wife, Jennifer, has endured many restless nights and continues to be a source of enlightenment, despite my resistance. My sons are my joy and inspiration. They make me proud every day, and it is the hope for a better future for them that gets me through the difficult times. Lastly, I want to acknowledge the countless men and women of law enforcement whose sacrifices are made for us all.

—Guy Antinozzi

Trademarks

Part 1

Overview and Long View

Just about everyone has a theory about crime: why it happens, who commits it, how to fight it, and how to prevent it. We begin by looking at some popular points of view and how these fit into the history of criminology and relate to the business of criminal investigation.

In this part of the book, you'll find prehistoric and early historical views of crime and punishment, as well as the birth and evolution of criminology as a field of scientific study, with emphasis on eighteenth-century rational idealism, nineteenth-century positivism, and the empirical approaches developed during the first half of the twentieth century.

Right and Wrong and Cops and Robbers

In This Chapter

- ◆ Crime: the popular view
- ◆ Criminology and criminal investigation defined
- ◆ Some leading theories of crime
- ◆ Relation of criminology to criminal investigation
- ◆ At the crime scene
- ◆ Fantasy cops vs. real investigators

To a question posed by the public opinion firm Zogby International—
"Have you or any member of your immediate family been a victim of nonviolent crime over the last five years?"—26 percent of Americans asked
answered yes, while an additional 9 percent said they had been victims of
violent crime. According to the public opinion analysts at Public Agenda
Online, crime tops the list of what Americans say are the most important
problems the United States faces in the twenty-first century. For most

Americans most of the time, crime looms with greater importance than moral values, health care, poverty, the economy, education, environment, drugs, jobs and unemployment, overpopulation, and war.

Clearly, crime is very much on our minds. And it has always been, in both a collective social sense and individually. Can you remember a time when you *didn't* know about right and wrong or cops and robbers? Yet, can you answer the following questions: What, exactly, *is* crime? And what causes it?

Everyone's Got a Theory

Well, maybe you believe you *can* answer these questions. But how do you know they're the right answers? Start talking to people about crime and the causes of crime, read the popular press, turn on the TV, or think about your own experience, and you will likely discover there are at least as many opinions concerning the nature of wrongdoing and criminality as there are actual misdeeds.

Authority Figures

For most of us, our first concepts of the nature of right and wrong come from our parents and other early authority figures. At first we believe that a thing is wrong because mom or pop or some other important adult says it's wrong or, perhaps, punishes us for doing that thing. Many people never really move beyond this concept, and many people see no reason to move beyond it. They are content to define crime as conduct forbidden by authority. End of story.

But what authority? For some, it is nothing less than God. For others, it may be government, it may be a king or tyrant, or it may not be a person at all, but custom and law. Act contrary to the "will" of any of these authorities, and you have committed a crime.

One of the earliest surviving documents of civilization is the Code of Hammurabi, king of Babylon, which dates from before 1750 B.C.E. The first three of the 282 laws of the Code of Hammurabi are …

> **By the Numbers**
>
> The FBI reported that 11,605,751 crimes were committed in the United States in 2000—4,124 crimes per each 100,000 inhabitants. Offenses included in the FBI statistics are the violent crimes of murder, non-negligent manslaughter, forcible rape, robbery, and aggravated assault, as well as the property crimes of burglary, larceny/theft, motor vehicle theft, and arson.

1. If any one ensnare another, putting a ban upon him, but he can not prove it, then he that ensnared him shall be put to death.

2. If any one bring an accusation against a man, and the accused go to the river and leap into the river, if he sink in the river his accuser shall take possession of his house. But if the river prove that the accused is not guilty, and he escape unhurt, then he who had brought the accusation shall be put to death, while he who leaped into the river shall take possession of the house that had belonged to his accuser.

3. If any one bring an accusation of any crime before the elders, and does not prove what he has charged, he shall, if it be a capital offense charged, be put to death.

Tabloids and TV

If most of us derive our earliest concepts of right and wrong—and, therefore, of criminality—from our parents, many of us go on to gather our first, and perhaps even our most enduring, concepts of the causes of crime from the media outlets of popular culture.

Novels, newspapers, tabloids, and television introduce us to a vast array of criminals or, at least, fictional portrayals of criminals. All of these media aim to present good stories. Now, a story may include plenty of exciting action, but such action alone is not sufficient to make a really *good* story. A good story always makes sense of the action it presents, neatly tying up any loose ends; therefore, most popular portrayals of criminal behavior include some explanation for that behavior.

Since the advent of the scientific study of psychology toward the end of the nineteenth century, many explanations have been psychological in nature. The criminal behaves as he or she does because of psychological forces over which the criminal has no control.

But the psychological explanation, although prevalent, is not the only common reason given for criminal behavior. TV and tabloids portray many people who turn to crime because they were raised in poverty or exposed to the "bad influences" of "peer pressure" in a "rough neighborhood." Some criminals are portrayed as the products of bad families, families that find crime acceptable.

> **Sworn Statement**
>
> There are two kinds of criminals: those who get caught and the rest of us.
>
> —Anonymous observation quoted in Leonard Roy Frank, ed., *Random House Webster's Quotationary* (New York, 1999)

Still other popular images of the criminal include those who are wicked for some unknown reason: a genetic flaw, perhaps, as in the 1956 film *The Bad Seed*, in which a little girl proves literally to be a born criminal. Another familiar criminal image is the product of the Judeo-Christian tradition, which divides the world into those who walk the godly path of righteousness, and those who, for some reason known perhaps only to God, turn away from the strait gate and follow the way of the devil.

Gloomiest of all the popular images of criminality is the explanation that wrongdoing is not aberrant at all, but rather part of human nature; that is, anyone would commit a crime if that person were certain he or she could get away with it.

Your Own Perspective

It is, of course, ultimately your own experience that filters all of the concepts, half-concepts, and vague thoughts about crime and criminality. You may come to favor this view or that, based on people you have known and things you have seen.

If you are a certain kind of person, you may try to look at everything from a fresh perspective. Maybe crime and criminality are not about bad individuals behaving badly, but about society labeling certain behavior as criminal and thereby *creating* criminals. Maybe treating someone as if he or she is deviant can, by and by, *make* that person deviant. Or perhaps at least some crime is merely a definition used by society's "haves" to control society's "have nots." In this connection, the writer Howard Scott wryly observed, "A criminal is a person with predatory instincts who has not sufficient capital to form a corporation."

Order and Law

While it is hardly difficult to find disagreement over the nature and causes of crime and criminality, just about everyone agrees that this behavior must be a central focus of any society and civilization. Crime, whatever it is, whatever its causes, must—somehow—be dealt with.

There was a time in which dealing with crime was simple. The king declared this and that wrong and, therefore, punishable. Or the high priest declared this or that a sin and, therefore, punishable. Doubtless, there are still places in the world where this system is still applied. But in a modern democracy such as ours, such simple tyranny does not hold. Crime and criminality, therefore, become proper—and urgent—subjects for rational, scientific inquiry: hence criminology.

Many people think about crime, but for most people, "criminology" never gets beyond an image like this: an urban cop from 1940.

(Image from Arttoday.com.)

What Is Criminology?

Defined at its broadest and most basic, *criminology* is the systematic inquiry into the causes of crime.

An eighteenth-century Italian, the Marchese Cesare Beccaria, is generally credited with having introduced the rational, systematic study of crime and punishment with a 1764 book titled —what else?—*On Crimes and Punishments*. We'll get into that, as well as the prehistory and early history of criminology, in the next chapter. The point to observe here is that criminology is a fairly youthful science, yet it has branched out to encompass many and varied approaches. However varied, criminology generally addresses three main areas:

Talking the Talk

Criminology is the systematic inquiry into the nature and causes of crime, typically with the object of creating social strategies to prevent crime and to respond more effectively to it.

1. Crime causation, sometimes referred to as criminogenesis, or the branch of criminology devoted to studying the causes of crime. Most criminologists consider this the heart of their discipline.

2. The sociology of law—that is, how crime and law relate to society and the particular values of a given society.

3. Social responses to crime—how the police, courts, and correctional institutions cope with crime.

In the first six chapters of this book, we will concentrate on the first area, the causes of crime, which is the heart of criminology.

What Is Criminal Investigation?

The principal objective of criminology is to create theories of crime causation. It is hoped that such theories will ultimately serve a practical purpose, suggesting ways in which crime can be prevented, predicted, and appropriately responded to by police, the courts, and lawmakers.

Talking the Talk

Criminal investigation is the process of discovering, collecting, identifying, preparing, analyzing, and presenting evidence, often directly from or related to a crime scene, to prove the truth or falsity of an issue of law.

Criminology looks at the big picture, identifying trends and searching for meaning. However, criminology is not about solving individual crimes. That is the province of the other major subject of this book, *criminal investigation*. Although the theories of the criminologist may assist and inform the work of the criminal investigator, criminal investigation is more practical than theoretical. Put simply, criminal investigation encompasses the tools, techniques, and processes of solving crimes—identifying the perpetrator or perpetrators and providing the legal evidence to bring him, her, or them to justice.

When It Comes to Crime, Everything's Relative

Now that we've defined criminology (as the study of the causes of crime in general) and criminal investigation (as the practical business of solving particular crimes), let's return to the issue we opened with: Just what *is* crime?

The Difference Between Right and Wrong

It is a cornerstone of our legal system that only individuals determined to be "competent to stand trial" can be validly judged guilty or not guilty of a crime. Among the most basic determinants of such competence is the ability to "distinguish right from wrong."

Yet the fact is that the difference between right and wrong is not always clear cut, even to sane and intelligent people. And the relation between what is right and legal and what is wrong and illegal is not absolute. For example, almost all societies in all recorded times have deemed premeditated murder both wrong and illegal. But earnest, well-meaning people disagree on whether abortion is premeditated murder and, therefore, both wrong and illegal. If the antiabortion lobby secures legislation outlawing abortion, does that make abortion wrong? Or if the pro-choice lobby succeeds in upholding the legality of abortion, does that make abortion right?

While most of us would agree that the definition of crime should relate in some way to concepts of right and wrong, the relation is not as absolute as most of us would like it to be. At any given moment, people may legitimately disagree on what is wrong and what is right and, therefore, on what is criminal and what is not. When the perspective of history is taken into account, the issues become even more complex. For instance, in seventeenth-century Europe, the most common of all crimes was witchcraft. Today, many people would dismiss witchcraft as mere superstition, and those folks who still take it seriously might regard witchcraft as a sin, but not as a crime.

Just as we may venture outside of our own point of view or out of our own historical period to get a radically different perspective on the definition of crime, so we might travel to a different culture. Theft, most of us would agree, is a crime. Yet if we lived in a communal society such as that of the aboriginal people of Australia, who have no concept of private property, theft would not only not be a crime, it would not even be a concept, because it would be totally without meaning.

Case in Point
Recently, the state of Oregon and the United States Department of Justice have come to loggerheads over the legality of physician-assisted suicide. The citizens of Oregon voted to permit doctors to aid terminally ill patients to end their lives, but U.S. Attorney General John Ashcroft has decided that this is a violation of federal law. Is physician-assisted suicide inherently criminal?

Is That Legal?

If absolute concepts of right and wrong cannot be looked on as the foundation for an absolute definition of crime, what about taking the less ambitious approach of simply defining crime as whatever the state calls crime? That is, if an act is against the law and is subject to a specific, state-sanctioned penalty, it is, therefore, a crime. Criminologists call this the "formal legal" definition of crime, which holds that crime is defined by the laws of a particular state.

While such a definition may serve in a pragmatic and immediate context, it is not very satisfactory in a moral or philosophical sense. In Nazi Germany, for example, it was a "crime" to give aid and protection to Jews, Gypsies, homosexuals, and other "undesirables." Closer to home, in 1955, Rosa Parks, an African American, was arrested for the "crime" of sitting in the white-only section of a Montgomery, Alabama, city bus. Until very recently, in Afghanistan, under the rule of the fundamentalist Taliban government, it was a "crime" for a woman to seek an education. By the formal legal definition, these are all crimes. But who among the readers of this book would truly consider them so?

Where's the Harm?

An alternative to an absolute right-versus-wrong definition of crime and a narrow formal legal definition is the "social harm" concept, which defines a crime as any action (or, for that matter, inaction) that causes some type of harm. Assault causes harm and is, therefore, a crime, but so is negligence—the failure to act in a given situation—because it, too, causes harm.

Talking the Talk

In criminology, **cross-cultural norms** identify certain acts as universally deemed crimes, regardless of cultural or historical context.

Right Is Right!

In our quest for a definition of crime, we might revisit the right-versus-wrong argument and make it less absolute. While there may be no universal standard for unfailingly telling right from wrong, there are certain *cross-cultural norms* by which some acts (not all) are always (or almost always) deemed crimes. Murder, for instance, is a crime from Atlanta to Zimbabwe.

Check the Label

A more radical perspective altogether rejects crime as a thing in itself and holds that crime exists when a social response to an act or activity brands that activity as criminal. This is known as the "criminal labeling approach." In civilized society, crime is defined by society. In the absence of a label, a given act is not a crime.

Right Is Human

For some, the only significant definition of crime is an act that violates human rights. The "human rights perspective" defines crime as any act that violates human rights, regardless of whether a particular state authority or jurisdiction deems the act a crime. From this perspective, the persecution of the Jews in Nazi Germany, the Montgomery, Alabama, segregation ordinances, and the Taliban's strictures against female education are all crimes—even though they were perfectly legal in Germany, Alabama, and Afghanistan.

Deviance Is Normal

Yet another approach defines crime as deviance, but also defines deviance as a normal response to oppressive or inherently unequal circumstances. That is, the dominant group in a society attempts to restrict human diversity of language, experience, or culture in order to retain its dominance. This restriction is achieved by classifying certain manifestations of diversity as deviance and by further deeming deviance as criminal. This definition of crime as a concept societies use to maintain the status quo is sometimes called the "human diversity approach."

Sworn Statement

While it's unlikely criminologists will ever agree on a single definition of crime, it doesn't mean criminology is a failed science. Of greater value than defining crime once and for all is the ongoing *attempt* to define it. This ensures that thought on the nature and causes of crime will continue to evolve, perhaps yielding more effective approaches to preventing and dealing with criminal behavior.

The Professor and the Cop

Can the cop on the beat or the judge on the bench afford the luxury of theorizing about the nature and causes of crime? Is there a point at which criminology and criminal investigation meet? Does criminology have immediate, practical value?

Criminology in Theory

As an academic pursuit, criminology is a specialized branch of sociology. Formulating theories of crime and criminality is, in part, an academic end in itself, its goal neither more nor less than attaining a fuller understanding of society. But most academic criminologists attempt to reach beyond the merely academic. They try to evolve the big picture of crime and its relation to society, not for the purpose of helping the patrol officer in the squad car, but for viewing momentous social issues in new ways. For example, a criminologist might speculate on the wisdom of building more and bigger prisons when imprisonment has failed to achieve a dramatic reduction in crime. The object of such speculation, on a theoretical level, is not to improve this or that aspect of the penal system, but to invite profound rethinking of society's entire approach to crime and punishment.

Criminology in Practice

Not all criminologists are theoreticians. So-called vocational or professional criminology does not shy away from theory, but, in contrast to strictly academic criminology, does seek to apply theory directly to practices employed by various professionals within the criminal justice system, including criminal investigators, beat cops, prosecutors, judges, and lawmakers.

Sleuths and Scientists

While criminologists ponder the causes of crime, criminal investigators focus on the results of crime for the purpose of identifying and apprehending the perpetrator, and ultimately bringing him or her to justice. In the process, side benefits of a particular investigation may include deriving some lessons on how to prevent certain crimes in the future and how to identify patterns of criminal behavior that might assist investigators in solving future crimes. However, the main purpose of criminal investigation is implied in the verb *investigate* and, in particular, in the Latin root from which it is derived: *vestigare*, "to track or to trace."

Police officers and detectives conduct criminal investigations, but they are often aided by technical and professional specialists whose roles are detailed later in this book.

Crime Scene

Most criminal investigations begin at the scene of a crime. Virtually all human activity, including crime, leaves a trace of some sort. Television and movie depictions to the contrary notwithstanding, most criminal activity is carried out in the heat of desperation. Perpetrators make mistakes. They leave fingerprints, they make noise (which a witness hears), they leave something behind. Crime is often a messy business.

Even those criminals who go about their activities with cool competence create evidence in the very act of committing the crime. There may be bloodstains, footprints, body hairs, clothing fibers, and other examples of *trace evidence*.

An experienced investigator or investigative team regards the crime scene as a kind of book. The print on the page may be faint and incomplete. The language may be strange and difficult. But still, the scene is there to be read—if one possesses the skill, experience, and tools to read it.

Talking the Talk

Trace evidence is extremely small matter left at a crime scene, such as bloodstains, body hairs, and clothing fibers.

Just the Facts, Ma'am

In addition to "reading" the crime scene, criminal investigators seek suspects, victims, and witnesses. They ask them questions, and they listen first and foremost to the spontaneous statements that are made as close to the time of the crime as possible.

Goals of Criminal Investigations

Criminal acts vary widely, as does the quality of crime scenes and the presence and reliability of witnesses. But all criminal investigations have similar general goals:

1. To determine, first of all, if a crime has been committed

2. To obtain, legally, evidence and information to identify the person or persons responsible for the crime

3. To find and arrest the suspect or suspects

4. To recover property, if any has been stolen

5. To present the prosecuting attorney with the best possible case

Get Real: The Truth About Criminal Investigation

We've seen all this a thousand times on television and in the movies: Sherlock Holmes in his deerstalker cap or Columbo in his wrinkled trench coat with his eagle eyes riveting on this piece of evidence or that, the one clue that, for the super sleuth, immediately reveals the identity of the criminal.

Real investigations are typically much harder work and much less instantly revealing. It is also a fact that many crimes cannot be solved, even by highly skilled investigators. Some crime scenes present insufficient evidence and offer no witnesses. That is a hard reality not very conducive to an exciting hour of television.

Police professionalism grew up alongside the academic development of criminology and the professionalization of criminal investigation. Reform-minded bureaucrats and politicians (like Teddy Roosevelt, who was appointed a New York City police commissioner in 1889) did much to bring scientific knowledge and discipline to modern police work. This contemporary political cartoon shows Commissioner Roosevelt as the ever-watchful Cheshire Cat.

(Image from Arttoday.com)

Fantasy Cops

The classic criminal investigator of pulp fiction and pulp film operates on sheer intuition and an uncanny ability to "think like a criminal."

While it is true that intuition and empathic imagination—an ability to put oneself in the place of another—are valuable qualities in an investigator, they are hardly enough. Real-life detectives are patient, careful, and observant of detail. They have a talent for obtaining and also retaining information. They have a detailed familiarity with the mechanics of crime, with the way particular criminal acts are usually done. Yet they remain open minded and objective. They deal with intensely emotional situations in a logical way. While they obtain vast amounts of information, they are selective and systematic and refuse to be overwhelmed. Their work is occasionally exciting, but it is always hard.

Pressures, Dangers, and the Nitty-Gritty

Gathering information, scrutinizing the crime scene, finding and following up on leads, and doing research is hard work. But hard as gathering, evaluating, sorting, and analyzing evidence are, and as demanding as finding witnesses and suspects can be, all of this is only part of what makes the work of a criminal investigator difficult.

There's the added grind of the nitty-gritty, of ensuring that all the paperwork is executed correctly and completely, that no suspect's civil rights have been violated, and that no evidence has been obtained or handled in a legally questionable manner. There are a hundred traps to avoid, and while the legal system is set up to ensure that the innocent are not erroneously punished, it is all too easy for some oversight, some investigative lapse, to set a guilty person free. That is the reality of criminal investigation.

We'll return to criminal investigation in Part 3. But the rest of this part of the book and the next, Part 2, focus on criminology, its history, its present, and even a glimpse into its future.

> **Sworn Statement**
>
> Criminal investigations are carried out under pressure—pressure from prosecutors and defenders, pressure from politicians, pressure from the press, pressure from the public—and the work can be dangerous. Suspects don't generally sit still and politely await arrest.

The Least You Need to Know

- Crime is a big part of civilized life, yet it is a phenomenon surprisingly difficult to define.

- Criminology studies the causes of crime, whereas criminal investigation discovers, collects, prepares, identifies, and presents evidence relating to a particular crime.

- Criminologists present a variety of theories on the nature and causes of crime, ultimately with the object of helping society and the criminal justice system deal more effectively with crime.

- The fantasies of novelists and screenwriters notwithstanding, crime scene investigation is hard and painstaking work, rarely glamorous, and often dangerous.

2

Criminology Classic

In This Chapter

- Pre–eighteenth-century theories of crime and criminality
- Beccaria and Bentham develop classical criminology
- Outline of classical criminology
- A critique of classical criminology
- Some early fringe theories

Classical criminology, first developed by Cesare Beccaria and Jeremy Bentham in the eighteenth century, is a body of theory aimed at providing a criminal justice system with a way to bring the greatest good to the greatest number within society.

Although today's criminologists regard classical criminology as the origin of modern criminology, it was hardly the beginning of all thought about crime and the causes of crime. Doubtless, this began long before the days of Beccaria and coincides with thought, theories, and mythologies intended to explain the very nature of good and evil. In this chapter we'll take a closer look at classical criminology and the work of Beccaria and others.

Criminological Prehistory

As far as can be determined, many early societies equated crime with sin and sin with some form of supernatural evil influence. According to some authorities, evidence that criminal behavior was ascribed to demonic possession may be found as early as 5000 B.C.E. Notions that the zodiac and planetary influences can cause crime date as far back as 3500 B.C.E. and persist into the seventeenth century. Theological explanations that crime is somehow related to the will of God may be found as early as about 1200 B.C.E. Medical explanations for crime—the idea that some people commit crimes because of a physical disorder—appear about 3000 B.C.E.

The Demons Made Me Do It

Demonic possession, the state in which a person becomes inhabited by a demon or demons and, therefore, cannot exercise his or her own will, dates to ancient times and is noted in both the Old and New Testaments.

Look at this case of demonic possession from the New Testament (Mark 5: 1–13):

1 And they came over unto the other side of the sea, into the country of the Gadarenes.

2 And when he was come out of the ship, immediately there met him out of the tombs a man with an unclean spirit,

3 Who had his dwelling among the tombs; and no man could bind him, no, not with chains:

4 Because that he had been often bound with fetters and chains, and the chains had been plucked asunder by him, and the fetters broken in pieces: neither could any man tame him.

5 And always, night and day, he was in the mountains, and in the tombs, crying, and cutting himself with stones.

6 But when he saw Jesus afar off, he ran and worshipped him,

7 And cried with a loud voice, and said, What have I to do with thee, Jesus, thou Son of the most high God? I adjure thee by God, that thou torment me not.

8 For he said unto him, Come out of the man, thou unclean spirit.

9 And he asked him, What is thy name? And he answered, saying, My name is Legion: for we are many.

10 And he besought him much that he would not send them away out of the country.

11 Now there was there nigh unto the mountains a great herd of swine feeding.

12 And all the devils besought him, saying, Send us into the swine, that we may enter into them.

13 And forthwith Jesus gave them leave. And the unclean spirits went out, and entered into the swine: and the herd ran violently down a steep place into the sea, (they were about two thousand;) and were choked in the sea.

In the Old Testament, demons were fallen angels; in the New Testament, they are "malignant spirits." Many demons, some of which have names, were associated with temptations toward lust, mischief, and outright crime. The most active demon was called Asmodeus, who could assume male or female form and would imbue the person he or she inhabited with insatiable lust for adultery, sodomy, and child molestation. The most famous demon was Beelzebub, which, contrary to popular usage, is not another name for Satan or Lucifer, but a demon in his own right who was associated with murder and cannibalism. Another motivator of murder was the bat-winged demon Sammael and, from Indian religious traditions, Rakshasas, a vampire demon.

The demon Asmodeus, from a Renaissance woodcut.

(Image from the author's collection)

There are others. Widespread interest in demonology, including its relation to crime, ended by the late seventeenth century, although, in some places and among some people, demonology doubtless remains an active belief.

> **By the Numbers**
>
> A Gallup Poll conducted during May 10–14, 2001, found that 41 percent of Americans believe "that people on this earth are sometimes possessed by the devil." Sixteen percent were "not sure," and 41 percent did not believe in possession by the devil. The same poll found that 28 percent of Americans believe in "astrology, or that the position of the stars and planets can affect people's lives." Eighteen percent were "not sure," and 52 percent did not believe in astrology.

In the Stars

Various cultures have looked to stars and planets for guidance of all kinds—personal, spiritual, and political. The earliest forms of astrology date from at least 3500 B.C.E., but Westerners are most familiar with Western tropical astrology, which has its origin in Mesopotamia, circa 2300 B.C.E. From this region, astrology was imported into ancient Greece, perhaps as early as 600 B.C.E.

The idea behind all astrology is that the stars and planets exert an influence on human behavior, both individually and collectively, and that, by studying the changing positions of the stars and planets relative to one another, it is possible to predict operative influences and, perhaps, even the resulting behavior.

The term "behavior" takes in all human behavior, including crime. Astrological explanations of the causes of crime did not end in the early seventeenth century, although most people stopped taking astrology seriously by then. Even today, astrologers write books analyzing the zodiacal influences on such serial killers as Jeffrey Dahmer and John Wayne Gacy; see, for example, Jan Warren Allen's *Blueprint for Murder*, available from the Astrology Center of America (www.astroamerica.com), which looks at the lives and careers of Dahmer, Gacy, and two additional notorious serial killers, Ed Gein and Dennis Nilsen.

God's Will and Satan's Work

Theologians, who are responsible for explaining how God works through his creation, the universe, have wrestled with the nature and the very existence of crime since time immemorial. The problem is this: If God is absolute good, how can we account for crime in the realm of his creation?

This book is hardly the place to enter into a detailed discussion of the various theological explanations of crime; however, in the Judeo-Christian tradition, such explanations have centered on three theories:

1. **Crime is the product of original sin,** which was brought into the world when Eve ate of the forbidden fruit in the Garden of Eden and then induced Adam to do the same.

2. **Crime is part of God's plan.** God endows each human being with free will, the ability to choose between good and evil. For free will to have any meaning at all, there must be *both* good and evil in the world—otherwise there would be no real choices to be made.

3. **Crime is not of the realm of God,** but of the devil, God's enemy and antithesis.

Theological explanations of crime date as far back as 1200 B.C.E. and, among many people, persist to this day.

Humor Me

Speculation that crime—or, at least, some criminal behavior—is the product of natural illness or congenital disorder was recorded as early as 3000 B.C.E. Since at least the era of the "father of medicine," Hippocrates (460?–377? B.C.E.), physicians have believed that attaining and maintaining good health was largely a matter of balancing bodily fluids, known as the four *humors*. These were blood, phlegm, yellow bile, and black bile. Too much of one humor or too little of another caused various disorders, including a predisposition to commit crimes.

Blood, which Hippocrates believed was manufactured by the liver, was responsible for "sanguine disorders" when present in excess. People with too much blood were unrealistically optimistic and overconfident. In a word, they were "sanguine." A very sanguine person might lack the inhibitions that keep most of us on the strait and narrow. Without "normal" inhibitions, crime becomes increasingly likely.

Too much phlegm, a humor associated with the lungs, was thought to create a phlegmatic personality, one characterized by sluggishness. An

Talking the Talk

Humors are bodily fluids; the Greek physician Hippocrates believed that the balance among the four basic humors—blood, phlegm, yellow bile, and black bile—substantially determined an individual's personality and the state of his or her physical and mental health.

excessively phlegmatic individual, too lazy to earn his own bread, might well turn to theft or larceny.

Yellow bile, believed by Hippocrates to be a product of the gallbladder, could, in excessive quantities, bring on "choleric disorders," which cause one to be angry and ill-tempered. Today, we still call a testy person "bilious," reflecting the earlier belief that ill temper was caused by too much yellow bile. Choleric persons might be inclined to commit violent crimes and crimes of passion.

Hippocrates thought black bile was made by the spleen. Too much of this humor was said to bring on melancholia (*melas* is Greek for "black," and *khole* is Greek for "bile"), which today we call depression. Insofar as depression may bring on desperation, a melancholic person might be driven to commit certain crimes.

Although the theory of the four humors was pretty thoroughly put to rest by the end of the eighteenth century, medical explanations for at least some types of criminal behavior continue to be important.

Case in Point

Perhaps the most controversial medical explanation for a crime was the infamous "Twinkie defense." On November 27, 1978, Dan White, who had recently resigned as a San Francisco city supervisor, walked into Mayor George Moscone's office and demanded his job back. When Moscone refused, White shot him four times, reloaded, walked down the hall to the office of another city supervisor, Harvey Milk, and killed him with five gunshots. White's attorneys argued that White was addicted to junk food (such as the popular Twinkie snack cake) and that too much sugar could have chemically exacerbated White's depression. A jury found White guilty not of murder, but of voluntary manslaughter, and he was sentenced only to six years in prison. Paroled in 1985, White soon committed suicide.

Hail, Cesare!

Cesare Bonesana, the Marchese di Beccaria, was born in 1738 to a noble Milanese family of modest means. Bridling under the rigors of an early Jesuit education, he left the Jesuits to study law and received his degree from the University of Pavia in 1758. He returned to Milan, where he became an ardent activist in the cause of general social reform. In 1764, Beccaria produced *On Crimes and Punishments*, the volume most historians call the starting place of classical criminology.

Cesare Bonesana, the Marchese di Beccaria.

(Image from the University of Pavia, Italy)

Beccaria's book made its most immediate impact as a scathing indictment of criminal justice in eighteenth-century Italy and, by extension, throughout most of the so-called "civilized" world. Beccaria criticized the penal system, the use of torture in punishment as well as during interrogation, the universal corruption of officials, and the often grotesquely severe penalties meted out for relatively minor offenses.

Human Nature and the Social Contract

Beyond criticism of the current state of criminal justice, Beccaria presented a theoretical basis for reform. This came in the form of a pioneering theory of criminology.

Beccaria rejected the notion that crime was the equivalent of sin, and proposed instead that it was an injury to society. As Beccaria saw it, submission to society—that is, the creation of government—was a transaction, something advanced eighteenth-century social thinkers called a *social contract*. Individual human nature is self-interested and hedonistic; that is, individuals tend to act in order to

Talking the Talk

A **social contract** is a view of the relationship between individuals and the state (or society) that defines this relationship as a rational exchange of rights and obligations.

benefit themselves and to minimize pain and cost. But, according to Beccaria, people are also rational and, before taking action, can calculate what *really* is in their self-interest. This rationality gives people a significant measure of freedom from their desires and from their environment. It allows them to enter into a social contract, creating governments and legal systems to avoid the conflicts produced by self-interest.

Government and Laws

The nature of any contract is an equitable exchange of value. The contracting parties each give and each gain. As Beccaria reasoned, the best social contract, the most effective government, provides the greatest good for the greatest number. In terms of the criminal justice system, laws should be restrictive enough to prevent injury to society (that is, crime) yet should create a minimum of encroachment on humanity's natural freedom and rationality.

Preventive Punishment

As for judicial punishment, it should be crafted to create the greatest good for the greatest number. Instead of seeking revenge, punishment should deter future crime.

> **Sworn Statement**
>
> The end of punishment ... is ... to prevent the criminal from doing further injury to society, and to prevent others from committing the like offence. Such punishments ... ought to be chosen, as will make the strongest and most lasting impression on the minds of others, with the least torment to the body of the criminal.
>
> —Cesare Beccaria, *On Crimes and Punishments*

The idea of punishment as deterrence carries an important implication for the role of a criminal justice system in society. To function as a deterrent, punishment for crime must be a certainty, an invariable consequence. Achieving this level of certainty requires establishing a permanent, professional police force and judicial system.

Of course, the further implication of punishment as deterrence is that prevention of crime is ultimately a more desirable goal than punishment for crime. Therefore, in a rational society, Beccaria argued that popular knowledge of the law was essential. Moreover, laws had to be standard, clear, equitable, and rational. If people knew the law, they would be less likely to break it.

Bentham's Head

The classical view of criminology, as first articulated by Beccaria, was developed further by the Englishman Jeremy Bentham (1748–1832). Although Bentham is remembered as the founder of that most rational of philosophies, utilitarianism, he was sufficiently eccentric to request in his will that his body be preserved, dressed in his own clothes, and kept in a cabinet at the University of London. His will was largely respected; however, something went wrong in the process of preserving Bentham's head—the nose came off—and a wax facsimile perches atop the dressed skeleton that still resides in the wooden cabinet in the institution now known as University College London. Fortunately, the thoughts that had raced through that head have been more successfully preserved.

Greatest Good for the Greatest Number

Like Beccaria, Bentham proposed that the chief purpose of society and all social institutions was to create the greatest good for the greatest number. In the context of criminal justice, this, Bentham held, could be achieved only by rendering law and punishment in as rational terms as possible.

Jeremy Bentham.

(Image from Arttoday.com)

An Antidote to Hedonism

Bentham believed that all behavior could be reduced to the seeking of pleasure and the avoidance of pain. The main question for criminal justice, therefore, was how to make crime more painful (to the criminal!) than pleasurable. From the perspective of the would-be wrongdoer, crime should offer more pain than breaking the law is worth.

Crime, as Bentham saw it, was a choice—a free choice made, as all free choices are made, out of self-interest. That same self-interest dictated that, if punishment outweighed the potential benefit of a crime, the rational choice would be to re-frain from committing the crime.

Classical Criminology Distilled

All classical criminology is based on a concept of individual rights and a basic human capacity to make rational choices. Among these choices is a social contract by which individuals relinquish some portion of freedom in exchange for the benefits of government, law, and order.

Definition and Focus

In classical criminology, crime is defined in essentially legal terms as a violation of law and a violation of the social contract, which is, therefore, an injury to society itself. Classical criminology focuses its attention on the criminal act, with the object of formulating appropriate laws to prevent certain criminal acts. Punishment is tailored to the specific crime and is designed to outweigh the benefit of the crime, to deter the offender, as well as others from committing the crime, and to yet do no gratuitous or excessive injury to the offender.

Causes of Crime and Criminality

Classical criminologists see people as rational beings capable of free choice. Crime is a matter of choice. In a properly ordered society with a rational system of criminal justice, any crime is, by definition, the product of an irrational decision.

For the classical criminologist, the criminal is a person who makes bad—flawed, ill-informed, or downright irrational—choices. This is an assumption that was applied (albeit perhaps in bad faith) in the former Soviet Union, where those tried for the "crime" of political dissidence were often judged to be insane. No sane person, it was rationalized, could possibly find fault with Soviet communism.

Response and Prevention

In the classical view, the best punishment is always rationally proportioned to the crime. For each crime, a prescribed punishment is fixed and never left to the whim of a particular judge or other authority. To function as a deterrent, punishment must be both just and certain.

Prevention of crime, in this rational view, is preferable to punishment for a crime already committed. Deterrence based on the pleasure-pain principle—the potential pleasure of the offense must be outweighed by the potential pain of the punishment—must be in the context of a thoroughly accessible legal system. In order to make the rational decision to refrain from crime, everyone must know the law and be aware of the nature of the penalties for various offenses.

A Flawed but Persistent View

Classical criminology did much to purge criminal justice systems of cruelty and inconsistency, yet the classical view does suffer from profound flaws—although elements of this view remain very much a part of most modern criminal justice systems.

Flunking the Reality Test

It is unrealistic to assume that everyone is endowed with an equal capacity to make rational decisions. Classical criminology fails to deal with intellectual disability or mental illness.

Classical criminology does not admit of the possibility that, sometimes, breaking the law is actually a rational choice. If you are starving and penniless, is it not rational to steal bread? If society were truly perfect, crime might, in fact, always be an irrational choice. But in an imperfect society, it is unrealistic to assume that breaking the law is inevitably irrational.

Efficiency Versus Justice

The prescriptive, cut-and-dried aspects of classical criminology have done much to simplify and rationalize the world's legal systems; however, the emphasis of classical criminology is on the efficiency of criminal justice as a social system and not on ensuring that justice is done. Classical criminology fails to consider mitigating circumstances in judging and punishing most crimes.

Status Quo

Viewed from the broadest social perspective, classical criminology does not inquire deeply into the nature of crime or the values of society. By defining crime as an injury to society, it reinforces the status quo and, in this sense, does not promote rigorous critical inquiry that might lead to sweeping or radical reform.

Just Desserts

Although the theory of classical criminology emphasizes deterrence as the principal goal of punishment, in practice, punishment tailored to the offense does not produce deterrence so much as it creates a sense of meting out "just desserts." In this respect, the theory of classical criminology is more or less incompatible with its practice.

And Now for Something Completely Different ...

Whatever its shortcomings, classical criminology introduced scientific reasoning into an important area that had long been the subject of irrational speculation. This does not mean that classical criminology instantly swept aside all of the less plausible approaches.

Bumps on the Head

During the late eighteenth century, the Viennese physician Franz Josef Gall (1758–1828) created *phrenology*, the study of the topography of the human skull. He proposed that the irregular bumps and bulges on an individual's cranium were the outward expression of that person's character and proclivities. Gall's protégé, assistant, and collaborator, Johann C. Spurzheim (1776–1832), began to apply the master's work most specifically to criminology.

Talking the Talk

Phrenology is the systematic study of the topography of the surface of the human skull and is based on the assumption that various bumps and irregularities are the outward expression of the individual's personality, character, and intellectual and emotional proclivities.

Spurzheim refined Gall's original description of cranial topography by dividing the brain into 35 different "faculties," each responsible for different behavioral and emotional patterns. He identified in particular certain features that denoted a tendency toward criminal behavior, so that, by assessing the bumps on a skull, a trained practitioner might identify a potential murderer or thief and, by timely counseling, alter the destiny of a future offender.

The fatal flaw of phrenology? It is entirely without scientific basis.

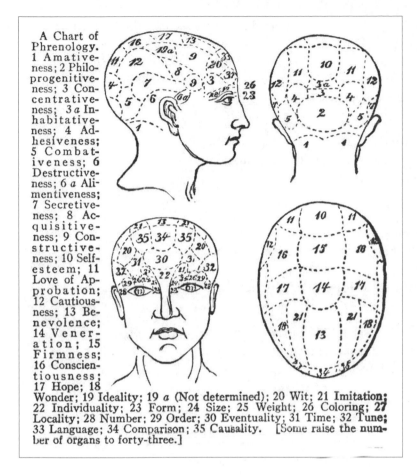

A Chart of Phrenology. 1 Amativeness; 2 Philoprogenitiveness; 3 Concentrativeness; 3 *a* Inhabitativeness; 4 Adhesiveness; 5 Combativeness; 6 Destructiveness; 6 *a* Alimentiveness; 7 Secretiveness; 8 Acquisitiveness; 9 Constructiveness; 10 Self-esteem; 11 Love of Approbation; 12 Cautiousness; 13 Benevolence; 14 Veneration; 15 Firmness; 16 Conscientiousness; 17 Hope; 18 Wonder; 19 Ideality; 19 *a* (Not determined); 20 Wit; 21 Imitation; 22 Individuality; 23 Form; 24 Size; 25 Weight; 26 Coloring; 27 Locality; 28 Number; 29 Order; 30 Eventuality; 31 Time; 32 Tune; 33 Language; 34 Comparison; 35 Causality. [Some raise the number of organs to forty-three.]

A phrenological chart from a nineteenth-century edition of Webster's Dictionary.

(Image from the author's collection)

It's the Weather

Early in the nineteenth century, any number of writers speculated on the relation between climate and crime. Among many northern Europeans, for example, it was taken as an article of faith that the peoples of warmer climes, in southern Europe and in Latin America, were "hot blooded" and, therefore, given to violent crime.

While it is true that more violent crimes tend to occur in hot weather than in cold, no useful theory of criminology predicting criminal behavior has ever been formulated by connecting crime with climate.

In Your Bones

In the 1890s, the development of osteopathy (a system of medicine based on the theory that disturbances of the musculoskeletal system affect other bodily systems and create disorders seemingly having nothing to do with bones and muscles) led to intense speculation that criminal behavior could result from specific musculoskeletal problems. Not only could a trained osteopath predict criminal behavior based on the disposition of bones and muscle, he might be able to prevent such behavior by executing the appropriate manipulations.

At about this time, some chiropractors made a similar claim concerning problems of the nervous system, which might predict or even cause criminal behavior, but which could be treated by the correct chiropractic manipulation.

He's Just Slow

In the early 1950s, when intense attention was focused on the problem of juvenile delinquency, some criminologists theorized that poor academic performance in school was an accurate predictor of criminal behavior and, indeed, a leading cause of it. The feelings of failure induced by learning disabilities were believed to make crime attractive as a field in which the slow learner could find success and peer approval.

While many criminals fail to find fulfillment in academics or any other socially acceptable pursuit, few really useful links have been identified between learning disorders and the causes of crime.

Follow the Crowd

Some criminologists have reached the apparently common-sense conclusion that much crime is the product of environment and example. If the crowd you hang around with approves of criminal behavior, the chances are that you will commit crimes.

Peer pressure and modeling are difficult concepts to dispute, but they don't get us very far. They may predict the behavior of a given individual in a certain environment, but they don't account for the behavior in the first place. Joe Blow behaves badly because all his friends do. But why do his friends behave badly? Who started it, anyway?

And one more thing: How does the theory account for criminals who were raised among "nice people"?

The follow-the-crowd explanation of crime and criminality is a useful illustration of just how difficult it is to create adequate criminological theory. A good theory must account for the origin of crime *and* must also predict criminal behavior. In reality, few theories manage to do both of these things persuasively and reliably. Nevertheless, criminologists continue to accept the challenge, and the inquiry continues.

The Least You Need to Know

- ◆ Prior to the work of Cesare Beccaria in the eighteenth century, there was no rational, systematic inquiry into the causes and nature of crime.

- ◆ Most early explanations of crime equate it with sin, demonic possession, or physical disorder.

- ◆ In the eighteenth century, Beccaria and Jeremy Bentham developed classical criminology with the aim of reforming the criminal justice system so that it would contribute to creating the greatest good for the greatest number.

- ◆ Classical criminology is based on the assumption of a social contract, and the fact that crime violates that contract and, therefore, injures society. Deterrence of crime must include punishments that, from the perspective of the potential criminal, clearly make the consequences of crime more painful than the anticipated benefits.

- ◆ Although valuable as a force for reform, classical criminology does not fully account for the practical realities of individual variation and social inequality.

3

Power of Positive Thinking

In This Chapter

- ◆ Lombroso and the concept of positivist criminology
- ◆ Are criminals born or made? Biological vs. psychological positivism
- ◆ Forensic psychology and psychiatry
- ◆ Control theory
- ◆ The role of society
- ◆ A critique of positivist criminology

Theories, theories about almost anything, are products of their time. Beccaria's ideas about classical criminology were developed in the eighteenth century, the so-called Age of Reason, when the leading philosophies expressed an almost boundless faith in the potential of human rationality. Not surprisingly, then, Beccaria's view of crime and criminality was based on the concept of individual choice. As he saw it, in a properly ordered society, the rational choice was always to obey the law, whereas the choice to commit a crime was invariably an abandonment of rationality. In either case, the issue was a matter of individual choice.

The nineteenth century began to turn away from blind faith in individual rationality and free will. Philosophy became less important than science. Philosophy dealt with thought and spirit, science with brain and body—what could be seen, felt, measured, and manipulated. The industrialization of Europe (and other places) during the nineteenth century put additional emphasis on the technological and the empirical. The growth of mass production and mass consumption of manufactured goods shifted the focus from the inner world of the individual to the outer world of society and social forces.

Not surprisingly, the leading criminological theories born of this new century differed sharply from Beccaria's classicism. Whereas eighteenth-century criminology focused on individual choice, nineteenth-century criminology explained crime by reference to forces and influences beyond the individual.

Lombroso: The "Father" of Criminology

The most important criminologist of the nineteenth century was, like Beccaria, an Italian and, also like Beccaria, a Cesare—Cesare Lombroso. Those historians who do not credit Beccaria as the founder of criminology almost invariably give the honor to Lombroso.

Cesare Lombroso, from a photograph made late in his life.

(Image from the author's collection)

He was born in 1835 in Verona and studied medicine at the universities of Pavia, Padova, Vienna, and Genoa. He became less interested in the conventional practice of medicine, however, than in applying medical and biological science to the study of society, in particular the study of crime. The idea that social issues and problems may be usefully examined with the tools and methods of natural science is called *positivism*.

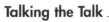

Talking the Talk

Positivism holds that social issues and problems, including crime, may be usefully examined with the tools and methods of natural science.

The positivist sees himself as a completely objective (value-free) observer of the world, whose primary responsibility is to record data and draw conclusions from analysis of that data. The principal method of the positivist is to classify and quantify human behavior and experience using objective tests. Underlying this responsibility and this method is an assumption that the social world, like the natural world, obeys certain natural laws of operation. Through careful observation and analysis, these laws can be discovered and, thereby, the causes of various behaviors can be determined, the behaviors predicted, and, in the case of negative behaviors, perhaps prevented, avoided, corrected, or at least ameliorated.

The Idea of the Born Criminal

In two highly influential books, *L'Uomo delinquente* (*The Delinquent*), 1876, and *L'Homme criminel* (*The Criminal*), 1895, Lombroso developed the theory of the born criminal, arguing that criminality was first and foremost the product of heredity.

Lombroso distinguished between two broad categories of born criminal: the epileptic criminal, who was susceptible to criminal behavior because of epilepsy, and, of greater significance, the insane criminal. This type of criminal was mentally deficient because of *atavism*, a pathological, antisocial throwback to primitive behavior.

Talking the Talk

Atavism is a throwback to a primitive state. The criminologist Cesare Lombroso believed that most criminality resulted from an inborn atavism in certain individuals that caused them to revert to an earlier phase of evolution, which created presocial (and therefore antisocial) behavior.

The Criminal as Outcast

The antisocial behavior of the born criminal, whether he is of the epileptic or insane variety, tends to make him a social outcast, and this circumstance only serves to deepen and intensify his criminality. In this way, society germinates the seed planted by nature.

Lombroso did not claim that all offenders were born criminals. He recognized what he called the occasional criminal, a criminal type that existed in two varieties: the pseudocriminal and the criminaloid.

The pseudocriminal betrayed none of the atavistic antisocial traits of the insane or epileptic criminal; however, from time to time, he might commit a petty crime from motives apparently beyond his control, but without the intent of harming society.

The criminaloid was inherently abnormal—and outwardly seemed so—yet his deviance did not result from biological heredity, but from society's treating him as an outcast. This cause alone warped him.

The Two Strands of Positivist Criminology

From its origins in the work of Lombroso, positivist criminology divided into two strands, one leading most directly from Lombroso and biological issues—physical causes and physical predictors of criminality—and another derived from psychology.

Biological Positivism: Criminologist as Anthropologist

In addition to his medical training and his faith in the scientific method, Lombroso was also influenced by the work of Charles Darwin, formulator of the theory of evolution. For Lombroso, the atavism that created the born criminal was a kind of glitch in evolution, a freak of nature that doomed the criminal to behave as primitive people behaved in the days before ordered societies came into existence.

Along with his evolutionary point of view, Lombroso believed that human beings could be classified racially and biologically, and that some readily distinguishable physical characteristics were directly associated with criminality. To a degree, Lombroso embraced phrenology (see Chapter 2), but he went beyond this to develop a physical anthropology of the criminal, and he drew up a roster of physical features typical of the born criminal. For the most part, these features suggested resemblance to an ape—or, at least, to humanity at an earlier evolutionary stage:

- Unusually short or unusually tall

- Small head, but large face

- Small, sloping forehead

- Receding hairline

- Wrinkled forehead

- Wrinkled face

- Unusually large sinus cavities

- Bumpy face

- Large, protruding ears

- Bumps on head

- Cranial bump(s) in the "destructiveness center" (region above the left ear)

- Bumps or protuberances in the back of the head

- Bumps or protuberances around one or both ears

- Unusually high cheekbones

- Bushy eyebrows that meet

- Deep-set eyes in large eye sockets

- Beaklike nose (may turn up or down)

- Flat nose

- Prominent, strong jaw line; however, small or weak chin

- Lower lip fleshy, upper lip thin

- Very prominent incisors

- Generally abnormal teeth

- Thin, even delicate neck

- Sloped shoulders, but a large chest

- Disproportionately long arms

- Toes and fingers either pointy or snubbed

Sworn Statement

... [T]he criminal woman is ... a monster. Her normal sister is kept in the paths of virtue by many causes, such as maternity, piety [and] weakness; and when these counterinfluences fail, and a woman commits a crime, we may conclude that her wickedness must have been enormous before it could triumph over so many obstacles.

—Cesare Lombroso, quoted in Christine E. Rasche's, *Criminal Justice and Behavior* (1974)

Additionally, born criminals often bore tattoos on their bodies, Lombroso associated tattooing with primitive peoples and cultures.

Two illustrations from Lombroso's L'Uomo delinquente (The Delinquent), *1876, showing brutish, atavistic criminal facial features.*

(Image from the 1876 book)

Lombroso saw the female criminal as a special case. Criminality was essentially aggressive, whereas women were by nature passive; therefore, the female criminal was biologically more like a man than a woman.

Psychological Positivism: Criminologist as Psychiatrist

Early in the twentieth century, another form of positivism emerged in criminology. Whereas Lombroso's biological positivism regarded most criminals as "born that way," psychological positivism identified most crime as the result either of externally caused biological problems (traumatic illness or injury) or strictly psychological problems (mental illness). Criminals were not born, they were made, their criminality the result of acquired medical or psychological conditions. Whereas medically or psychologically treating the born criminal was fruitless, psychological positivism held out the hope that acquired conditions could, in fact, be treated. If criminal offenders were "sick," the obvious thing to do was to "cure" them.

Psychological positivists have attempted (and some continue to attempt) to associate specific types of emotional trauma with specific kinds of criminal behavior. The tools used for treatment might include …

 ◆ **Psychoanalysis,** in an attempt to get at the unconscious causes of certain criminal behaviors.

 ◆ **Analysis of personality traits,** in an attempt to relate, for example, aggressive tendencies to criminal acts.

 ◆ **Analysis of environment and upbringing,** in an attempt to identify various nurturing patterns or specific childhood traumas that may have contributed to later criminality.

Positivist Criminology Distilled

Whether biological or psychological, positivism rests on the assumption that a scientific understanding of crime and criminality is both possible and desirable. All positivism also assumes definable and significant differences between what is normal and what is deviant, and all positivism also assumes that the individual has little or no choice concerning his criminality. In some cases, he may choose not to *act* on his criminal impulses, but the impulses themselves are the result of forces and factors beyond the control of the individual.

Definition and Focus

For the positivist, the causes of crime may be found in the biological or psychological makeup of the individual. Criminal behavior itself is defined as deviance from social norms, a violation of social consensus. The positivist focuses on the criminal, not on society or even on the nature of the crime. The principal objects of study are the characteristics of the offender.

The emphasis on the offender highlights another key difference between positivism and classicism. Whereas classical criminology tends to assume that all human beings are endowed with a similar capacity for making rational judgments, positivist criminology recognizes that offenders vary, that individual differences exist among them, including the degree of their rationality, impulse control, and so on.

Case in Point

Factors that contribute to criminality include hereditary biological factors (such as atavism), social conditioning (paramountly, treatment as an outcast), and (for the psychological positivist) acquired injuries and disorders of a particularly traumatic nature.

Causes of Crime and Criminality

For the positivist, most crime is pathology, either hereditary (according to the biological positivist) or acquired (according to the psychological positivist). Crime is not sin, and it is neither immoral nor moral, any more than a birth defect or an illness is sinful or immoral. In most cases, crime is not the product of individual choice. Criminal offenders, according to the positivist, are either born or created, and if they are not invariably doomed to a life of crime, they are predisposed to one.

Response and Prevention

For the born criminal, the prospects for treatment are bleak. If an evolutionary glitch has made a person behave more like an ape than a human being, there is little that can be done.

The psychological positivist takes a more optimistic view. Criminals should not merely be punished, but diagnosed on an individual basis. Medical and psychological treatment appropriate to the individual and his disorder can then be prescribed.

Informed observation can prevent criminal behavior. If an individual is diagnosed and classified in a timely manner, it may be possible, through treatment, the supervision of behavior, the management of the environment, or some combination of these, to prevent the individual from acting on his criminal impulses.

In any event, under the positivist approach, the response of the criminal justice system to an offender must be morally neutral. The emphasis should be placed on measurement and evaluation on a case-by-case basis.

Positivist Criminology Today

Today, some aspects of the positivist approach seem antiquated and highly dubious, particularly the reliance on phrenology and the concept of atavism; however, the positivist strain is still very much a part of some modern approaches to criminology. In modern forensic psychology, the foundation of positivism is quite apparent. Forensic psychology applies psychology, the study of mind and human behavior, specifically to the fields of criminology, criminal investigation, and criminal justice. Generally, forensic psychologists hold Ph.D. degrees, while forensic psychiatrists always hold an M.D. degree.

Another modern approach, biosocial criminology, is also based in the positivist tradition. Biosocial criminology approaches crime and criminality as a biosocial process, proposing that criminal behavior may be explained as the product of a combination of psychological and environmental influences.

The Science of Forensics

"Forensic" is an adjective applied to a number of fields to indicate their specific application to the criminal justice realm. Forensic psychologists (nonphysicians) and forensic psychiatrists (medical doctors) apply psychology and psychiatry to the study of criminal behavior. In practice, these experts are routinely called upon to render opinions on an offender's mental competence to stand trial, to provide presentencing reports (to guide judges in determining the most appropriate sentence for an offender), to render opinions to facilitate parole decisions, and to treat incarcerated offenders. Some forensic psychologists also assist in criminal investigation as criminal profilers (see Chapter 8).

Some forensic psychologists concentrate on theoretical criminology. *Control theory* is perhaps the leading recent line of criminological inquiry in forensic psychology. It stands on its head the question traditionally posed by criminologists—"Why are some people criminals?"—and asks instead, "Why isn't *everyone* a criminal?" The answer is that, by developing self-control, most of us learn not to offend.

Control theorists agree with Sigmund Freud, who, toward the end of the nineteenth century, theorized that human beings are by nature antisocial and impulsive, but that most become socialized by systematically repressing various natural desires. For control theorists, it is the failure of such repression in certain areas that produces criminal behavior. The general psychological characteristics of a criminal are, first and foremost, impulsivity, followed by a desire to engage in high-risk behavior, a lack of concentration and perseverance, an egocentric outlook, a tendency to become frustrated easily, and a preference for physical over mental activity. According to current theorists, most defects in self-control are the result of an adverse childhood environment.

Talking the Talk

In contemporary criminology, **control theory** views crime and criminality as the result of an absence or failure of the self-control mechanisms adequately socialized people successfully develop.

Crime as a Biosocial Process

Hans Eysenck (1916–1997), a Berlin-born professor of psychology at the University of London, provided the most influential explanation of crime as a biosocial process, proposing that criminal behavior could be explained as a combination of psychological and environmental influences. All behavior, Eysenck suggested, including criminal behavior, is determined by two principal variables:

1. **The differential ability to be conditioned.** This is our genetically inherited ability to be permanently influenced by factors in the environment.

2. **The differential quality of conditioning.** For Eysenck, this referred to the effectiveness and efficiency of the family in using appropriate conditioning techniques, that is, the effectiveness of child-rearing in a particular family.

In short, we are all born with certain biologically determined potentials, which, after birth, interact with the environment, especially as that environment is shaped by our parents. Taken together, these two factors determine behavior, including a propensity toward crime.

That word "propensity" is important. In contrast to Lombroso, few modern positivists see a one-to-one correspondence between a given biological factor and criminality. Instead, certain biological and social factors are identified as putting an individual at risk for criminal behavior. No one is born a criminal, and no environment, no matter how negative, absolutely dooms an individual to become a criminal; however, factors that contribute to a predisposition to crime can be identified and studied.

By the Numbers

A 2000 Gallup public opinion poll on the causes of crime does not even include "born criminal" as an option. Those polled were asked to respond to lack of good jobs for young people, poor quality of schools, fatherless homes, lack of moral training in the home, TV violence, decline of religion, drug use, availability of guns, and racism in American society. However, the results of a 2001 poll conducted by about.com suggest that the idea of the born criminal still lives—at least where rape is concerned. Fifty-eight percent of respondents (1,365 of 2,370) believed that a "judge should have the right to order castration" as part of a rape sentence.

Genes and Hormones

While the biosocial explanation of crime is a dominant form of contemporary positivism, some recent forensic psychologists give more weight to genetic and hormonal factors in criminal behavior. Researchers are currently investigating the relation of various intellectual defects to criminality. Other researchers are engaged in projects assessing the possible influence of hormonal activity and metabolic processes on criminal behavior.

Just Say No

That illicit drugs and crime go together is hardly a revelation. Wherever a market for a legally forbidden substance exists, there will be criminals to serve that market. More complex, however, is how the use of drugs (legal and illegal) influences criminal behavior. Forensic psychologists examine psychopharmocological inducements to crime, including the effects of alcohol, cocaine and cocaine derivatives, amphetamines, and other substances.

Positivism: Problems and Pluses

As an attempt to apply rigorous science to the subject of crime and criminality, and to divorce this highly charged field from emotion and from particular religious and moral prejudices, positivism has made valuable contributions to criminology. Positivism has done much to promote the development of forensic psychology, which has become vital to criminal investigation, to criminal prosecution, and to the treatment of incarcerated offenders. As originally conceived by Lombroso, however, positivism draws certain rigorous connections between particular physical facts and criminality that must be rejected as one-dimensional. There are other problems to note as well.

Running in Circles

The single most serious criticism leveled against positivism is that it typically confines its research to incarcerated populations. This leads to circular reasoning. If, as the positivist asserts, criminality is the result of biological or psychological abnormality, all incarcerated populations are by definition biologically or psychologically abnormal. The positivist assumes that the abnormality produced the criminal behavior. But how can a researcher determine with certainty whether the abnormality caused the criminal behavior or the criminal behavior caused the abnormality? How can a researcher be certain that imprisonment did not create an abnormality? How can a researcher determine whether individuals in the general population who have a particular abnormality also identified in the incarcerated population will likewise offend?

> **Sworn Statement**
>
> Another problem with thinking of criminality as sickness is that positivist researchers tend to reduce potential reasons for a particular criminal behavior to a single biological or psychological cause. This reductionist approach may blind researchers to the varied wealth of influences that occur over a lifetime.

Sick? Bad? Misbehaved?

Another shortcoming is the failure of many positivists to distinguish adequately between sickness and criminality. If this distinction is blurred, it becomes all too easy simply to equate criminal behavior with sickness and, therefore, to assume that all criminal behavior, like sickness, is uniformly undesirable. Undetermined is the point at which deviation from a social norm must be considered criminal behavior or sickness or both.

Hello, Big Brother?

One of the great promises of forensic psychology and other forms of positivism is that, once biological or psychological causes of particular kinds of crime have been identified, it should be possible to identify criminal potential in individuals who fit certain profiles. Yet, is this truly a promise or is it more of a threat?

The American legal system is premised on the constitutional guarantee of presumption of innocence. All are presumed innocent until proven guilty by due process of law. If forensic psychology convincingly provides the tools for predicting criminal behavior, the state will have to decide whether to permit intrusive intervention in people's lives *before* any crime is committed. This would surely seem to encroach on the presumption of innocence.

Perhaps, then, one of the most valuable contributions positivism makes to the criminal justice system is in compelling us to consider just how far a free and ethical society should allow criminology to be applied to all of our lives. Given the means to predict crime, at what point does the application of those means become a graver threat than crime itself?

The Least You Need to Know

♦ Cesare Lombroso (1835–1909), sometimes called the "father of criminology," developed positivist criminology, premised on the concept of the born criminal.

♦ Lombroso believed that the born criminal was an atavistic throwback to a presocial stage of evolution and that, therefore, criminal behavior was antisocial.

♦ Society contributes to the development of criminality in the born criminal by treating him as an outcast.

♦ In biological positivism, criminals are born; in psychological positivism, they are created—typically by some acquired mental or emotional disorder or emotionally traumatic injury.

♦ Despite serious shortcomings, positivism is most evident in contemporary criminology in the work of forensic psychologists and psychiatrists.

Chapter 4

Strain Theory

In This Chapter

- Durkheim pioneers strain theory
- Social pathology: egoism and anomie
- Role of social change in producing crime
- Shaw and McKay on juvenile delinquency
- Merton's crime-generating "American Dream machine"
- A critique of strain theory

As you've learned, classical criminology locates the cause of crime in individual choice, whereas positivist criminology attributes crime to causes beyond the choice of the individual. Nevertheless, both schools of thought focus on the individual, either as a maker of choices or as a biological and psychological being subject to hereditary or acquired pathologies that doom or, at least, predispose him or her toward crime.

In contrast to both classical and positivist criminology, strain theory focuses not on the individual, but on society, specifically on how certain social forces create criminal attitudes and criminal behavior. If positivism attributes crime to individual pathology, strain theory attributes it to social pathology, certain economic and cultural "strains" created by society.

The Focus Shifts

The focus of criminology from the individual to society coincided with the development of sociology as an academic discipline beginning in the mid-nineteenth century and continuing into the early twentieth. As positivism was the product of a belief that the approaches, assumptions, and techniques of the natural sciences could be applied to the study of the behavior of individuals, so sociology applied the tools of natural science to the study of society.

Why study society scientifically? To challenge the status quo and allow social scientists, free of moral, cultural, and religious prejudices, to suggest new solutions to social problems, including the problem of crime.

The French Connection: Emile Durkheim

Emile Durkheim was born in Epinal, eastern France, in 1858, and was educated in his hometown, at the University of Epinal, and then in Paris, at the Superior Normal School. In 1882, he served in various professorial positions throughout France before accepting a permanent appointment at the University of Bordeaux in 1887. There he taught the first course in sociology ever to be offered by a French university. Fifteen years later, he joined the faculty of the University of Paris.

Emile Durkheim.

(Image from Arttoday.com)

As a sociologist, Durkheim was a pioneer of the early mainstream. He articulated the key sociological assumption that the individual does not create society, but is, in fact, the product of society. Following from this, he concluded that society does not respond to the actions of the individual, but, rather, that the individual conforms to society's norms and expectations.

Positivist criminologists, of course, also treated crime in relation to society, but defined it as a transgression of social norms and expectations. Most of Durkheim's fellow sociologists would have agreed. Durkheim, however, saw crime not as deviance from social expectations, but as inherent in society, something as normal as birth and death. A crime-free society was probably impossible and certainly undesirable, Durkheim argued, because it would require a degree of moral and conceptual standardization that would create a race of automatons.

Durkheim went even further. He suggested that, viewed objectively, crime was actually *beneficial* to society, just as the challenges of survival are beneficial to a biological species. As environmental adversity forces a species to evolve in response to the challenge, so crime compels societies to evolve in terms of improving its systems of law and criminal justice. Without crime, there would be no law.

Sworn Statement

Crime brings together honest men and concentrates them.

—Emile Durkheim, *The Division of Labor in Society*, 1893

Sick People or Sick Society?

Durkheim delved deeper than these broad generalizations. He proposed that, by nature, the desires of the individual were without limit, and that it is society that gives direction and control to desire. From this assumption, he developed two key concepts.

Although crime is normal in society, it is possible for crime to assume disproportionate dimensions in pathological societies. *Egoism* is the label Durkheim gave to the desires of the "presocial self," the desires society must shape and limit if civilization is to survive and develop. In some pathological societies, there is an undue

Talking the Talk

Egoism, as used by Emile Durkheim, describes desires of the "presocial self," desires society must shape and limit if civilization is to survive and develop. **Anomie,** as used by Durkheim, describes the absence of social regulation of individual desires due to the lack of strong social values.

emphasis placed on egoism, and individuals are encouraged to pursue their desires with little or no restriction. The norms of such a society are in themselves deviant and foster crime.

The second concept Durkheim derived from his assumptions concerning the role of individual desire in society is *anomie*, the absence of social regulation, so that individual desires, while not encouraged as normative social values, are not sufficiently held in check. An emphasis on egoism is a deep-seated social value, whereas anomie characterizes societies in flux, where rapid changes outpace the society's ability to formulate new values and controls.

Feeling Strained: Normal Folks in Abnormal Situations

Pathological societies—societies dominated by egoism or by anomie—typically create abnormally high levels of crime. This is because such societies are plagued by social strains, especially during periods of intense change, such as the rapid influx of immigrants, economic hardship (economic depression and unemployment, for instance), or the moral effects and aftereffects of war (for example, the gangster culture that developed during the "Roaring Twenties," following World War I). It is not that people become abnormal during such periods of strain, but that normal people find themselves suddenly thrust into abnormal situations.

Strain Theory Distilled

As we will see in the next chapter, strain theory has continued to develop and is an important school of criminological thought today. Through all of its permutations, however, it has retained certain basic assumptions, beginning with the principal notion that crime is a social phenomenon, related to and shaped by broad social structures and processes.

Definition and Focus

For the strain theorist, crime is natural. While crime is a normal feature of society, it is defined by society as a violation of social consensus. Because crime is a social phenomenon, the strain theorist focuses his or her inquiry not on the individual—his personal pathology or his specific biological traits—but on how society creates crime by applying certain factors, forces, and strains to create a situation in which the individual has severely limited social options available.

The strain theorist examines the structure of opportunities a particular society offers. For example, in many American urban immigrant neighborhoods early in the twentieth century, available opportunities included a limited array of low-paying, undesirable labor or participation in gangs and organized crime.

Also subject to study are the nature of social learning—how individuals absorb the values of their society—and various subcultures, especially subcultures affecting young people.

Causes of Crime and Criminality

Strain theorists locate the cause of crime in dysfunctional or pathological social structures and value systems. In short, crime is a symptom of social pathology.

Most strain theory analyses focus on the strains created between perceived social values and the inadequate or inappropriate means or opportunities available to attain those values. For example, we all see many TV images depicting great wealth and privilege, but few of us are able to access the educational and other opportunities that traditionally afford entry into this realm of wealth and privilege. In the absence of these opportunities, crime becomes an alternative route to wealth and privilege.

Response and Prevention

Assuming that social strain produces crime, the most effective means of responding to crime or preventing it in the first place is to enhance available opportunities. For example, government agencies may provide free educational programs in impoverished neighborhoods.

> **By the Numbers**
>
> A Gallup Poll conducted in August–September 2000, suggests that strain theory strikes a chord with about a third of the general population. Twenty-three percent of those asked if lack of good jobs for young people was important in causing crime responded that its importance was critical. Thirty-five percent thought it very important, and 31 percent somewhat important. Only 10 percent believed lack of jobs was not important. However, the majority of respondents (59 percent) thought drug use was *the* most important cause of crime.

Another means of reducing crime is to resocialize offenders or potential offenders by, for example, providing an alternative to the environment that fostered criminality.

This is the assumption behind most parole arrangements, which prohibit the parolee from associating with known criminals. It is also the idea behind any number of neighborhood youth associations, such as the Boys' Clubs and Girls' Clubs, which seek to keep kids off the streets.

Under strain theory, crime prevention and response strategies combine individual rehabilitation with broad social programs.

Modern Problems

Strain theory is very much the product of modern times; that is, times characterized by rapid and even accelerating change. Social commentators have frequently pointed to the lag, during the last 100 years, between the accelerating pace of technological and economic development versus the reliance on the status quo that characterizes the development of social values. This lag creates social strain.

The World Between the World Wars

The American novelist Ernest Hemingway attributed to the Paris-based American writer, art collector, and all-round cultural den mother Gertrude Stein the phrase "lost generation" to describe the young people who had experienced the devastation of World War I. This unprecedented, destructive, and fruitless war wrecked traditional values yet provided no adequate moral replacement for them. The 1920s fostered self-indulgent egoism as well as anomie, a social climate conducive to an explosion of crime.

Society in Crisis

The collective emotional crisis that followed World War I was played out in a time of relative economic abundance. Business boomed during the 1920s, especially in the United States. However, industry produced more goods than consumers could afford to purchase, and, in 1929, the economy collapsed in a precipitous stock market crash.

Poverty, Immigration, and Crime

The Great Depression of the 1930s plunged the nation and most of the world into profound economic and social crisis. Whereas the social strain of the 1920s had been chiefly a dearth of compelling social values, the strain of the 1930s was primarily economic—a severe and sudden reduction in available opportunity. Organized crime, which had been born in the self-indulgent 1920s (in the United States, especially, in connection with national Prohibition), became more thoroughly institutionalized as gangsterism.

During the 1930s, social strain theorists focused on how poverty and unemployment affected crime, as well as on the role of immigration. During this period, the economic position of the individual in society came to be regarded as perhaps the single most important factor in the commission of crime.

The Chicago School

Early in the 1940s, Clifford R. Shaw and Henry D. McKay, criminologists based in Chicago, studied juvenile delinquency during three periods—1900 to 1906, 1917 to 1923, and 1927 to 1933—and developed a theory of *social disorganization*. They found that crime was often concentrated in certain neighborhoods at certain times and that it was related to shifts in basic social organization, intensifying during a period of relative disorganization and diminishing again as reorganization took hold. Shaw and McKay concluded that delinquency should be viewed as a natural part of immigrant settlement, because, during initial settlement, social controls that normally foster conformist behavior are disrupted.

In their *Juvenile Delinquency in Urban Areas* (1942), Shaw and McKay used the "concentric zone model" of urban development, published by Robert E. Park and Ernest W. Burgess in 1925. Studying Chicago, Park and Burgess distinguished five natural urban areas:

♦ A central business district at the city's core

♦ A surrounding transitional zone occupied by recent immigrant groups and characterized by deteriorated housing, factories, and abandoned buildings

♦ A working-class zone surrounding the transitional zone, characterized by single-family tenements

♦ A residential zone of single-family homes, with yards and garages, surrounding the working-class zone

♦ The commuter zone in the outermost ring, described as the suburbs

Talking the Talk

Social disorganization is a phrase coined by sociologists Clifford R. Shaw and Henry D. McKay, who concluded that criminal behavior intensified during periods in which immigrants were in the process of settling urban neighborhoods. At these times, the local structure of society was in flux—disorganized; over time, as the local structure was reorganized (and as immigrant groups resettled in "better" neighborhoods), crime diminished.

Shaw and McKay concluded that juvenile delinquency rates corresponded to the five natural urban areas. Over time, delinquency rates remained high in the transitional zone surrounding the central business district, no matter which immigrant group lived there. That is, immigrant Group A showed a high delinquency rate when it lived in this zone; the rate for Group A diminished when it resettled in one of the outer zones; however, the new residents of the transitional zone, Group B, showed high delinquency rates, comparable to the earlier rates of Group A.

Crime in the "Age of Anxiety"

The onset of World War II brought an end to the Great Depression by sharply increasing demand for production and providing extensive employment. The first two decades following the war were economic boom times and, in the United States, a period marked by an emphasis on political and social conformity. Despite economic well-being and conformity, however, crime not only remained a serious problem, but, in the United States, actually increased.

The poet W. H. Auden called the 1950s outwardly prosperous and placidly conformist, the "age of anxiety." Clearly, there was trouble below the surface.

Case in Point

The popular culture of the 1950s reflected an underlying social anxiety. Films such as *The Wild One* (1954), *The Blackboard Jungle* (1955), and *Rebel Without a Cause* (1955) portrayed restless youths whose delinquency, in various ways, reflected either a paucity of constructive opportunity or a weakness of social values. The point was this: Even in times of relative peace and prosperity, social forces were at work creating the kind of social strain that was productive of crime.

Crime and Prosperity: Robert K. Merton's "Dream Machine"

Beginning in the late 1930s and carrying his work well into the mid-1950s, the criminologist Robert K. Merton investigated the persistence of crime in a nation enjoying flush times.

Merton built solidly on strain theory. He pictured society as a machine in which cultural goals—what the society proposes that its members should strive for—interact with the means that are believed to be legally and morally legitimate ways of attaining those goals. If the social machine is well built and properly adjusted, the legitimate means will always be available to deliver all members to their socially sanctioned goals.

Robert K. Merton.

(Image from Columbia University)

Merton argued that, in American society, the controlling goal is the "American Dream," a vision of how life should be. In the 1950s, this vision of success included a good job, wealth, respect, and a house in the suburbs. Integral with the American Dream is the socially sanctioned belief that anyone who works hard can attain success. Failure to realize the American Dream is a failure to work hard enough. Work harder and be patient, and the dream will be yours.

In fact, American society prescribes more than hard work. It calls for hard work in obtaining an education and then hard work on behalf of an employer, who will reward the effort with progressively better jobs and salary.

If the machine of American society really did operate this smoothly, prescribing the goals and invariably providing the means to achieve them, there would be little crime. However, not everyone enjoys equal access to good education and worthwhile employment. Many find their paths to the American Dream blocked, because the benefits of American society are distributed unequally.

It is these inequalities, even amidst relative affluence, that create social strains. As Merton pictured it, five responses are possible when a gap exists between socially approved goals and the available means of achieving them:

1. **Conformism.** Some accept the socially defined goals and find access to the institutionalized (socially legitimate) means of attaining them.

2. **Innovation.** Some accept the socially defined goals, but do not find access to the institutionalized (socially legitimate) means of attaining them. These individuals may resort to innovative means of attaining the goals, some of them illegal—robbery, for example.

3. **Ritualism.** Some accept the socially defined goals, but realize that they cannot hope to attain them. Despite this realization, they continue pursuing the institutionalized (socially legitimate) means of attaining them, even though the means fail to produce the promised outcome.

4. **Retreatism.** Some reject the socially defined goals as well as the institutionalized (socially legitimate) means of attaining them. These individuals drop out of society in various ways, some of which involve crime (the use and trade in illegal drugs, for instance).

5. **Rebellion.** Some substitute their own goals and their own means for attaining them. They march to a different drummer. This may involve the commission of crime, or this may result in creating alternative lifestyles that exist within the law. The hippie movement of the 1960s is a prime example. Hippies lived on the margins of society—and, often, of the law as well.

Strained to the Limit?

Social strain theory compels us to examine the phenomenon of crime in a new and fresh light, and it offers greater flexibility, allows for greater complexity, and admits of more positive response to crime and criminality than either classical criminology or positivist approaches do. However, strain theory is open to criticism on various fronts.

Swallowing the Status Quo

Although strain theory requires an examination of accepted social values, it tends, ultimately, to accept the status quo uncritically. That is, strain theory assumes that all people in society either want to achieve the same general goals or (as in the case of Merton) at least define themselves in relation to these goals.

Oversimplification as Explanation

The more or less uncritical acceptance of the status quo leads to another criticism of social strain theory: that it oversimplifies social structures, social values, and the relation between individuals and social values. The tendency to oversimplify is carried over into the remedies for crime strain theory typically suggests— programs to improve educational and vocational opportunities, and efforts to resocialize offenders and potential offenders. The assumption is that the conditions that create crime are "fixable" and that crime can be tinkered away by appropriate social engineering.

> **Sworn Statement**
>
> A major criticism is that strain theorists tend to focus exclusively on working-class crime. Researchers who adopt strain theory typically work from official crime statistics, which suggest that most offenses are committed by the working class. There is little attempt to study white-collar crime, much of which never appears on police blotters.

Opening New Vistas

Whatever the shortcomings of strain theory, it did open up an important new area of inquiry: the role of society in generating crime. This took the criminological debate to a new level, away from an exclusive focus on the offender and toward exploring the means by which society influences the behavior of groups. The new focus invited an unprecedented degree of activism in coping with crime and criminality. Instead of merely responding to crime with punishment or with intrusive attempts at psychological intervention, strain theory suggested introducing a variety of social programs and economic reforms to prevent crime.

The Least You Need to Know

◆ In contrast to classical criminology and positivist criminology, strain theory focuses not on causes of crime within the individual, but causes of crime within society.

◆ The social strains that create crime are the result of social pathologies, such as egoism and anomie, and the frustrating disjunction between the values society proposes as desirable and the scarcity of means society offers for attaining those values.

◆ According to strain theorists, rapid social change (as in new urban immigrant communities) can produce strains that create an environment conducive to crime.

◆ Robert K. Merton argued that the relatively high crime rate in prosperous America resulted from social inequality: unequal access to the "American Dream."

Part 2

In Theory

Part 1 surveyed the history of criminology through the first half of the twentieth century. Part 2 of the book explores criminology as it is practiced today. Leading schools of thought on crime and the social response to crime include Strain Theory, Labeling, Marxist Theory, Feminist Criminology, Realism on the right and on the left, the Restorative Justice approach, and most radical of all, Critical Criminology.

Each approach to criminology offers answers, but also leaves questions. After more than 200 years of hard thinking, the field of criminology remains a work in progress.

Chapter 5

Current Criminology: Some Leading Perspectives

In This Chapter

◆ Focus of contemporary strain theory

◆ Social ecology and other recent strain theory concepts

◆ Criminology addresses youth gangs

◆ Crime as a social label and stigma

◆ Marxist approaches to criminology

◆ Feminist criminology: an attempt to level the field

Historically, the great movements in the development of criminology are the classical approach pioneered by Beccaria and Bentham at the end of the eighteenth century, the positivist approach introduced by Lombroso in the nineteenth century, and strain theory, first proposed by Durkheim late in the nineteenth century and carried by others into the twentieth and twenty-first.

All of these approaches remain influential in various aspects of contemporary criminology. Much of our criminal justice system today is founded on the classical idea that people are individually responsible for their own actions. Many criminologists as well as criminal investigators bow to positivism in their reliance on the work of forensic psychologists and psychiatrists.

Perhaps most currently active of the three major historical streams of criminology is strain theory, which is bolstered by extensive contemporary academic interest in sociology. It is just one of several contemporary approaches to criminology, which are the subjects of this chapter and the next.

Strain Theory Today

Contemporary strain theorists focus on four specific areas within the overall assumption that the causes of crime and criminality are to be found in the effects of social strains on individuals and groups. The four areas are social ecology, social disorganization, social development, and the phenomena associated with youth gangs. In the following sections we'll take a closer look at each.

Social Ecology

For many theorists, social ecology is virtually synonymous with strain theory. Social ecology is the study of the social and physical features of a particular environment for the purpose of determining how individuals and groups act and interact with these features. Theorists believe that anyone who proposes to look for the sources of crime in the social environment must carefully study the social ecology of the city, neighborhood, or place in question.

Social ecology includes the social as well as the physical features of an environment. Researchers in this field study the spatial features of criminal offenses by carefully examining the environment of particular neighborhoods. Researchers note how individuals and groups act and interact in various parts of the environment at various times of day. They attempt to draw conclusions concerning the processes of social regulation in a given neighborhood or even in a specific residential or commercial site.

The results of the social ecology approach may be used to make broad theoretical assumptions about the nature of crime, especially in urban settings. The research may also be applied to particular neighborhoods or parts of neighborhoods in order to develop practical crime prevention and policing programs tailor-made to the specific situation.

Conclusions based in large part on the approaches and assumptions of social ecology have sometimes had dramatic effect. During much of the two decades following World War II, many American cities rushed to house the poor in high-rise "projects," which replaced low-rise residential buildings in many neighborhoods. Many of these projects rapidly degenerated into "vertical ghettoes," environments that fostered and intensified crime, especially violent crime. In a number of cases, social ecologists concluded that the only effective way of reducing crime in the projects was to eliminate the environment, to tear the buildings down—a drastic step that, in several instances, was in fact taken.

Case in Point

Chicago's Robert Taylor Homes opened in November 1962 as the world's largest public housing project, a complex stretching more than two miles along State Street on Chicago's South Side. Begun with high hopes, the Robert Taylor Homes soon became a national symbol of urban squalor. For years, unofficial tenant leaders tolerated but regulated such enterprises as drug dealing and prostitution, but when gang leaders began to transform youth gangs into full-time drug-dealing enterprises, the gangs quickly overwhelmed the tenant leaders. Shootouts and other violence became routine, and the police refused to enter the project except to conduct massive, ineffectual raids. By 1992, with the project half empty and plagued by crime and desolate poverty, the city of Chicago decided to raze the Robert Taylor Homes and its other high-rise housing projects.

Social Disorganization

Another approach to the analysis of the social environment is to examine and evaluate social disorganization on the level of a particular community. Social disorganization describes such disruptive factors as poverty, broken families, inadequate housing, and general isolation from the cultural mainstream, all of which contribute to the creation of crime.

Criminologists who study social disorganization typically focus on inner-city neighborhoods in an effort to define a "culture of violence" created by a combination of such disruptive factors as poverty, broken families, and inadequate housing, as well as general isolation from the cultural mainstream. Such conditions create an urban underclass, which, blocked from achieving success in the social mainstream, looks to the forces and values of the neighborhood itself for social status. In such neighborhoods, violent crime is not only acceptable, but often rewarded. It may well be perceived as the only available means of survival.

The social disorganization approach offers a compelling answer to the question of why some socially disadvantaged or marginalized young people have a greater tendency to commit crime than others in similar socioeconomic situations. If the neighborhood reinforces and rewards criminal behavior, the crime rate will rise. If the neighborhood does not provide this reinforcement, the crime rate is likely to be lower, even if that community consists of a disadvantaged population.

Social Development

Social development theorists combine strain theory with positivist approaches (that is, biological and psychological research) to formulate models of how personal, family, and community factors influence life decisions, including the decisions that result in criminal behavior.

Whereas social ecologists and researchers who focus on social disorganization typically study very specific environments, the social development theorist seeks more broadly to identify general risk factors associated with crime, especially crime perpetrated by youthful offenders. Typical risk factors identified and studied include the following:

- **Predisposing biological factors,** such as prenatal influences (for example, substance abuse during pregnancy), hyperactivity, attention deficit disorder, neuropsychological disorders, and the like

- **Level of intelligence,** including the effect of low nonverbal intelligence, problems with abstract reasoning, and learning disorders

- **Family life,** including the level and nature of parental discipline, parental praise, and parental violence; large family size may result in overcrowding, insufficient attention, and poor supervision

- **Broken homes,** including the absence of a father or mother, or parental criminal behavior

- **Socioeconomic hardship,** including outright poverty, poor housing, inadequate nourishment, and inadequate clothing

- **Peer-related factors,** such as peer pressure to use drugs or commit crimes

◆ **School-related factors,** including the use or absence of praise, punishment, the quality and quantity of attention from teachers

◆ **General community influences,** such as deterioration of the physical environment, overcrowding, type and adequacy of housing, availability of positive neighborhood activities, and availability of transportation

The social development approach to criminology is rich, complex, and ambitious. While it may produce some specific suggestions for steps to reduce crime, the attempt to evaluate a broad array of factors may also produce an overwhelming result, implying that the only truly effective means of reducing crime in a particular place is to change just about everything in that place.

Youth Gangs

Youth gangs have been of interest to criminologists at least since the 1950s, but only recently have they become an area of intensive study. Instead of regarding gang activity as merely group delinquency, criminologists use strain theory, especially the approaches of social ecology and social disorganization, to make precise observations and definitions concerning specific types of youth gangs, their origin, and their behavior. Recent studies have concentrated on the formative role of racism and ethnic divisiveness, in addition to such factors as poverty and unemployment.

Police organizations have been especially supportive of recent criminological efforts to understand gang behavior. As organized, community-focused, violent crime, gang activity has long been a major and highly resistant policing problem. By learning more about the nature of gangs, police hope to create more effective policies.

> **By the Numbers**
>
> In 2000, the Los Angeles Police Department released a survey of citywide gang crime. Four hundred seven gangs were counted, with a total membership of 64,771. According to *The New York Times* (April 11, 2002) there were 331 gang-related deaths in Los Angeles in 2000 and 346 gang-related deaths in 2001. LAPD officials fear that the casualty count in 2002 will be the highest in a decade.

Labeling: Crime as a Social Process

As different as classicism, positivism, and strain theory are from one another, they make at least one assumption in common. They all regard crime as a given, as

Talking the Talk

Labeling is an approach to criminology that treats crime not as an objective given, but as a social process. What most call crime is actually the label that the social mainstream applies to behavior it deems threatening or deviant.

something that exists, that happens, and that can be observed, recorded, and, perhaps, prevented, controlled, or otherwise coped with. Much of the question of what constitutes a crime is either taken for granted or addressed by the concept of consensus—the idea that all crime in some way violates certain core values and norms jointly honored by social consensus. In any given society, for example, just about everybody would agree that murder and robbery are crimes.

A recent approach to criminology, *labeling*, refuses to take crime as a given.

Is It a Crime?

The labeling theorist sees crime not as an objective phenomenon—a given that exists "out there" in the world—but as a social process; that is, as the outcome of specific kinds of human interaction. "Crime" is the label that the social mainstream—the relatively elite and the relatively powerful—apply to behavior it deems deviant or threatening. Crime is not an absolute *object*, but a *perception* of some type of behavior.

The Powerful ...

In practical terms, according to labeling theory, crime is what the criminal justice system says it is. That is because the criminal justice system is operated and controlled by the segment of society that holds all the power.

... and the Powerless

Those who lack power in a society—the poor, the underprivileged, victims of ethnic or racial discrimination and oppression—may act in ways deemed criminal by those who do hold power.

But labeling theory goes beyond this simple relationship. An important aspect of the labeling analysis is the stigmatization that occurs because of the labeling itself. A person labeled a criminal typically begins to act in conformity with the role prescribed by the label. Thus, according to the theory, labeling does not merely designate crime, it actually creates it.

Labeling alters the self-image of the offender. Even worse, the label sticks to him, altering the way others see him. Labeled a criminal, outcast from the mainstream, the offender tends to seek the company of others similarly labeled. In this way, his criminal behavior is reinforced, and a criminal subculture develops.

In strain theory, criminal behavior may result from blocked opportunities; society proposes certain desirable goals, but then blocks access to them. In labeling theory, social opportunities are blocked by the labeling process itself.

The Concept of Decriminalization

The most challenging and controversial implication of labeling theory is the proposition that the potentially negative consequences of labeling—that is, stigmatization—may outweigh the social benefit of intervention in certain behaviors. That is, by labeling a given act a crime and arresting the "criminal," the resulting stigma may propel the individual into a career of such activity. To avoid this, labeling theorists suggest a broad program of decriminalization, which redefines certain offenses as noncriminal or reduces the penalties for them.

Decriminalization aims to avoid stigmatization, especially in young offenders. The underlying assumption is that, for most people, certain behaviors traditionally labeled as crimes are, in fact, transitory. Why, then, risk expanding and extending the consequences of such acts by labeling them? Instead of saddling a young offender with a criminal conviction for drug use, he or she should be given counseling. Instead of sending a young property vandal to juvenile hall, assign him or her to perform non-punitive community service, without recording the arrest or conviction.

Labeling theorists suggest that the proper response to a whole range of so-called victimless crimes should be tolerance, and criminal labeling should be reserved only for the most serious and harmful offenses.

Crime as Class Warfare

Labeling theory is built on the assumption that society consists of the relatively powerful and the relatively powerless. The source of the elite's power is economic, and one important means by which that economic power is jealously guarded is by labeling certain acts of the powerless as crimes. Thus, labeling theory sees society as necessarily torn by conflict between the haves and have-nots. It is not a very long leap from the labeling perspective to other theories of crime as the product of class warfare.

The Marxist Challenge to Traditional Criminology

The analysis of society developed during the nineteenth century by Karl Marx (1818–1883) and Friedrich Engels (1820–1895) has exerted a profound, complex, and extremely wide-ranging influence over modern social and political thought. Marxism has driven revolutions in Russia, China, Vietnam, Cuba, and many other places. It has also driven a revolution in the thinking of some contemporary criminologists.

Marxism holds that creativity—the capacity to work objects of nature to satisfy one's needs—is the single characteristic that most uniquely defines humanity. A person, however, is a being who labors not just for himself, but for the species. Ideally, everything produced by human beings should be enjoyed by all human beings. But the advent of capitalism distorted this ideal situation. In a capitalist society, one class of people (the proletariat) works to create goods and services consumed by another class (the bourgeoisie) in exchange for wages.

> **Sworn Statement**
>
> The ruling ideas of each age have ever been the ideas of its ruling class.
>
> —Karl Marx and Friedrich Engels, *The Communist Manifesto*, 1848

This inherently unnatural situation creates a world built by the proletariat but owned by the non-laboring bourgeoisie. Thus the mass of humanity is alienated, and the resulting society is in a perpetual state of conflict, which routinely produces (among other negative outcomes) crime.

According to the Marxist criminologist, the bourgeoisie, who control the means of production and own the products of labor, also have the power to control the criminal justice system.

Crime and Human Rights

Because the definition of crime as codified in society's laws is biased, reflecting the interests of the ruling class and supporting the continuation of capitalism, many types of social harm are inadequately accounted for in conventional criminal law. Therefore, the Marxist definition of crime is, first and foremost, any activity that assaults human rights and causes social injury.

Crimes of the Powerful

For the Marxist, the most serious crimes are often those least recognized by capitalist criminal codes. These are the crimes of the powerful, the owners of the means of production, and are driven by economic motives. Economic crimes include exploitation of labor (for example, violation of labor laws), destruction of the natural environment for profit, fraud perpetrated on consumers, price gouging, price fixing, unfair competition, and the like. All are motivated by some form of individual (or corporate) greed, a desire to augment one's wealth.

A second class of crimes committed by the powerful involve the state—either officially or through the action of corrupt officials. Such crimes include malfeasance in office, corruption, bribe taking, misappropriation of public funds, violation of civil rights, and so on.

Crimes of the Oppressed

The Marxist criminologist by no means ignores the crimes of the less powerful, the proletariat. The cause of such crimes, however, is seen as economic, social, or a combination of these factors. For example, there is a host of subsistence-related crimes, including shoplifting, burglary, robbery, and even welfare fraud. These and the like are primarily economic in motivation. Other crimes are more sociocultural in nature—in effect, acts of social protest and revolution. Crimes of this type include vandalism, certain instances of assault, rioting, and various disturbances of the peace.

Who Is a Criminal?

Whatever the nature of the crime, its cause is always to be found in the unequal structure of class relations in capitalist society. Thus, the powerful commit crimes intended to maintain or enhance their position of dominance, while the underclass commits crimes in response to inequality. They need money or goods, or they need to vent frustration and outrage.

Whether powerful or powerless, a criminal exhibits certain behaviors in response to the essential inequality of capitalist society.

Response and Prevention

While the Marxist criminologist accounts for crimes perpetrated by the powerful as well as for those committed by the underclass, it is clear that the crimes of the powerful are of greater consequence because they cause much greater economic and social harm than mere "street crime." Therefore, the Marxist calls for a shift in the conventional focus of the criminal justice system, which typically prosecutes more working-class crime than white-collar crime—let alone corporate crime—and which treats street crime with greater severity than crimes committed by the powerful.

Ultimately, however, the best and most thorough response to crime is not to make a few adjustments to the criminal justice system. Rather, it is to redress social inequality by rejecting capitalism. Crime flourishes under inequality; therefore, redistribute the resources of society according to human need, not human greed, and collectivize ownership and control of the means of production.

Opponents of Marxist criminology point to the fact that, historically, such redistribution and collectivization have been effected only by state-sanctioned coercion of the most oppressive and violent sort, in which human rights are ruthlessly trampled. Moreover, the maintenance of Marxist governments has also, historically, required a sustained policy of human rights abuse and has resulted in inefficient and inadequate economies.

Feminist Criminology

Like Marxist criminology, feminist criminology focuses on power: who wields it in society and who most feels its impact. Whereas Marxist criminology sees crime as the product of the inequalities built into capitalist society, the leading premise of feminist criminology is that Western society is essentially patriarchal and that female subordination is part and parcel of such a society. This inequality makes its presence felt in the criminal justice system.

Crime in a Man's World

Feminist criminology is concerned primarily with crimes against women and with the status of female offenders. To begin with, feminist criminology addresses the almost total neglect of women in criminological thought and research. The field of criminology is dominated by male researchers. To what degree can decades of research derived from studying male offenders be applied to female offenders?

By the Numbers

In 2000, 22.2 percent of those arrested in the United States were women. Of those arrested for violent crimes, 17.4 percent were women.

Second, feminist criminology calls for recognition that the criminal justice system—police personnel, lawyers, judges, legislators, prison officials—is overwhelmingly male. This surely skews the perspective of the system.

The National Crime Victimization Survey (NCVS), begun in 1972, is one of two Justice Department measures of crime in the United States. In 1992, the NCVS questionnaire was extensively redesigned in response to research by feminist criminologists. New questions addressing rape resulted in a 157 percent increase in rape and sexual assault victimization rates and a 155 percent increase in reports of victimization by relatives.

Sexualization

Sexualization describes the process by which a male-dominated criminal justice system deals with female offenders and female victims, unconsciously but invariably applying to them gender-related criteria based on appearance, behavior, and marital status, all reflecting male ideas of what properly constitutes "femininity."

Because of sexualization, the patriarchal criminal justice system typically prosecutes prostitutes more vigorously than it does their male customers. Feminist criminologists attribute this inequity to a male-dominated view of morality and the nature of what is deemed sexually deviant for women but sexually acceptable for men.

Female victims also suffer at the hands of the male-controlled criminal justice system. In the case of rape victims, police and prosecutors are often influenced by their perception of whether or not the victim was "deserving" or "undeserving." Did she somehow "invite" the assault? And how does the assault fit into the pattern of her past behavior?

Case in Point

On February 10, 1992, an Indianapolis jury found World Heavyweight boxing champion Mike Tyson guilty of rape and two lesser charges. The sensational case highlighted issues feminist criminologists had frequently raised, especially relating to "date rape." Prosecuting attorney Barbara Trathen argued that, on July 19, 1991, Tyson lured an 18-year-old Miss Black America beauty pageant contestant to a hotel room and raped her. Physical evidence presented included vaginal abrasions, which suggested that the sex was not consensual. Tyson's attorney, Vincent Fuller, countered that Tyson made his intentions known to all contestants at the pageant. Fuller also pointed out that the woman had removed a panty shield in Tyson's bathroom (suggesting that she was preparing for sex). Prosecutor Trathen argued: "Mike Tyson used his fame and reputation in the same manner a thug in an alley uses a knife or a gun." Tyson was handed a six-year sentence and paroled in 1995, after serving three years.

Sex, Gender, and Crime

Feminist criminology calls for a reevaluation of attitudes toward women as offenders and as victims. The criminal justice system sexualizes offenses committed by women, but it does not do the same in the case of offenses committed by men. This introduces a prejudicial double standard. For example, young female shoplifters may be more vigorously prosecuted than young men who commit the same offense, because theft is deemed unladylike, but "boys will be boys."

Some crimes may be prejudicially related to male notions of female sexuality, biological drives, and "hormones." Male prosecutors, defenders, and judges may operate from assumptions about the essentially passive, weak, or inherently deceitful "nature" of women.

In the case of victims, males may excuse or mitigate violence committed against women by attributing such acts to provocation or the "irresistible" force of the male sex drive. Men in the legal system may indeed believe that women "naturally" have fewer or lesser rights than men, that women are the weaker sex and are incapable of the same level of judgment as men.

Response and Prevention

The feminist approach to criminology seeks to expose the unconscious and institutionalized assumptions of a male-dominated criminal justice system operating within and on behalf of a patriarchal society. Key issues include …

- The double standard, by which female offenses are prejudicially sexualized, while male offenses are not.

- The intent and use of various laws to control female behavior by criminalizing certain offenses as gender specific.

- The status of many women as victims, whether of physical and emotional abuse or of economic dependency.

- The status of women as victims of male violence—most of which goes unrecognized.

- The relative powerlessness of many women to protect themselves against violent crime.

At the very least, feminist criminology seeks to open up an area of study that, through most of the history of criminology, has been ignored. Researchers in the field also seek to raise consciousness at all levels of the criminal justice system, so that women do not become the victims of unconscious but deeply entrenched male biases.

Ultimately, as with Marxist criminology, the feminist approach suggests that the essential inequalities of contemporary criminology and the criminal justice system cannot be significantly corrected by supplying a few pieces of new data or revising a few procedures. While affirmative action policies might be used to induct more women into the criminal justice system, much more is necessary to prevent many crimes committed by women and to prevent many that are committed against them. The conclusions of feminist criminology suggest that society as a whole must be reformed, so that women are accorded greater social, political, and economic equality. Like the Marxists, the feminists see the biases and blind spots of criminology and the criminal justice system not as aberrations, but as reflections and embodiments of the larger society these fields serve.

The Least You Need to Know

◆ Strain theory, first developed in the 1930s, continues to exert a powerful influence on contemporary criminological thought.

◆ Recent strain theorists have used social ecology and other approaches to make intensive studies of youth gang behavior.

◆ Labeling theory challenges the idea of crime as an objective phenomenon and argues instead that it is the product of social labeling and resulting stigmatization.

◆ Marxist criminology approaches crime as the product of inequalities inherent in capitalist society.

◆ Feminist criminology sees women as a permanent underclass, who are treated prejudicially by a male-dominated criminal justice system that serves a patriarchal society.

Chapter 6

Current Criminology: Right and Left

In This Chapter

- The New Right perspective

- New Right conservatives and libertarians

- The Left Realist alternative

- The concept of restorative justice

- The most radical challenge: critical criminology

The contemporary approaches to criminology outlined in the previous chapter had their early development, for the most part, during the 1960s and 1970s, a period of rapid, predominantly liberal social change. Strain theory, Marxist criminology, and feminist criminology approach the field from liberal, even radical perspectives, and each poses a challenge to the status quo.

Not all recent criminological thought has emerged from left of center, however. A "New Right" criminology has emerged to call into question the various liberal approaches. Partially in response to the New Right, even more innovative movements have developed in the field of criminology. We will review all of these, right and left, in this chapter.

Contemporary Criminology Under Indictment

New Right criminology makes what it deems an appeal to common sense; however, "common sense" seems to be defined as the popular, media-influenced picture of crime in contemporary society. That is, the New Right criminology assumes that various liberal approaches to the problem of crime have failed—and have failed precisely because of their liberal political assumptions.

Talking the Talk

New Right criminology is a recent movement that offers either a conservative moral approach to crime (strict moral values, strict law enforcement, personal responsibility for behavior) or a libertarian approach (defense of personal liberty and private property, least official intervention possible, personal responsibility for behavior).

What is the evidence of this failure?

◆ High crime rates

◆ A sense that the criminal justice system is generally "soft" on crime

◆ A sense that the criminal justice system bends over backward to favor the accused

◆ A sense that police forces are understaffed and hampered by liberal policies that restrict their power

◆ A sense that victims' rights are neglected and that victims deserve court-sanctioned retribution for crimes committed against them

Law and Order

The New Right puts fresh emphasis on law and order. Laws should be unambiguous and rigidly enforced. The consequences of transgression should not be an attempt at treatment or reform of the offender. These approaches are considered ineffectual. Instead, the New Right stresses punishment for crimes, punishment as social retribution, as a means of getting offenders off the streets, and as deterrence to future crime. While justice remains important, the major emphasis is on order and discipline. Crime flourishes where social discipline is lax.

The New Right Points a Finger

The New Right harks back to one of the chief tenets of classical criminology in that it does not hesitate to point the finger of blame at the offender. People make choices. If they choose the path of crime, they must pay for the choice freely made.

Rejected are positivist notions that the causes of crime are beyond the control of the individual. Rejected is the leading proposition of strain theory, that crime is created by the social environment. Rejected are Marxist and feminist perspectives, which trace the roots of crime to essential flaws in society. And emphatically rejected is the notion that crime is a social "label" or, indeed, anything other than an absolute, objective evil.

The Conservative View

The most conservative advocates of New Right criminology define crime as a violation of the law. But this is no merely legalistic definition. Because it is held that the law is the embodiment of the society's morals (which, in turn, reflect absolute religious notions of right and wrong), crime is an offense against morality.

The causes of crime are found in a combination of the inherent evil or wickedness of the offender and his failure to exercise sufficient self-discipline, self-control, and respect for authority. The only effective way to deal with such bad people is to bring strong coercive forces to bear against them in the form of long prison sentences, which emphasize punishment rather than rehabilitation, and, for capital offenses, capital punishment. Moreover, to create effective deterrence, punishment must follow the offense swiftly and surely. If anything, the criminal justice system should be weighted against the offender.

By the Numbers

Does the public attitude mesh with the criminology of the New Right? Judging from an August–September 2000 Gallup Poll, the answer is yes—and no. Asked whether they believed the criminal justice system is too tough, not tough enough, or about right in handling crime, only 3 percent of respondents answered that it was too tough, while 70 percent thought the criminal justice system was not tough enough. Twenty-two percent thought it was about right. However, asked whether it was better to cope with crime by attacking social problems or providing more law enforcement, 68 percent of respondents favored devoting more resources to attacking social problems, while only 27 percent favored more law enforcement.

In the broader picture, the New Right believes that crime may be prevented by the repeated assertion of strong social authority founded on a basis of traditional morality. Children and youths should be taught to respect authority and freely subordinate themselves to it. Successful socialization requires that respect for authority be thoroughly internalized as self-discipline.

Libertarians Speak Out

While the majority voice of New Right criminology is conservative, the libertarian view also makes itself heard. Often, the libertarian view clashes with that of the conservative right wing. For example, whereas conservatives define crime as violation of laws and, by extension, violation of morality, the libertarian defines crime as that which violates certain "natural rights" of others.

In the libertarian view, crime is an assault on personal liberty and on private property rights. This emphasis introduces a strong possibility for conflict arising from how the criminal justice system deals with crime, since some of the power and authority the conservatives would invest in police and the courts encroaches on personal liberty as well as private property rights.

While conservative and libertarian views on the definition of crime differ sharply, there is much greater concurrence on the nature of the offender. Like the conservative New Right criminologist, the libertarian believes people are fully responsible for their own actions. This being the case, punishment, retribution, and deterrence are valid responses to crime. Rehabilitation and treatment are rejected as ineffectual. However, restitution to compensate the victim of crime is strongly favored.

Although the conservative and libertarian approaches to punishment closely coincide, their views on crime prevention again sharply differ. The conservative stresses the importance of morality and self-discipline, whereas the libertarian advocates a program of decriminalization, the reduction of criminal offenses to those acts that encroach upon natural rights, paramountly individual liberty and the right to private property. Laws relating to so-called victimless crimes should be stricken altogether.

Talking the Talk

Left Realism, a recent school of criminological thought, focuses on the working class as both crime victim and offender.

Realists from the Left

Left Realism developed during the 1980s as a direct response to the emergence of the New Right perspective. Even as it moved to counter New Right conservatism, Left Realism also sought an alternative to Marxist criminology, which, it was felt, failed to address the practical realities of working-class crime.

Focus on Street Crime

Like the New Right, Left Realism takes what it believes is a common-sense, even pragmatic approach to crime. In contrast to the Marxists, the Left Realists are little concerned with determining the nature of crime. Instead, they are content to accept crime as violation of the legal code; however, the Left Realists focus on street crime, gathering data principally from local victim surveys and mainly targeting inner-city locations.

Crime: By and Against the Working Class

Whereas the New Right conservatives see crime as a threat to morality and the social establishment, and whereas Marxists stress crimes of the powerful, which victimize the working class, the Left Realists focus on street crime as crime committed *by* the working class *against* the working class.

This is the controlling perspective of the Left Realism: The working class is studied both as offender and as victim. In contrast, the New Right tends to see most criminals as working-class individuals who pose a threat to what is in effect the ruling class, and the Marxists see the working class as victims of the ruling class.

Role of the Police

While Left Realism is little concerned with defining crime other than in strict legalistic terms, it does assume that crime is caused by deprivation among the working class *combined with* ineffective policing. According to Left Realist research, police responses in inner-city neighborhoods typically antagonize, rather than aid the community. The result is not reduction of crime, but a further breakdown of social values.

Case in Point

Community policing is consistent with Left Realist recommendations for reform of the criminal justice system. Here is a success story from Aurora, Colorado. An antidrug effort called HICOP (High Intensity Community-Oriented Policing) instituted a zero-tolerance approach to drugs in response to local citizen complaints that the number-one neighborhood problem was crack. Police interrupted traffic flow in critical areas by having the patrol officers do their routine paperwork conspicuously in front of crack houses. Another tactic involved securing the cooperation of apartment-house owners and managers in evicting drug dealers in rental units.

The Left Realists call for extensive reform of police practices. The police must be highly responsive to the needs of the local community, which should have a strong voice in how the police operate. This means that the local community should identify what problems the police should particularly address, and the community should become actively engaged in cooperating with local police to address these problems.

Response and Prevention

In addition to close cooperation between the local community and the police, with the community having a strong hand in the activities of the police, an effective approach to crime should include programs to address the needs of the victim, the one person who is typically given little attention by the conventional criminal justice system. Furthermore, by closely integrating the criminal justice system into the community, it should be possible to place more emphasis on the prevention of crime in the first place.

Finally, many Left Realists have begun to suggest that the punishment of at least certain offenders should also be more closely integrated into the community. Community-based corrections might include sentencing to perform appropriate community service; for example, an offender who vandalized property might be sentenced to assist with the necessary repairs.

Restorative Justice

Most criminological approaches call for responses to crime that are preventative, punitive, or rehabilitative. The recent idea of restorative justice takes a more holistic view, integrating victim-related issues with issues related to the offender. The object of restorative justice is to respond to crime with actions and methods that restore the losses suffered by victims, that hold offenders accountable for the harm they have caused, but that attempt to build peace within communities by reconciling victims and offenders.

Republican Theory Defined

Restorative justice flows from republican theory, which holds that the role of the government is to preserve a just public order, while the role of the community is to build and maintain a just peace. Thus, the criminal justice system should embody the authority of the government and the voice of the community. It should operate to restore those who have been harmed by crime and it should allow victims to become directly involved in the response to the crime committed against them. In short, the criminal justice system should promote the goal of republican liberty or, expressed another way, "personal dominion"—control or sovereignty over oneself within a social context.

Dominions Under Attack

As interpreted by republican theory, crime is a denial of personal dominion. Crime challenges and threatens that dominion by asserting the will of the criminal over that of the victim. A successful crime diminishes or destroys the victim's dominion. Robbery, for example, diminishes dominion, whereas kidnapping, rape, or murder destroys the victim's dominion.

Sworn Statement

Crime is not just an assault against an individual. Because republican society is charged with protecting the dominion of each individual, an assault on an individual's dominion is also an assault on the community and on collective confidence in the ability of the community to protect its members. Crime is a communal evil.

Response and Prevention

It is in the areas of crime response and prevention that republican theory and restorative justice have made the most innovative suggestions.

In sentencing offenders according to the principles of restorative justice, courts must take into account three elements:

1. The offender should be guided to the recognition that he has violated the victim's dominion. This requires the offender's acknowledgment of the victim's right to that dominion.

2. The sentence imposed must include some form of recompense to restore the victim's personal dominion.

3. The sentence should reassure the community that the negative impact of the crime can be, at least to some degree, undone, so that confidence in the community's competence to protect individual dominion is restored.

In general, sentencing should use the least restrictive measures possible. Ideally, sentencing focuses on reintegrative shaming, a sentence that publicly rebukes the offender, but does not cast him out from society. The idea is ultimately to forgive the offender and reintegrate him into the community. However, part of the process of reintegrative shaming is the direct involvement of the victim in all judicial proceedings and, if possible, some additional means of compensating the victim for the harm done.

The overall aim of reintegrative shaming is to restore equilibrium to the community, such that the victim is compensated and the offender is properly rebuked, but also reintegrated into society. Communities are likely to accept reintegrative shaming only for nonviolent offenders. Republican theory can do little to address violent and capital crimes. Republican theory also emphasizes crime prevention through fostering self-sanctioning conscience in each member of the community. This is developed by creating "communitarianism," an overall sense of community based on openly discussed social values or valued norms. Programs that provide community-related work and social and educational opportunities are believed to be valuable vehicles for enhancing communitarianism.

Cutting Edge: Critical Criminology

Critical criminology borrows from other recent, radical criminologies, including, paramountly, Marxism and feminism, as well as Left Realism and republican theory, and combines these approaches with a broad interest in contemporary political economic theory and critical theory. The purpose is to locate the genesis of crime and the interpretation of justice within structures of power. Driven by its Marxist and feminist orientation, critical criminology generally views law, the definition of crime, and punishment for crime as products of a system of social inequality. Moreover, these features of criminology and the criminal justice system are the means by which essential social inequality is maintained and reproduced.

Talking the Talk

Critical criminology represents the cutting edge of criminological thought and uses a number of sociological and critical disciplines to deconstruct the present operation of the criminal justice system, to expose the underlying power relations, and to show how they shape the content of the law and the administration of the law.

In effect, the critical criminologist seeks to deconstruct the present operation of the criminal justice system, to expose the underlying power relations, and, similar to the Marxist approach, to show how they shape the law, both in regard to content and administration. The practical purpose of this analytical exercise is to develop strategies to transform not merely the criminal justice system, but the society it serves. As with Marxism and feminism, therefore, the orientation of critical criminology is, at bottom, revolutionary.

Critical criminology is very much a cutting-edge field, a work in progress, and a discipline under construction. Because it draws on such diverse areas as linguistics and anthropology as well as sociology, it is particularly complex and resistant to quick summary. However, at least two main streams of critical criminology can be recognized: structuralist critical criminology, which emphasizes the ways in which political, social, and economic structures influence individual behavior; and postmodernist critical criminology, which borrows from modern linguistic theory to study concepts and definitions of crime as functions of language.

Structuralism

The structuralist defines crime as oppression and focuses analysis on the structure or institutional function of such oppression. The groups most vulnerable to oppression—the victim groups—include the working class (proletariat), women (especially the poor), ethnic and racial minorities, and, in some colonial societies, indigenous peoples. Like the Marxists, the structuralists recognize crimes of the powerful (the bourgeoisie, big business, and the state and its agents) as well as crimes of the less powerful (the working class or the proletariat).

Crimes of the powerful develop from the structure of capitalist society and relate to the negative (that is, oppressive) effects of status quo ideology, such as law-and-order politics, various forms of capitalist economic exploitation, and out-and-out oppression by the state (for example, an approach to government that is managerial rather than truly democratic).

Of more original interest is the structuralist view of the crimes of the less powerful. The focus here is on how different layers of the working class interrelate and, sometimes, oppress one another, thereby creating crime. More critically, the structuralist attempts to show how two forces, marginalization and criminalization, shape society's picture of crime among the working class. Marginalization describes the status of being cut off or isolated from the social mainstream and the opportunities it offers. Criminalization describes the effect oppressive intervention by state authorities has on increasing crime within marginalized communities.

The crimes of the powerful are products of pressure to acquire and maintain wealth and power, including state power. The crimes of the less powerful, however, grow from marginalization—being cut off from the social mainstream and its opportunities—and the relation of marginalization to criminalization, the oppressive intervention by state authorities.

Another related factor structuralist criminology recognizes is the racialization of crime, the process by which the social mainstream, especially through the mass media, identifies and targets certain communities and groups as meriting special police attention. By marshaling society's resources against particular groups, the least power-ful and most vulnerable individuals in a society are lumped together or homogenized, so that they come to constitute a disproportionate fraction of offenders and repeat offenders.

The structuralist response to crime is twofold. First, like the advocate of restorative justice, the structuralist advocates implementing a strategy of social empowerment, whereby people are directly involved in the criminal justice process, including how police are used in their community and how offenders are prosecuted. Second, like the Marxist and feminist, the structuralist believes that crime is ultimately a function of entrenched social inequalities. The appropriate response to crime, therefore, is to reform society by redistributing resources to communities on the basis of social and economic need. On the largest scale, crimes of the powerful must be responded to or prevented by a system of public accountability for all officials of the state. The emphasis of these officials and their acts must be on the protection and preservation of basic human rights.

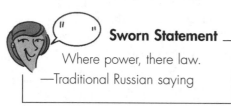

Sworn Statement

Where power, there law.
—Traditional Russian saying

Postmodernism

The postmodernist approach to critical criminology is the most radical and, at least at first blush, perhaps the strangest. In the postmodern view, language is seen as the medium that defines social relationships and institutions. Crime, therefore, is also mediated through language. In effect, crime is whatever those who control the means of expression define crime to be.

But who controls the means of expression?

For the postmodernist, the social world is inherently chaotic, fragmented, and in per-petual flux. The only *apparent* structure in all this is whatever relations language defines or mediates. The only *real* constant, however, is the struggle of individuals to assert power over other individuals.

Within society, researchers can identify any number of "microprocesses of power," including, for example, among the operations of police and the courts. Within each microprocess, the key to obtaining and wielding power over others is to control the means of expression.

As in any power relationship, controlling the means of expression is a dynamic rather than a static process. Those who wield power are met by those who resist power. The postmodernist sees this relationship of dynamic opposition as a conversation or discourse among various groups and, most significantly, between the more powerful and the less powerful, between mainstream society and the marginalized. Thus the postmodernist focuses on analyzing the everyday social discourse, how language is used (often quite unconsciously) to construct social relationships that give one group a power advantage over another.

Narrowing the focus to the criminal justice system itself, the postmodernist researcher may examine the roles language assigns to each "actor" within the system. That is, a police officer communicates and behaves as a police officer—or what language tells him a police officer is—rather than as a father or mother or husband or even a fully rounded human being. Others in the system (lawyers, offenders, judges, even victims) communicate and behave according to their linguistically mediated roles as well. The result, according to postmodern theory, is that the participants in the criminal justice system really *are* actors, who work from a kind of unwritten but shared script and who, therefore, are "decentered," not in control of their own thoughts, let alone their own behavior.

Who is the author of this script? The postmodern theorist answers that those who control the means of expression collectively constitute the author. And who are these controllers of expression? The Marxist would call them the bourgeoisie; the feminist would call them the social patriarchs. The main point is that, while the powers that be control the means of expression, the script, once it is entrenched in the form of legal jargon, official criminal categories, and the like, is really within no one's control. People—offenders, lawyers, judges, police officers, legislators, the general public—work strictly from the script, with very little conscious, let alone critical, thought and no ad libs.

The goal of the postmodern critical criminologist is to deconstruct the script, to expose it, to make it a matter of conscious discussion, debate, and revision. Only by this means can the nature of crime and the response to crime be rethought, and the criminal justice system redesigned and reformed.

The Least You Need to Know

- Criminologists of the New Right attempt to return criminology to a law-and-order orientation and fix responsibility for crime on the individual offender.

- The Left Realists seek an alternative both to the New Right (too conservative) and to the Marxists (too theoretical) by analyzing street crime in practical terms as crime committed by the working class against the working class.

- So-called republican theorists have introduced the concept of restorative justice, in which crime is seen as a violation of individual dominion and community equilibrium, and the appropriate response to crime is to restore dominion to the individual, reintegrate the offender into society, and return the community to equilibrium.

- Critical criminology represents the cutting edge of the discipline and attempts to deconstruct the criminal justice system and the society it serves in order to expose to study and possible revision unconscious assumptions and inequalities.

Part 3

The Usual Suspects

In the first two parts of this book, we explored criminology, a scientific inquiry into crime. Now we will begin to look into criminal investigation, the process of inquiry into particular crimes. Whereas criminology is the work of sociologists, criminal investigation is the work of cops and the other professionals—mostly scientists and physicians—who support them.

In this part, we explore the classification of crime and the profiling of criminals.

Crimes to Order

In This Chapter

- ◆ Why classify crimes?
- ◆ The major crimes against persons
- ◆ The major crimes against property
- ◆ Drugs and crime
- ◆ The white-collar offenses
- ◆ Victimology: a new focus on the victim

A brontosaurus was lumbering in the background while a pterodactyl soared overhead. Vines clung from trees in a primordial mist. Lugg clubbed Ugg on the head and dragged her by her hair into his cave. The local law enforcement officer who responded to the scene after Ugg woke up did not complete a Domestic Violence Incident Report. While there may have been a need for record keeping and criminal statistics in the Stone Age, there were so many other needs that this mundane practice didn't become popular until much later.

Today it seems that we have become obsessed with numbers and statistical record keeping. From elections to grocery shopping, many of our daily activities are recorded, processed, disseminated, and utilized to affect our lives in countless ways. And that includes how we classify crime—the topic of this chapter.

Classifying Crime

For today's law enforcement professional, numbers are everything. How many tickets does a traffic officer write? How many cases does a detective close? Where should uniform patrol be increased? Where can it be decreased in order to increase it somewhere else? What are the crime patterns? Do property crimes increase in a particular area when school is out of session or as the holidays approach?

You get the idea. It may seem as if we are drowning in numbers and losing focus on the important issues. But the way to achieve tangible results is to set realizable goals, then go out and realize them.

What's the Point?

There was a time when an officer's career could have been made or unmade by the number of traffic citations he or she wrote—or to whom they were written. Those days are mostly gone, but the numbers are still important. If an officer works diligently in an area with moderate to heavy vehicle traffic, the number of observable traffic violations is legion. The issue becomes one of common sense. A prudent officer will enforce the traffic laws and make a useful impact on the safety of the driving public, but the officer will not be so zealous as to be seen as heavy-handed. A gentle touch is often best. Besides, the traffic pullover is the most dangerous of police-initiated encounters with the public.

Case in Point
Nothing is ever routine, including the traffic pullover. The vehicle must be guided to a stopping point that will provide the officer with room to maneuver. This is not to say that the driver will in fact stop. If he flees, the officer must follow the SOP (standard operating procedures) of the department when deciding whether or not to give chase. If he slows but fails to pull over promptly, the officer must expect a "bush bond," in which the driver exits the rolling vehicle and flees on foot. Even if the driver does pull over, the situation may still be dangerous. A sizable fraction of people stopped for traffic violations are, in fact, guilty of something far more serious and do not want to be caught.

Setting Priorities

During the 1980s, driving under the influence of alcohol (DUI) became the focus of a passionate crusade both inside and outside of law enforcement. The crime that was once seen as a social faux pas now became a heinous offense. Earlier, police officers had given rides home to drivers who had had too much to drink. Now DUI enforcement became a high priority. Officers were establishing traffic safety checkpoints—roadblocks typically set up to check drivers for alcohol intoxication and for such violations as failure to wear safety belts or to possess a valid driver's license, registration, and insurance identification card—to apprehend and jail offenders. Some civil libertarians have challenged the checkpoint as a violation of the constitutional presumption of innocence.

Another example of making and revising priorities is the so-called war on drugs. In the nineteenth and early twentieth century, before passage of the Pure Food and Drug Act of 1906, cocaine was considered an innocuous pick-me-up and was even an ingredient of Coca-Cola—just the thing to make it the "pause that refreshes." During the last two decades, however, the war on drugs, especially cocaine and its derivatives, has consumed an incredible proportion of the time and budget of law enforcement agencies. The point is not that this priority is invalid, but it is a relatively recent priority, and, like every priority, it exacts a price on law enforcement at every level, from the cop on the street to the courts to the corrections system. Focusing on one type of crime inevitably removes the focus from some other type.

Predictions as Prevention

When we decide that certain behaviors are negative, we also decide that actions should be taken to suppress them. New York City was the first of the nation's law enforcement jurisdictions to determine that *quality of life offenses* should be prosecuted vigorously. This was a huge leap for a municipality that many had written off as a wasteland of crime and an example of the degradation of modern society. As many see it, police policies under former mayor Rudolph Giuliani made the city not only more livable, but may well have served as a basis for the reconstruction necessary after the attack on the World Trade Center on September 11, 2001. It is conceded, even by many skeptics, that policies focusing on quality of life offenses

Talking the Talk

Quality of life offenses generally include such misdemeanors as littering, defacing property with graffiti, and panhandling. During the last decade of the twentieth century, New York City pioneered the vigorous prosecution of such offenses—a controversial policy, which, some argued, drained law enforcement resources and others claimed greatly improved the livability of the city.

at the very least compel municipal leaders to seek alternatives to the graffiti, panhandling, and public disorder that were once thought to be inevitable features of urban life.

The Stat Keepers

The crime analysis and police management process known as COMPSTAT was developed by the New York City Police Department. The essence of the process is to collect, analyze, and map crime data and other essential police performance measures on a regular basis and hold police managers accountable for their performance as measured by these data.

The four principles of COMPSTAT express the rationale for keeping accurate crime statistics:

1. **To obtain accurate and timely intelligence.** Officers at all levels of the police department must understand when (time of day, day of week, week of year) various types of crimes have been committed as well as how, where, and by whom they have been committed.

2. **To formulate effective tactics.** Having collated, analyzed, and mapped intelligence, the department's commanders must develop effective tactics for dealing with the problems that are revealed. To bring about permanent change in crime conditions, tactics must be comprehensive, flexible, and adaptable to changing trends. They must also involve other law enforcement agencies such as the FBI, DEA (Drug Enforcement Agency), and ATF (Bureau of Alcohol, Tobacco, and Firearms), prosecutors, probation services, other city agencies not directly connected to law enforcement, as well as the public (such as community groups, schools, and neighborhood associations).

3. **To enable the rapid deployment of personnel and resources.** Once a tactical plan has been developed, the deployment of personnel must be rapid and focused. To be effective, the response to a crime or quality-of-life problem demands that patrol and special units coordinate their resources and expertise and act with a sense of urgency.

4. **To promote relentless follow-up and assessment.** All actions must be relentlessly followed up and assessed to ensure that the desired results

By the Numbers

The Federal Bureau of Investigation's Uniform Crime Reporting program and the U.S. Department of Justice's Bureau of Justice Statistics are two key sources of crime statistics in the United States. You can access both of these sources at www.fedstats.gov.

have been achieved. This is the only way of ensuring that recurring or similar problems are dealt with effectively in the future.

COMPSTAT is now being used in many police departments around the country and is having a profound influence on the way policing is done, even where the process has not been formally adopted. Today, even small to medium-sized departments break down their crime statistics by geographic area, time of day, and type of crime. What was once a "rash of break-ins" is now a statistically analyzed recurring set of similar incidents.

Even before COMPSTAT, all law-enforcement jurisdictions recognized certain broad classifications of crime. The rest of this chapter discusses them.

Crimes Against Persons

In our society, top priority is given to preventing and punishing crimes committed against persons. The most serious of such offenses is homicide.

Homicide

Homicide is the general term for the killing of a human being. *Murder* is a specific type of homicide: the killing of another human being "with malice aforethought" or during the commission of a felony. Another form of homicide is *voluntary manslaughter*, the killing of another human being as a result of a sudden and violent passion arising from a serious provocation. There are also two types of *involuntary manslaughter:* a killing caused by the commission of a nonfelonious unlawful act, and a killing caused by the commission of a lawful act in an unlawful manner likely to cause death. The single common element to all homicidal offenses is the death of a human being.

By the Numbers

Most murderers and victims are well acquainted. According to the Bureau of Justice Statistics, between 1976 and 1999, 14 percent of murders were committed by strangers to the victim, whereas 52.4 percent were committed by spouses, relatives, friends, or other acquaintances. (In 33.5 percent of the cases, the relationship of perpetrator and victim was undetermined.)

Robbery

A person commits the offense of *robbery* when, with the intent to commit a theft, he takes property by the use of force, intimidation, threat of force, coercion, or by sudden snatching. In *armed robbery*, the offender employs an offensive weapon, or a replica, article, or device having the appearance of such weapon. The offender who seeks to hedge his bet by using a toy gun, hoping to evade an armed robbery charge if caught, is in for a rude awakening.

Assault

Simple assault is the deliberate violent injury to the person of another or the commission of an act that places another in reasonable apprehension of immediately receiving a violent injury. *Aggravated assault* is assault with the intent to murder, rape, or rob with any weapon or any object, device, or instrument likely to result in serious bodily injury.

Sex Offenses

A man commits the offense of *rape* when he has carnal knowledge of a female against her will. "Carnal knowledge" means penetration of the female sex organ by the male sex organ. The meaning of *sexual assault* varies with jurisdiction. In some states, it is virtually synonymous with rape, but may also encompass an assault with the clear intent to commit rape. In some jurisdictions, sexual assault is defined far more narrowly and is deemed to have occurred when any person who has supervisory or disciplinary authority over another person engages in sexual contact with that other person. *Sexual battery* is intentional physical contact with the intimate parts of the body of another person without the consent of that person. *Aggravated sexual battery* is the intentional penetration, with a foreign object, of the sexual organ or anus of another person without the consent of that person.

> **" "** **Sworn Statement**
>
> Give me a kid who knows nothing about sex, and you've given me my next victim.
>
> —Child molester quoted in the Child Lures Prevention website (www.childlures.com)

Crimes Against Children

Child molestation is any immoral or indecent act against, with, or in the presence of any child under age 16 with the intent to arouse or satisfy the sexual desires of either the child or the adult. *Aggravated child molestation* is molestation that physically injures the child or involves an act of sodomy.

The Serial Offender

Perhaps the most grotesquely intriguing criminal is the serial offender. While there is no universally accepted definition of this criminal, he is more often than not white, male, intelligent, attractive, and personable. (Even after these sociopathic monsters are convicted and sentenced to a life behind bars—or even to death—they are often besieged by marriage proposals from enamored female suitors.)

Serial offenses committed range from property crimes to sexual sadism to murder, or any combination of these. But the crimes committed by any one offender are typically quite consistent. The fetishes and quirks are very personal to the offender. What turns on one serial sexual sadist may disgust another. Roy Hazelwood, the former FBI special agent and profiler, describes serial sexual crimes as existing in the fantasy world of the offenders. The more complex the crime, the more complex the fantasy, and the more intelligent the offender.

Crimes Against Property

Crimes against property are second in priority only to crimes against persons. Note that robbery is classified as a crime against a person, whereas burglary is deemed a crime against property.

Burglary

A person commits the offense of *burglary* when, without authority, with or without force, and with the intent to steal, he enters any structure, including a dwelling or a vehicle used as a dwelling.

Environmental Crime

Criminal codes relating to natural resources regulate such areas as parks, historic sites, and recreation areas; mineral, water, and forest resources; soil erosion and sedimentation; waste management; air pollution; asbestos safety; underground storage tanks; oil spills; and sewage holding tanks.

Environmental laws are complex and vary greatly from jurisdiction to jurisdiction. For example, in many states it is a misdemeanor to operate without authorization any motorized vehicle or machine on sand dunes or beaches. Similarly, it is unlawful to enter a park without complying with all the rules, regulations, and permits regarding use of the park. It is unlawful to violate laws regulating the archaeological exploration or excavation of a historic site.

Arson

The basic definition of *arson* is simple: It is the willful and malicious burning of property. The crime, however, is often quite complex, because the motives of arson are many.

Some arsonists are motivated by excitement. They may be thrill seekers, attention seekers, or even driven by sexual perversion (achieving sexual gratification by setting and watching fires). Some arsonists are motivated by revenge, perhaps personal retaliation for some wrong, perceived or actual, perhaps retaliation against a corporation or institution, or perhaps retaliation against society itself. Arson may be used to conceal other crimes, including murder, suicide, breaking and entering, embezzlement, fraud, and so on. Some arsonists destroy their own property in order to make an insurance claim.

Sworn Statement

Two special types of arson are *extremist motivated*—that is, terrorism, hate crimes, or rioting—and *serial*. Some arsonists, especially those who derive sexual gratification from the offense, indulge in spree or mass arsons.

The evidence of arson is often quite apparent—the presence of an accelerant (such as gasoline) or an explosive device—at the crime scene. But because so much of the physical evidence is destroyed by the crime itself, it is often extremely difficult to trace the particular act of arson to a particular perpetrator.

The Drug Cycle

The "war on drugs" has been an essential part of law enforcement for about two decades. Are we winning the war? This would be easier to determine if what constitutes "victory" were clearly defined. The fact is that the objectives of the war seem to change as frequently as they are discussed.

From a tactical point of view, today's police officer is better trained and more capable of handling the dangerous situations the war on drugs often entails. Weapons are better, and training is better, but does this translate into better law enforcement?

It all depends on who you ask. Few police officers live where they work, and the war on drugs has left many cops feeling like an invading army in a very real war zone. It is hard to tell the good guys from the bad guys, and drug use is so prevalent that it alone cannot be the determinant of good versus bad. Drug dealers themselves are frequently the victims of violent crimes.

Most jurisdictions do make distinctions among different controlled substances. They are classified according to their potential for abuse, their medical importance, and their level of safety.

The Georgia Controlled Substances Act of 1974 is an example of an attempt to classify drugs according to their potential for abuse. Crimes involving drugs higher up on the schedule are deemed more serious than those involving drugs lower down:

- **Schedule I.** High potential for abuse, no currently accepted medical use, and a lack of accepted safety; for example, nonmedicinal opiates and hallucinogens

- **Schedule II.** High potential for abuse, current accepted medical use, and if abused may lead to severe physical or psychological dependence; for example, medicinal opiates, cocaine, coca leaves, and depressants

- **Schedule III.** Less potential for abuse, medically accepted uses, and moderate to low physical dependence, but high risk of psychological dependence; for example, certain stimulants, certain depressants, and anabolic steroids

- **Schedule IV.** Low potential for abuse, currently accepted medical uses, and limited physical and psychological dependence; for example, seratonin inhibitors

- **Schedule V.** Lower potential for abuse than Schedule IV drugs, currently accepted medical uses, and if abused may lead to limited physical or psychological dependence; includes substances with very limited narcotic concentrations

Generally, it is more serious to sell than to possess controlled substances, but distinctions are also made on the basis of seemingly arcane issues. For example, sellers as well as users of powdered cocaine are generally treated with greater leniency than sellers and users of the popular rocklike street version commonly known as "crack." Moreover, for many offenders, drug dealing is a way of life, and "three strikes, you're out" sentencing in some jurisdictions has put even low-level drug dealers behind bars for decades.

White-Collar Crime

White-collar crime encompasses business-related or occupational offenses such as embezzlement and fraud. Although often very serious—and costly—they are not violent crimes.

Fraud

Arguably, *fraud* is the most frequently perpetrated crime. Offenses range from the complicated telemarketer scam in which thousands of persons are tricked into purchasing five years of subscriptions to magazines they may never read at a price exponentially greater than they would have paid from a reputable distributor, to multimillion-dollar fraudulent insurance claims, to billion-dollar embezzlement schemes. Some authorities believe that about one third of all insurance claims have at least an element of fraud in them. For instance, following a collision, it is very common for a person to report existing damage as damage caused by the collision under claim.

The victims of fraud are often multiple. In the case of the insurance company that pays a fraudulently inflated claim, the company is certainly victimized, but so are policyholders, who end up making up the insurer's losses by paying higher premiums because actuarial tables become skewed.

Computer Crime

Who can calculate the benefits computers have brought to commerce and the economy? Yet as wonderful as the computer is, the technology has also provided a new vehicle for criminals of many kinds. From money scams to financial transaction card fraud to child pornography on the Internet, the surge in computer use has aided perpetrators and frustrated law enforcement officers. Many jurisdictions now have units specifically tasked to combat the crimes made popular—or even possible—by computers.

Talking the Talk

Victimology is the study of the victim's role in a particular crime and particular classes of crime. The objective of victimology is to use victims' experiences to prevent future crimes and to find ways to restore crime victims to wholeness.

Victimology

For centuries the focus of law enforcement has been exclusively on the perpetrator. The victim was left to fend for him- or herself. Recently, the focus has broadened. One of the most dynamic areas in recent criminology and criminal investigation is *victimology*. The hope of this new field is that studying the victim will produce better results in crime prevention and prosecution.

Crime is never the victim's fault, but it is often the case that certain actions or behaviors on the part of the victim might have made the victim vulnerable. Learning from victims' actions may aid in preventing crime.

Victimology also strives to help the victim heal after the offense. More and more jurisdictions are offering victims financial assistance, psychological counseling, and other help.

Victimology promises to be an increasingly active area in criminology as well as in all phases of the criminal justice system.

The Least You Need to Know

◆ To begin to understand crime, it is first necessary to obtain reliable statistics on crime, pegged to time, place, and circumstance, and to organize and analyze the data obtained.

◆ Police agencies and the criminal justice system as a whole give top priority to addressing crimes against persons, which put lives at jeopardy.

◆ Crimes against property are the most common and numerous offenses.

◆ The "war on drugs" is a relatively new priority for law enforcement, which, many feel, consumes an inordinate proportion of police, court, and penal resources.

◆ White-collar crimes are nonviolent but costly, ranging from scams perpetrated against individuals to embezzlement (typically a crime against a corporation) to massive frauds committed by some of the nation's wealthiest and biggest companies.

◆ Increasingly, crime statistics are being analyzed not just to understand criminals, but to learn more about victims in order to address their needs; this is known as victimology.

Chapter 8

Profiling the Bad Guys

In This Chapter

- Criminal profiling: Hollywood myth vs. nitty-gritty reality
- Evolution of profiling: from Jack the Ripper to the Boston Strangler
- FBI profiling practices
- Profiling serial offenders: the Canter method
- Turvey's Behavioral Evidence Analysis method
- How effective is criminal profiling?

If you're a fan of old detective movies, crime shows of television's Golden Age, or pulp detective fiction of the '40s and '50s, you've doubtless heard and read a lot about "M.O." It's short for *modus operandi* (Latin for "method of operating") and refers to a once commonly held assumption that individual criminals or types of criminals almost invariably behave in the same way. That is, a given repeat offender or class of offender always leaves a recognizable signature on each crime committed. The clever detective arrives on the scene of the crime, looks around, instantly recognizes a familiar M.O., then goes out and gets his or her man. Piece of cake.

Most criminal investigators today regard the concept of *modus operandi* as too simplistic to be of much practical use. But far from obsolete is the idea that offenders motivated by certain emotional drives, offenders shaped by certain elements in their current life and in their background, leave a recognizable signature on the crimes they commit. In contemporary criminal investigation, the *modus operandi* concept appears as the much more sophisticated and refined process of criminal profiling, which we'll discuss in this chapter.

Criminal Profiling: Fact vs. Fiction

Let's get the inevitable pun out of the way fast: These days, *criminal profiling* is a high-profile investigative technique. The public is fascinated by it and sees TV news magazine stories about it, watches movies about it (such as the 1999 Denzel Washington vehicle, *The Bone Collector*, or Morgan Freeman in *Kiss the Girls*, 1997, and *Along Came a Spider*, 2001) and TV cop shows built around it (*Profiler*, for example, about a sexy forensic psychiatrist, haunted by the murder of her husband, but possessing an uncanny knack for nailing "the criminal mind").

Welcome to Hollywood

As portrayed in popular fiction, film, and TV, detectives are cops who operate on (invariably brilliant) hunches, while "profilers" are detectives whose hunches are raised to the *n*th degree by a combination of nerdy scientific savvy and paranormal psychic ability. They arrive at a crime scene, slip on the latex gloves, pick up a few pieces of evidence, stand back and survey the scene, frown, grimace, then raise their eyebrows and declare, "The doer is a white guy, early twenties, brown hair, brown eyes, and a fan of *Seinfeld* reruns. Let's go get him!" (See Chapter 22 for more on psychic detectives.)

> **Talking the Talk**
>
> **Criminal profiling** uses crime scene evidence and other (mainly psychological) data to indicate the type of person likely to have committed a crime under investigation.

And if it's never quite this simple on *Profiler*, well, the loose ends *are* almost always tied up before the last commercial break.

A Dose of Reality

Thus spake Hollywood. In reality, however, profiling is, first and foremost, painstaking detective work, which begins with a by-the-book analysis of physical evidence at individual crime scenes. By deductive reasoning—that is, reasoning that uses specific physical facts to build generalizations—the criminal profiler begins to identify the tendencies and typologies that characterize various classes of offender.

It is only after carefully analyzing many crime scenes that the criminal profiler can, with some confidence, attempt to reconstruct the behavior of a perpetrator at a particular crime scene and, from this reconstruction, draw inferences about his motivation.

No reputable criminal profiler believes in the old-time definition of M.O., that a certain type of criminal behavior is always and inevitably the result of the same motivation. On the contrary, it is assumed that a given behavior may have resulted from any number of motives. Say an investigator finds a body with its eyes covered by a cloth. Does this reveal a significant psychological kink in the offender? Or does it mean that the offender knew the victim and didn't want to be recognized?

Usually, the most that can be expected from criminal profiling is a narrowing of the range of suspects. Although this is no investigative silver bullet, it is a valuable tool, because it allows police agencies to focus their limited resources more efficiently. If the perpetrator is likely to possess characteristics A, B, and C, detectives don't have to hunt for suspects who partake of the rest of the alphabet.

Sworn Statement

The criminal profiler should … have [some] understanding of … psychology: the study of individual behavior; sociology: the study of group behavior, groups being comprised of individuals; criminalistics: a general term for the scientific study of recognition, collection and preservation of physical evidence as it is related to the law; … forensic pathology: a branch of medicine that applies the principles and knowledge of the medical sciences to problems in the field of law …. Anyone without specific training from qualified experts, or experience in at least the above fields is not, in my opinion, capable of the complex processes involved in rendering a criminal profile.

—Brent E. Turvey, M.S., in "What Is Criminal Profiling?"

A Short History of Criminal Profiling

Ask most law enforcement professionals who "invented" criminal profiling, and the credit will probably be given to the Behavioral Sciences Unit (BSU) of the Federal Bureau of Investigation, based at the FBI Academy in Quantico, Virginia. While it is true that a number of FBI special agents, including Roy Hazelwood and Robert

Ressler, among others, have pioneered contemporary profiling, the idea of creating criminal profiles was born long before the FBI even came into existence.

Looking for the Ripper

The most famous early historical example of profiling is the work of London Metropolitan Police surgeon Dr. Thomas Bond, who, in 1888, performed the autopsy of Mary Kelly, the last victim of Jack the Ripper. Bond's autopsy led to the conclusion that, contrary to what many believed, the Ripper had no knowledge of surgical technique. But Bond went beyond this to reconstruct certain aspects of the crime and, based on wound patterns and the use of a sheet to cover the victim's face, he advised police to seek a quiet and inoffensive-looking man, neatly dressed, and in his middle age.

Based on his examination of all of the Ripper's victims, Bond concluded that the crimes were the work of the same perpetrator, a man of "great coolness and daring."

While Bond's analysis was thought provoking, it did not assist police in tracking the Ripper. He was never brought to justice.

> **Sworn Statement**
>
> In each case the mutilation was inflicted by a person who had no scientific nor anatomical knowledge. In my opinion he does not even possess the technical knowledge of a butcher or horse slaughterer or any person accustomed to cut up dead animals.
>
> —London Metropolitan Police surgeon Dr. Thomas Bond, in reference to the work of Jack the Ripper

A Profile of Der Führer

Something very like modern profiling was employed in the study of another infamous murderer, Adolf Hitler. During World War II, the precursor agency to the CIA, the Office of Strategic Services (OSS), called on psychiatrist Walter Langer to "profile" Hitler in an attempt to gain a strategic edge against German forces. "If Hitler is running the show," OSS officials asked Langer, "what kind of person is he? What are his ambitions? We want to know about his psychological make-up—the things that make him tick. In addition, we ought to know what he might do if things begin to go against him."

This 1888 cartoon from the British humor magazine Punch *is titled "Blind Man's Buff" and depicts what the public perceived as the utter confusion of the police in their failed pursuit of Jack the Ripper.*

(Image from ArtToday)

Langer made a number of fascinating speculations, the most intriguing of which involved predicting what would happen to Hitler in the end. Langer believed that Hitler was too healthy to die of natural causes. While he did not rule out the possibility of assassination, he did conclude that Hitler, in defeat, would never seek refuge in another country, because the dictator was convinced that he was the savior of Germany. Langer predicted that Hitler would commit suicide if defeat seemed inevitable. This, of course, is precisely what Der Führer did.

Mad Bomber of New York

On November 16, 1940, someone walked unseen into the 64th Street offices of Consolidated Edison, New York City's electric power generating company, dropped his toolbox, and walked out again. Workers opened the toolbox and discovered an unexploded pipe bomb with a note wrapped around it: "Con Edison crooks, this is for you." The NYPD Bomb Squad was summoned, but, finding no fingerprints or other evidence, let the matter lie.

One year later, an unexploded alarm clock bomb was found in a gutter just outside another Con Ed building, this one on 14th Street. Three months after this, the police received a letter: "I will make no more bomb units for the duration of the War—My patriotic feelings have made me decide this—Later I will bring the Con Edison to justice—they must pay for their dastardly deeds."

True to his word, the perpetrator the press dubbed the "Mad Bomber" planted no more bombs during the war, but he did continue to send letters (each signed "F.P.," for "Fair Play") to various individuals, newspapers, movie theaters, Con Edison, and the police. Then, on March 29, 1950, a bomb was discovered in Grand Central Station. During the next half-dozen years, 30 more were found, in phone booths, in the public library, in subway stations, and in movie theaters (here the Mad Bomber would slit a seat, tuck in a bomb, then disappear through a fire exit). Up to this point, none of the Mad Bomber's devices had actually exploded, but, on December 2, 1956, the detonation of one in a Brooklyn movie house injured six people, three critically. At last the police were driven to take unconventional action. They called on Dr. James Brussel, a Manhattan forensic psychiatrist.

Brussel intensively reviewed the massive 16-year case file on the Mad Bomber, including his many letters. After some deliberation, Brussel delivered a remarkably detailed and specific "profile": The Mad Bomber was a middle-aged man, heavyset but meticulous in grooming, self-educated, and of Slavic, Roman Catholic background. Brussel believed that he was single and living with a brother or sister in Connecticut. He suffered from an *Oedipus complex*. Brussel also concluded that the bomber had worked for Consolidated Edison or one of its subsidiaries.

> **Talking the Talk**
>
> In psychoanalytic theory, an **Oedipus complex** is the unconscious sexual desire in a child, especially a boy, for the parent of the opposite sex. Unresolved, the Oedipus complex may result in an adult neurosis.

Dr. Brussel had some pointed recommendations for the detectives. He told them not to keep the profile confidential, but to publicize it widely, so that the bomber, antagonized, would be lured out of cover. In addition, he urged them to search Con Ed files pertaining to former employees. Just as the detectives were leaving with their marching orders, Brussel added: "One more thing. When you catch him, and I have no doubt you will, he'll be wearing a double-breasted suit. And it will be buttoned."

The police reluctantly followed Brussel's recommendation about publicizing the profile, and, as the doctor had predicted, the stories so irked the Mad Bomber that he revealed himself by sending to a newspaper a detailed account of his motive: an accident he had suffered while working for Con Ed and what he believed was the company's plot to cheat him out of workmen's compensation.

The police consulted Con Ed files and arrested George Metesky, a heavyset bachelor living in Waterbury, Connecticut. At the time of his arrest, he was wearing a double-breasted suit. It was buttoned.

Committed to an asylum, Metesky was released in 1974 and returned to Waterbury, where he lived, quietly, until his death, at age 90, in 1994.

Boston Strangler

In Boston, on June 14, 1962, the body of Anna Slesers, age 55, was discovered by her son. She had been strangled with her own belt. Before the end of June, three other Boston women—ages 85, 68, and 65—were discovered strangled to death.

The press began referring to the unknown assailant as the Boston Strangler, and police called in a team of forensic psychiatrists to create a profile of the killer. The psychiatrists concluded, among other things, that the murderer was acting out a hatred of his mother, and his next two murders, during August 1962, both of elderly women (75 and 67), seemed to bear this out. But, on December 5, 20-year-old Sophie Clark was found strangled, and, on the 31st, the body of Patricia Bissette, 23, was found.

Stymied, police again called on Dr. Brussel. Whereas the earlier profilers had concluded that the serial killer was between 18 and 40 and suffered from delusions of persecution and a hatred of his mother, Brussel believed that the murderer was about 30, of strong build and average height, clean shaven, with thick dark hair. He was, Brussel thought, of Spanish or Italian heritage and a paranoid schizophrenic.

Despite possessing this profile, the police turned up nothing as five more women, ranging in age from 19 to 69, were found strangled in Boston. The break in the case came not from the profile, but from the perpetrator himself.

On October 27, 1964, posing as a detective, Albert De Salvo entered a young woman's home. He bound her and began to assault her sexually. Then, as suddenly as he had attacked her, he stopped, said "I'm sorry," and left. The woman subsequently described him to police, and he was soon identified by other rape victims. He was apprehended for the rapes, but he was not suspected of being the Boston Strangler until he voluntarily confessed. The police were impressed not only by the detailed nature of his confession, but by how well he fit Brussel's profile.

Because there was no evidence to corroborate his confession, De Salvo was never tried for the stranglings, but he was tried for robbery and rape and sent to prison for life in 1967. Six years later, he was murdered in his cell.

Although he fit the forensic psychiatrist's profile to a tee, nobody personally acquainted with DeSalvo ever believed he was the Boston Strangler—not his wife, his former employers, his lawyer, his prison psychiatrist, and not even police officers who knew him as a small-time burglar. Furthermore, no physical evidence connected him to any of the murders, and there were no eyewitnesses to place him anywhere near any of the crime scenes.

Some experts now believe that the murders were perpetrated by more than one person. But why would DeSalvo have confessed to horrendous crimes he didn't commit? Some point out that he believed the rape convictions would send him to prison for life in any event. By confessing to the sensational Boston Strangler crimes, he could raise money to support his family. Besides, the high-profile stranglings were a "step up" for a petty criminal.

FBI Crime Scene Analysis

In the 1960s, Howard Teten, an investigator with the San Leandro (California) Police Department, worked with the School of Criminology of the University of California to develop a systematic approach to profiling. In 1970, after Teten became an FBI special agent, he initiated what would become the bureau's famous profiling program, working in conjunction with Pat Mullany, a specialist in abnormal psychology. The FBI's profiling methods were further refined in the late 1970s by John Douglas and Robert Ressler, who introduced the "organized/ disorganized method," still a cornerstone of the FBI profiling procedure.

FBI Crime Scene Analysis begins by distinguishing between an "organized" and "disorganized" crime scene. Organized offender characteristics include:

- Average to above average intelligence
- Adequate level of social competence
- Prefers skilled work
- Sexually competent
- High birth-order status
- Father had/has stable work
- Childhood discipline inconsistent
- Mood was controlled during the crime
- Used alcohol in connection with the crime
- Situational stress precipitated crime
- Lives with partner

- Is mobile; owns a car in good condition

- Follows crime in the news media

- May change jobs or leave town after the crime

Disorganized offender characteristics include:

- Below average intelligence

- Socially inadequate

- Works at unskilled labor

- Sexually incompetent

- Low birth-order status

- Father has/had unstable work

- Received harsh discipline as a child

- Mood was anxious during the crime

- Minimal use of alcohol in connection with the crime

- Situational stress played little role in precipitating the crime

- Lives alone

- Lives or works near the crime scene

- Not interested in following the crime in the news media

- Significant behavior change follows the crime; may resort to drug or alcohol use

Between 1979 and 1983, agents from the FBI's Behavioral Sciences Unit interviewed incarcerated offenders about their backgrounds, crimes, crime scenes, and their victims. They supplemented the interviews with reviews of court transcripts, police reports, and psychiatric and criminal records. Using this data, they developed a six-step "Crime Scene Analysis" procedure for building a suspect profile:

1. **Inputs.** The first step is collecting and assessing materials relating to the case under investigation, including crime scene and victim photographs, a thorough background check of the victim, autopsy reports, and other forensic data.

2. **Models.** The modeling phase requires arranging the data gathered in the input stage into a logical, coherent pattern for analysis.

3. **Assessment.** Using the sorted and arranged data, the profiler attempts to reconstruct the sequence of events and the behaviors of the perpetrator as well as the victim. The object is to determine the role each played in the crime.

4. **Profile.** Based on the reconstruction of the crime, a list of background, physical, and behavioral characteristics is prepared. This is the profile of the perpetrator. The profiler tries to advise police officials on how to identify, apprehend, and then interview the suspect.

5. **Investigation.** In this stage, the profile is fully integrated into the investigation of the crime. If the profile fails to turn up suspects—or if new evidence comes to light—it is reevaluated and, possibly, modified.

6. **Apprehension.** Any suspects who are apprehended are cross-checked against the profile to assess how closely the suspect's characteristics correspond with it.

Investigative Psychology: The Canter Approach

David Canter is a British psychologist long associated with the University of Surrey, where, under the auspices of Scotland Yard, he developed a leading method of psychological profiling designed especially to identify serial rapists and murderers.

Canter is best known for his work in nailing John Duffy, England's "railway rapist," during the 1980s. By identifying certain features of Duffy's crimes—location, timing, method—Canter established that the offender had a troubled, childless marriage, that he was interested in the martial arts, and that he was employed as a semi-skilled laborer. Using this and other information, police were able to pick Duffy out of a field of 1,999 suspects.

> **Talking the Talk**
>
> The **five-factor model** is the basis of the criminal profiling method developed by David Canter. It evaluates evidence of interpersonal coherence, the significance of the time and place of the crime, criminal characteristics, criminal career, and the offender's forensic awareness.

Canter's method is based on what he calls the *five-factor model*, analysis of five key aspects of the interaction between the victim and the offender: interpersonal coherence, significance of time and place, criminal characteristics, criminal career, and forensic awareness. Let's take a closer look at each.

Interpersonal Coherence

Canter believes that features of an offender's criminal activity relate to features of his activity in noncriminal situations. For example, the most infamous serial killer of the

1970s, Ted Bundy, apparently selected victims who somehow resembled a former girl-friend. Canter makes the assumption that offenders deal with their victims in ways that are similar to how they deal with people in their everyday lives.

Time and Place

Because the offender chooses the time and place of the crime, this information may reveal information about the perpetrator's mobility and where he lives or works. The choice of time and place may also suggest how the offender views his surroundings and may say something about the offender's usual schedule: when he is (legitimately) at work, for example.

Criminal Characteristics

This is a catchall category in which the investigator may list characteristics that seem significant and compare these to the evidence found at the crime scene. The FBI's organized/disorganized categories are examples of criminal characteristics that might be considered.

Criminal Career

Based on the crime scene evidence, does it seem likely or unlikely that the offender has committed other crimes? Is he a career criminal? A serial offender?

Forensic Awareness

This is strongly related to the "criminal career" category. The investigator looks for signs of the perpetrator's awareness of police techniques relating to the collection of evidence. Such awareness strongly suggests a serial offender as opposed to someone who committed an isolated or random crime on impulse or because of opportunity.

Behavioral Evidence Analysis: The Turvey Approach

Brent E. Turvey is a California-based private criminal profiler who has extensively interviewed convicted sex offenders and serial killers in an effort to understand characteristics common among them. He developed Behavioral Evidence Analysis (BEA), a four-step profiling method. It begins with a new concept called equivocal forensic analysis, the assumption that any given piece of evidence may suggest more than one interpretation, then narrows this down and proceeds through analysis of victimology, crime scene characteristics, and offender characteristics.

Equivocal Forensic Analysis

Turvey assumes that physical evidence found at a crime scene is typically equivocal in nature; that is, any given piece of evidence may suggest more than one interpretation. Therefore, the first step in analysis is to list the possible interpretations and assess the most likely one.

Victimology

After thoroughly evaluating evidence related to the crime scene, Turvey turns next to the victim, profiling him or her in much the same way and with the same thoroughness as the perpetrator is profiled. Assessing how, where, when, and why a victim was chosen suggests a wealth of information about the offender. For instance, the physical build of the victim implies much about the physique and strength of the offender and whether or not he worked alone or with others. The presence or absence of signs of struggle may suggest whether or not the victim and offender were acquainted with one another.

Crime Scene Characteristics

Crime scene characteristics are, according to Turvey, the "distinguishing features of a crime scene as evidenced by an offender's behavioral decisions regarding the victim and the offense location, and their subsequent meaning to the offender." Is there evidence to suggest that the scene of the crime has special significance for the offender? How does this crime scene compare with the scenes of prior, apparently related, crimes? Does the crime scene reveal little forensic information? This is significant, in that it may suggest that this scene is only one of several scenes involved in the crime under investigation.

Offender Characteristics

Using data and conclusions derived from the first three steps, the investigator now attempts to create a picture of the characteristics of the offender. The features that make up this picture typically include the following:

- Physical build and other characteristics
- Gender

- Presence and type of vehicle used

- Offender's residence or workplace in relation to the crime scene

- Level of skill

- Criminal history, repeat or serial offender

- Aggressiveness

- Medical history

- Marital status

- Race or ethnic origin

Profiling Scorecard

Because criminal profiling is almost always just one element in any criminal investigation, it is difficult to assess how effective or ineffective it is in bringing about an arrest. Moreover, the quality of the profiling depends on the quality of the crime scene and crime scene investigation. The skill, knowledge, experience—and, yes, luck—of investigators also vary widely.

Nevertheless, research conducted in the early 1990s strongly suggests that trained profilers provide more useful and more valid criminal profiles than general clinical psychologists or even detectives do. While it is clear that criminal profiling does not magically deliver the offender into police custody, profiling often significantly improves the odds of making an arrest and doing so with less time and less wasted effort than would be the case without the profiling information, especially when the perpetrator is a repeat or serial offender.

Sworn Statement

The FBI musters a few agents who specialize in criminal profiling. A number of private investigators market themselves as criminal profilers and are hired on a case-by-case basis by local police departments. In large urban departments, some detectives receive training as criminal profilers.

The Least You Need to Know

- Criminal profiling employs meticulous analysis of crime scenes in order to reconstruct offender and victim behavior and draw conclusions about the characteristics and identity of the perpetrator.

◆ Although the FBI Behavioral Sciences Unit brought profiling to a high level of sophistication in the 1970s, the technique was used at least as early as 1888 in the case of Jack the Ripper.

◆ Alternatives to "FBI Crime Scene Analysis" include the Canter method of investigative psychology and Brent Turvey's Behavioral Evidence Analysis approach.

◆ Criminal investigation involves too many variables to permit an unambiguous assessment of the effectiveness of profiling, but most experts believe that, especially in serial cases, criminal profiling is a significant aid to investigation.

Part 4

On the Scene (and in the Lab)

Edmond Locard, the French police official who established the world's first crime lab in 1910, proclaimed the chief assumption of forensic science. "Every contact," he said, "leaves a trace." Crime, especially violent crime, is a profound and terrifying contact between assailant and victim. Criminal investigators look for the traces of this contact, collect them, examine them, and use them to solve the crime and secure justice.

This part tells what patrol officers and detectives do when they arrive at a crime scene, how investigators "read" that scene and question witnesses, victims, and suspects, and how evidence is gathered, processed, and analyzed. A special chapter is devoted to the history and present practice of fingerprint identification and analysis.

Chapter 9

The Arrival

In This Chapter

- ◆ Crime scene roles
- ◆ Processing the scene
- ◆ Investigative pitfalls
- ◆ Learning from the O.J. Simpson and JonBenet Ramsey cases

As with any event, the entrance is often the most important moment in the crime-scene investigation. How investigators enter the scene sets the tone for the entire investigation. The initial responding officer, the lowest-paid officer holding the lowest rank, makes decisions that will affect the rest of the case or, more critically, whether or not a case can even be made.

Safety comes first. A hot crime scene may include injured victims and may yet harbor dangerous perpetrators. And once the scene is secured, it becomes a matter of keeping your eyes open and taking care not to compromise any pieces of evidence. This chapter covers the initial investigative assessment and processing of a crime scene.

Who's on Call

Responding to a crime involves a number of professionals, typically beginning with the dispatcher, who relays vital information to a responding officer or officers. In the case of any major crime, other investigators are called in, including detectives, investigators from the prosecutor's office, and, depending on the nature of the crime, the medical examiner and his or her staff.

Dispatchers

The first line of response in law enforcement is the dispatcher. These professional communications officers take the call for help and dispatch appropriate responding officers. Too often, their work goes unappreciated, by the public and even by other law-enforcement professionals.

Since the introduction of the *911 system* beginning in 1968 and extending through the 1970s, the dispatcher has become more important than ever. Although 911 has been a lifesaver, the system is abused perhaps as frequently as it is used properly. The dispatcher must filter through the information and properly assess urgency in an emergency context in which everything seems equally urgent.

Talking the Talk

The **911 system** is a standardized means of dialing directly for help in a police, fire, or medical emergency. The idea is that the 911 operator has the training to obtain the necessary information from the caller, dispatch the appropriate personnel, and, in some cases, provide emergency instructions to the caller.

The dispatcher's job is to determine *who*, *what*, *where*, *when*, and *how* the emergency has happened. In the case of a crime, the dispatcher must also determine if the perpetrators are still present, where they went, how many of them are there, what they were wearing, and whether they are armed. Often, it is up to the dispatcher to calm a desperate or injured victim, or the child who has found a parent severely injured, sick—or worse.

It takes a special kind of person to be a dispatcher—someone who is satisfied with a behind-the-scenes role, but who can project him- or herself into the setting to which he or she is sending the otherwise blind uniformed officer.

Once a call comes into the emergency operation dispatch center, the 911 operator gathers as much information as possible from the caller:

1. Where is the emergency? What address? What apartment number?

2. What has happened?

3. With whom am I speaking?

4. Are you the victim? If not, are you a witness?

5. Has anyone been injured? Is an ambulance needed? What are the injuries?

6. Who is the suspect?

7. Can you describe the suspect?

8. Is the suspect present?

9. If the suspect is not present, do you know where he or she may be?

10. Are weapons involved? If yes, what kind? Where are they located?

11. Is the suspect under the influence of alcohol or drugs? If yes, what substance?

12. Are children present?

13. Have the police been to this address before? If yes, how many times?

14. Does the victim have a protective order from a judge (in the case of a domestic violence incident)?

Even those of us who have never had to dial 911 have heard recordings on TV news and "true crime" shows. No exchange was more desperate and chilling than this call, received on March 20, 1999, by a dispatcher at the Jefferson County, Colorado, sheriff's communications center:

Caller: Yes, I'm a teacher at Columbine High School and there is a student here with a gun. He just shot out a window. I believe, um, I'm at Columbine High School. I don't know what's in my shoulder. If it was just some glass. I don't know what's going on.

911 operator: Has anyone been injured, ma'am?

Caller: I am, yes! And the school is in a panic and I'm in the library. I've got students down. Kids under the table! My kids are screaming, under the table, kids, and my teachers are trying to take control of things. We need police here.

911 operator: Okay, okay, we're getting them. Who is the student, ma'am?

Caller: I don't know who the student is. I saw a student outside …. I said what was going on out there. (Talking to students) I don't think that's a really good idea. (To 911 operator) And we were waiting to see what was going on. He turned the gun straight at us and shot and my God, the window went out and the kid standing there with me, I think he got hit.

911 operator: Okay, we got help on the way, ma'am.

Caller: Oh God! Oh God! Kids, just stay down. Do we know where he's at? I'm in the library. He's upstairs. He's right outside of here. He's outside this hall. There are lines of people … kids, just stay down! Do we know where he's at? He's outside in the hall. There's alarms and things going off and smoke. (yelling) My God, smoke is coming into this room. I've got the kids under a table. I don't know what's happening in the rest of the building. Shouldn't someone else be calling 911?

911 operator: Yes, we have a lot of people on. I need you to stay on the line with me. We need to know what's going on.

Caller: I am on the floor.

911 operator: You've got the kids there?

Caller: I've got every student in this library on the floor. (yelling) You guys just stay on the floor!

911 operator: Is there any way you can lock the doors?

Caller: Um, smoke is coming in from out there and I'm a little … my God, it's … (Bang. Bang. Bang. Bang. Bang. Bang.) My God, the gun is right outside my door. Okay, I don't think I'm going to go out there. We're not going to go to the door. I've got the kids on the floor. I got all of the kids in the library on the floor.

911 operator: We have paramedics and we have fire and we have police en route.

Uniformed Officers

Uniformed police officers hold the most important job in law enforcement. Underpaid, overworked, stressed, tired, and often young, they are also brave, dedicated, trained, and mature beyond their years.

When an officer leaves the academy, he or she is faced with a tangled web of complex law and even more complex human emotion, which make for a degree of confusion greater than what a rookie in any other field faces. In law enforcement, your mistakes shoot at you. You must make quick and positive decisions at the most inopportune of times. It is an awakening akin to a cold slap in the face when a new officer arrives at a violent domestic disturbance, a grisly murder scene, or a horrific traffic accident. The thought runs through that officer's mind that *someone, please,* should call 911. Then it hits the rookie: *Well, someone already did.*

The training calls for the officer to be calm, to look for and aid injured victims, to apprehend the perpetrator, and to preserve the crime scene. Sometimes the mere presence of the officer is a sufficient calming force to comfort the victims. As for the perpetrator, he may be sitting in a chair, dazed, surveying the damage he has just done, or he may be attempting to flee, or he may have fled. The emotions of all parties simmer, boil, and swirl. Amid the chaos, the uniformed officer must conduct a security sweep, secure the scene, care for the injured, and begin the process of calling for backup and investigative help, if needed.

In addition, the uniformed officer must act as the first investigator. The officer's trained eye and skill at recording events can mean the difference between a successful prosecution and the failure of justice.

One of the most difficult but most critical duties of the uniformed officer is to secure the crime scene and control access to it. This means keeping nonessential persons out— including the overly inquisitive fellow patrol officer, the caring neighbor, the distraught relative, the pushy media personality, and even the micro-managing police chief about to breathe down the investigator's neck.

Sworn Statement

How does a lowly uniformed officer keep a superior from mucking up the crime scene? By issuing a judicious reminder that, since all officers on scene may be called on to testify, the superior's presence will probably mean a subpoena to a court appearance. No overworked cop *likes* to appear in court, and a word to the wise is usually sufficient to discourage unwanted interference from on high.

Assuming the absence of an obvious threat—for example, gunfire—the uniformed officer begins by determining the location and condition of the victim or victims. If he or she is confronted by an "active shooter," the officer must attend to that danger first. If not, the officer next takes these steps:

◆ Determines if the suspect is still at the scene.

◆ Determines if any weapon is involved.

◆ Determines what, if any, crime has occurred.

◆ Summons an ambulance if the injuries require one.

◆ Separates the victim, suspects, and witnesses.

◆ Prevents communication between the parties. This includes removing the victim and witnesses from the suspect's line of sight and range of hearing.

◆ Takes care to disturb no evidence and summons other investigators, as required, if the dispatcher has not already done so.

While the uniformed officer does all of this, he or she must also keep in mind the report that will soon have to be written. Older cops tell this to the rookies: "If it is not in the report, it did not happen." That is, in court, little or no weight will be given to any police testimony that is not documented in the on-the-scene report.

> **Sworn Statement**
>
> One of the toughest judgments an officer must make is to employ a level of force appropriate to the situation. Take the job of separating the parties at the scene. Simple? Not always. The officer must go about this without provoking violence or further violence and in a way that keeps fellow officers in his or her line of sight and range of hearing. This is particularly critical in responding to domestic violence incidents. These calls are often the most volatile, unpredictable, and dangerous. It is common for the responding officers to be attacked not only by the offender, but by the victim they were sent to protect—once it dawns on her that her husband, boyfriend, or partner is about to go to jail.

Detectives

Many uniformed officers want to be detectives—or so they think, until they actually get that promotion. The hours are long, the frequent calls to crime scenes are burdensome, and the responsibility is tremendous. Detectives usually have at least three years of law enforcement experience before they are even considered for the position. In large jurisdictions they may be assigned to a specialized unit: Homicide, Burglary, Auto Theft, White Collar, or Narcotics. In many smaller departments they need to be expert in whatever crime they are called to investigate.

Upon arrival at the scene the detective gets the first explanation of the event from the responding uniformed officer. The better job the officer has done, the better understanding the detective will have of the crime scene and the events that took place.

All detectives have their own personal style. Some are gruff, some are smooth, but all the good ones have the practical knowledge of a seasoned street officer, a grasp of the forensic sciences, the legal knowledge of a prosecutor, and an ability to place people, events, and tangible and intangible evidence in space and time in order to put together an investigative scenario of the criminal event.

The detective begins by making certain that all of the duties of the patrol officer have been effectively completed or are on their way to being completed. A good detective not only knows that the case depends on what the responding patrol officer has done, but also remembers what it was like to be in uniform. Rapport and cooperation between patrol officers and detectives is essential.

After getting a rundown from the patrol officer, the detective does the following, generally in the following order:

- Determines if immediate judicial action is required, such as securing a search warrant.

- Reinterviews the victim(s).

- Determines the status of the alleged perpetrator. Is the perpetrator in custody? Is the perpetrator a juvenile? Has the perpetrator been read his or her Miranda rights? (We'll discuss Miranda rights in the next chapter.)

- Determines if the witnesses are only that or more deeply involved in the commission of the crime.

- Contacts crime scene technicians.

- Reports the early status of the investigation to supervisors, uniformed officers, detectives, and staff.

- Determines if other law enforcement agencies should be notified, such as federal, state, county, or municipal departments.

- Controls the flow of information and media access.

- Develops theories about the incident based upon the evidence.

The more serious and complicated the crime scene, the more time is taken to gather and document evidence. On a homicide scene, the detective may choose not to gather or disturb the evidence, but leave this to specialized crime-scene personnel and the medical examiner.

Police Lab Personnel

The technicians of the law enforcement world are the forensic investigators. In large departments, these are full-time investigators exclusively assigned to crime-scene evidence gathering and analysis. They are usually assigned to every busy shift and remain on call at off hours. Smaller departments rely on regular detectives to do crime-scene technical work.

Many investigators hold academic degrees in the forensic sciences. But their qualifications run deeper. These are the people who can leave a bloody homicide scene and wolf down a piece of cold pepperoni pizza in the car. They are as caring and committed as most folks—probably more so—but they are conditioned to be clinical and deliberate. If they ever complain, it is only about other law enforcement officers messing up *their* crime scene.

Medical Examiners' People

The role of the medical examiner has changed dramatically in the last several decades. The professional ME is now usually a physician specializing in pathology and specially trained in forensic science (see Chapter 14). The investigators working for the medical examiner are usually former detectives with a background in homicide investigation.

Once on the scene, the ME's personnel can generally determine whether or not the murder occurred at that location or somewhere else. They are able to differentiate between a homicide and a suicide by the evidence available, both tangible and intangible. These investigators live with death. It is a part of their daily lives. Personally, they range from profoundly focused to overwhelmingly morbid. Professionally, they perform invaluable work in determining the cause of the event and the responsible party.

Prosecutor's People

Once the work of the police and medical examiner is finished, the prosecutor's investigators evaluate the case to ensure that it is ready for trial. These investigators are usually former detectives. They are still certified law enforcement officers, with full powers of arrest, but they've found a job with regular hours.

> **Talking the Talk**
>
> A **criminalist** examines and identifies physical evidence in order to reconstruct a crime scene. Criminalists often specialize in serology (body fluid evidence), DNA typing, trace evidence, firearms and tool marks, impression evidence, or drug identification.

The trend today is for the prosecutor's office to get involved early in the case. Investigators from the prosecutor's office may be present during a traffic safety checkpoint (roadblock) or assigned to a homicide or narcotics task force. This proactive approach allows the early input of the office that has the ultimate responsibility and accountability for law enforcement.

Criminalists

Criminalists go beyond the work of forensic technicians to examine and identify physical evidence in order to reconstruct a crime scene. This evidence may be a weapon, a piece of clothing, a bloodstain, hairs, fibers, drugs, or even a vapor in the air. The object is to use the evidence to establish a link between the suspect and the victim. Typically, criminalists work at a crime laboratory and receive the collected evidence from crime scene investigators; however, some criminalists collect physical evidence at crime scenes, but they do so only as the investigation progresses. Typically, the criminalist is consulted early in a case only when detectives are stumped.

Pitfalls

Investigating crime is a high-stakes occupation. Do the job right and lives may be saved and justice served. Make a mistake—or a misjudgment—and people can get hurt or a criminal walk free. The job has to be done quickly and efficiently, but also painstakingly—not an easy combination.

Inside the Pressure Cooker

Try to imagine the pressure on a law enforcement officer assigned to solve a crime or end a crime spree. Maybe the case in question is a high-profile serial murder investigation. Maybe it's a "routine" rash of convenience store robberies. To the officer in charge, the responsibility is great in either instance.

Throughout the investigation, the officer is considering not only the present victims, but future ones as well. If the suspect is not located, properly treated, and fully investigated, the officer knows only too well that many more horrible things may take place.

Media Spotlight

These days, the media is rarely friendly to law enforcement. At one time, a local reporter was assigned to the police beat, and usually felt like "one of the boys." Today, the relationship between police and media is more adversarial. With the advent of *sunshine laws*, the reporter is no longer solely reliant on the willingness of the police to provide information. Since the reporter is no longer dependent on the police for access to information, the climate of cooperation has all but disappeared.

Talking the Talk

Sunshine laws is a general term for legislation mandating free and open public (including media) access to many aspects of the police investigative process. The idea is to eliminate any dark corners of the criminal justice system by "letting the sunshine in."

Why buy lunch for a detective when you can force the release of information by other means?

Police officials want to be responsible and responsive to the public, but the wrong information published at the wrong time can seriously compromise a case, either in the investigative stage or when the matter goes to trial. While the prospect of police acting omnipotently or in secrecy is appalling, unbridled criticism in the press undermines police effectiveness, not to mention department morale, and the public's trust and willingness to cooperate with law enforcement professionals.

Chain of Custody

Chain of custody is a concept that is drilled into police officers from their first days in the academy to the last day of their career. The idea is this: Evidence is subject to loss, damage, contamination, tampering, or the suspicion of any of these things. Therefore, it is critically important to control the evidence and to be accountable for that control. Chain of custody is a complete and seamless record of all investigative and judicial personnel who have had custody of a piece of evidence.

The chain of evidence concept is simple in theory, but it is often complicated in practice. Once evidence is obtained, the goal is to seize it properly and use it against the accused. If the evidence is tangible—for instance, a gun, fingerprints, or a bloody shirt—it is seized, logged, secured, and processed. It is secured and brought to trial to be used in the prosecution of the case. At each step, every time the evidence changes hands, it must be accounted for. The person who releases the evidence to the next person must sign a release, and the receiver must sign a receipt.

In the case of intangible evidence, such as a statement, the material must be reduced to writing or video and/or audio recording. Each time a transcript is shared or a tape passed on, the same releases and receipts must be signed.

Of O.J. and JonBenet

Throughout this book there are examples of cases investigated, solved, brought to trial, and successfully prosecuted. Sometimes, however, the public hears most about the cases that show everything that can go wrong and demonstrate just how high the investigative stakes are.

The nearly year-long trial of O.J. Simpson for the brutal murder of his ex-wife, Nicole Brown Simpson, and her friend, Ronald Goldman, in 1995 was nationally televised and followed like a soap opera.

The Los Angeles Police Department (LAPD) presented prosecutors with what lead attorney Marcia Clark called a "mountain of evidence" against Simpson. Blood stains found at the crime scene were tested to determine blood type and to provide DNA samples. Blood stains were found in Simpson's white Bronco, on a pair of socks in his bedroom, on a pair of gloves, at the crime scene, in his driveway, and in his house.

DNA samples taken from blood at the crime scene were compared to samples from O.J. Simpson, Nicole Brown Simpson, and Ron Goldman. While expert witnesses for the prosecution testified that the DNA definitively linked O.J. Simpson to the murders, defense witnesses supported the claim that crime scene samples were mishandled, contaminated, or even planted as part of a racist conspiracy.

Shoe print evidence found at the scene (see Chapter 13) indicated that the murderer wore size 12 Bruno Magli "Lorenzo" shoes, and snapshots by a photojournalist showed Simpson wearing such shoes—but the actual shoes were never recovered, and the jury seemed unimpressed.

One of the most critical pieces of evidence presented was a pair of bloody gloves. The left-handed glove was found outside Nicole Brown Simpson's residence, and the right-handed glove was recovered from O.J. Simpson's estate. During a June 15, 1995, court session, Simpson put on the gloves, which appeared to be too small. The prosecution pointed out that the gloves, having been drenched in blood, had shrunk. The defense turned the evidence against the prosecution, however, claiming that if the glove didn't fit, Simpson could not be the killer.

To the stunned dismay of many, O. J. Simpson was acquitted of murder charges, the "mountain of evidence" notwithstanding. Physical evidence could not overcome the jury's suspicion that the LAPD was a racist organization quite capable of framing a high-profile black celebrity.

> **Sworn Statement**
>
> If it doesn't fit, you must acquit.
>
> —O.J. Simpson attorney Johnnie Cochran, regarding the infamous glove evidence in his summation to the jury

Similarly dismaying was the tragic case of JonBenet Ramsey, a six-year-old girl found, on December 26, 1996, strangled and sexually assaulted in the basement of her family's Boulder, Colorado, home. Physical evidence abounded, including a purported ransom note, a ligature around the girl's neck, and the body itself. Yet the crime scene was poorly processed, access to it poorly controlled, and cooperation among local law enforcement agencies and between the police and JonBenet's parents—who were treated by some officials as suspects, but were not arrested—seemed to range from grudging to nonexistent. In this climate, the physical evidence proved insufficient to identify a suspect, and, despite the investigative resources devoted to the case as well as intense public pressure, the murder of JonBenet remains unsolved as of early 2002.

The Least You Need to Know

◆ A 911 call mobilizes an array of law enforcement professionals, beginning with the dispatcher and uniformed officers, then continuing to detectives and other investigative specialists.

◆ Although the uniformed patrol officer soon relinquishes responsibility for the crime scene to other investigators, his or her actions as the first to respond often determine whether or not the case will be solved, suspects apprehended, and offenders successfully prosecuted.

◆ Complex or serious crimes are investigated by forensic specialists, criminalists, and the medical examiner in addition to detectives.

◆ Investigating a crime requires individual expertise and collective cooperation among a variety of law enforcement officials. When the expertise is seriously in doubt or cooperation breaks down, crimes remain unsolved and suspects walk free.

Bringing Method to the Madness

In This Chapter

♦ The importance of recording the crime scene

♦ The police report

♦ Interrogation: techniques and objectives

♦ Searches and the law

So much goes on during a criminal investigation that it is essential to filter the information coming in. This is the only way to separate useful information from the garbage. Information gathered is—or can lead to—inculpatory evidence, facts that may be used to prove an allegation of guilt. An investigation may also turn up exculpatory evidence, which suggests that the accused is innocent of the charges or at least not guilty beyond a reasonable doubt—the only acceptable standard for conviction.

Whether inculpatory or exculpatory, evidence must be probative; that is, it must have more value in providing information than in creating a sensational or emotional effect. While the investigator will use and filter all the information provided, he or she must always weigh the value of the evidence and its usefulness in prosecuting the case at hand. This chapter explains how investigators develop compelling probative evidence.

Recording the Scene

The crime scene itself is the first piece of evidence that the investigator comes upon after the original call for assistance, which typically provides only the location and a few limited details. The scene is, therefore, a critical piece of the puzzle and may provide perspective for understanding the events that occurred. Who did what, where, and why may be explained to a large extent by the physical geography of the location. However, the only way that most juries, who are the final arbiters of fact in a criminal proceeding, will get to observe the crime scene is through photographic evidence. Therefore, it is essential for the investigator to be able to reproduce the crime scene for the jury in as much detail as possible and in a fair and probative manner.

Investigative Photography

Photographs are excellent evidence—if they are properly taken, produced, and explained. There is an accepted method of crime scene photography used in most jurisdictions in the United States. The purpose of photographing the crime scene is to make a record of the scene to create a vivid demonstration and description for a jury. The crime scene photographer sets out to photograph the scene much as an average person would approach that scene. Thus, the first photos are overviews, which present the big picture, the crime scene as it fits into the surrounding landscape or cityscape.

After documenting an overview, the photographer captures the midrange. These photos are of a particular room or area, and they constitute a sequence of photographs taken to show the immediate area of the incident. Midrange photographs may be taken of

> **Sworn Statement**
>
> One of the most important aspects of crime scene photography is perspective. The photographer uses objects of known size—rulers, pencils, quarters, and so on—to provide a sense of scale that puts the evidence into perspective. A photograph of a laceration next to a six-inch ruler provides a vivid and yet objective image of the extent of the injury.

each room in a house to show how the rooms relate to one another. Generally, the photographer moves logically, from outside to inside.

After the midrange photos have been made, the photographer turns to closeups, images of particular pieces of evidence. In domestic violence investigation, for example, these photographs may be of bruises and other injuries. In the case of homicide, blood-splatter patterns are especially important, as are closeups of such evidence as fingerprints (see Chapter 12).

Crime-Scene Sketches

On-the-scene sketches are helpful supplements to photographic evidence. Most useful is a carefully measured overhead plan of the scene, showing how one relevant element relates to another—for example, the position of a body relative to a gun on the floor and relative to windows and doorways.

Investigators do not attempt great feats of artistry in making crime scene sketches, but they do try to create a sketch that accurately portrays and conveys the physical facts, that clearly relates to the sequence of events at the scene, and that precisely establishes the location and relation of pieces of evidence.

Sketches have value in investigation, as aids to thinking through a problem. They also help the jury put together pieces of evidence into the big picture.

Computer-Aided Imaging

Today's investigators often make use of *computer-aided imaging* to render more accurate and realistic sketches. Special drawing software specifically adapted to the requirements of police officers and lawyers speeds up the sketching process and makes it more accurate. The presentation is often neater and clearer. Best of all, the software makes it easy to create three-dimensional full-perspective renderings from two-dimensional floor-plan sketches. Such sketches are typically easier for a jury to understand.

Talking the Talk

Computer-aided imaging employs CAD (computer-aided design) software to create accurate, clear, and rapid renderings of crime scenes.

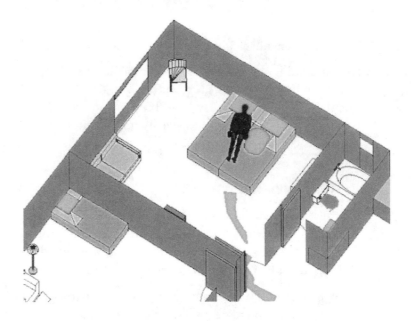

This computer-aided 3-D rendering of a crime scene employed Crime Zone software from the CAD Zone company.

(Image courtesy of CAD Zone, Inc.)

Taking Note

One of the first things police officers in the academy are cautioned about is this: *If it's not in the report, it didn't happen.* Seasoned investigators take ample notes, because they realize that if they don't write it down—now—it is probably not going to get into the final report. Gone are the days when police officers were trusted implicitly and their testimony taken as gospel. The juries of today give police testimony little, if any, more credibility than that of any other witness. The credibility comes not from the badge, but from the documentation, recording, and reporting. It must be routine, systematic, and reliable.

Those Pads—and What Investigators Write on Them

The paper pad is one of the most essential tools of police investigation. Of course, it does little good without a pen, but even in an era of tight city budgets pens are still being provided to police officers.

The investigator records the name, street address, date of birth, social security number, telephone number, and whatever other information relevant to the investigation the subject provides. Some pads have preprinted blocks for this information. It may seem like a very easy thing to do, writing down the personal information someone provides to you; however, it is remarkable how many people forget their birth date or even their own name when talking to a police officer, especially after a violent crime. Also, in many jurisdictions today, people of various cultures and nationalities coexist, and many languages are used. If the officer and the victim or witness do not speak the same language the same way, the possibility of confusion and misinformation is dramatically increased.

The practice of taking notes has become such an integral part of criminal investigation that defense attorneys often demand the policeman's pad as an actual part of the report. In the past, the notepads were discarded. Now they are kept in a safe location and indexed for use at a later time.

Reducing It to Words

Many officers would rather conduct an operation into a very dangerous location than write a report afterward. Usually, by the time detectives have achieved that rank they have found a style that helps them struggle through the mundane task of report writing. The preferred style is neither flashy nor complicated. It is not filled with police jargon or unfamiliar code signals. Like any good writing, it is clear, concise, and truthful.

It is very difficult, if not impossible, to present to a jury evidence that did not find its way into the police incident report. Another real-world fact is that the time between the event and the trial is often so long that unaided memory fails the testifying officer. Commonly, investigators are asked to relay their recollections of events based upon a review of their police report prior to testimony. If a report is not sufficiently clear and detailed in the first place, the testimony will be that much less convincing. Juries do not look favorably upon testifying officers who seem unsure of the facts or, worse, appear to be making up the evidence as they go along.

Asking Questions

The trained investigator is a difficult person to be around. The children of such a person can always be sure of some type of interrogation upon returning home after being out: "Where were you? Who were you with?" The assumption is that everyone is lying, at least a little bit. Whether or not this assumption is warranted is arguable. What is not arguable is that a generous helping of skepticism can go a long way in testing the veracity of another person.

It's amazing the things people lie about. The secrets we wish kept are often of such a trivial nature that one would think they mean nothing. To the police interrogator—

and that is what a good investigator needs to be—these lies are the doors that open to the truth.

If you can get to what people are lying about, then you can get to the truth: Who is being protected and why? What motive is there for not coming clean? These are the questions the experienced investigator seeks to answer.

"You Have the Right to Remain Silent"

Miranda v. *Arizona* was the United States Supreme Court case that affirmed an accused person's right to be explicitly informed of the Fifth Amendment right to avoid self-incrimination by remaining silent.

When an accused person is in custody and is subjected to police interrogation, a *Miranda warning* is given to remind the accused of his or her Miranda rights. If the Miranda warning is not given and the right to remain silent is not freely and voluntarily waived, then any statement made by the defendant or any subsequent evidence garnered by his statement cannot be used against him in court.

Most police officers carry the Miranda warning on a printed card:

> You have the right to remain silent.
>
> Anything you say can and will be used against you in a court of law.
>
> You have the right to an attorney.
>
> If you cannot afford an attorney, one will be appointed to represent you if you wish.

> You can decide at any time to stop answering questions if you wish.

Talking the Talk

A **Miranda warning** is issued to any suspect taken into police custody and subjected to police interrogation; it advises the suspect of his constitutional rights to remain silent (to avoid self-incrimination) and to legal representation. The warning is named after the landmark 1966 Supreme Court decision in the case of *Miranda* v. *Arizona*.

Miranda can be tricky. Key terms to remember are *custody* and *interrogation*. Miranda applies only when the suspect is actually in custody or, more commonly, under arrest, and responding to police questions. It is not necessary, nor is it good police practice, to "Mirandize" everyone at a crime scene automatically and perfunctorily.

The most remarkable thing about Miranda is that so many accused individuals still talk. Is it because they are sure that they are much smarter than the police officer? Or do they have a sudden, urgent need to bare their souls? Whatever the motive, suspects talk, and talk a lot. Often, the over-worked and weary investigator secretly longs to say, "You have the right to remain silent. Why don't you exercise it?" Of course, he or she says no such thing and goes right on listening, sometimes late into the night.

Productive Questioning

One of the most valuable lessons an investigator learns is to avoid asking questions to which he or she does not already know the answer. It is critical to direct the flow of information. Rare is the subject who freely divulges truthful, useful, and concise information. It is far more common for the suspect to talk around the questions. This can lead to the truth, but not without some nudging.

Often, the first task is simply to get the person talking. The detective must figure out what sort of persona he or she needs to project in order to get through to the suspect— a parental figure, a confessor, an intimidator, or even something of a friend and ally. The detective tries to be whatever it takes to get the tongue wagging. In this role playing, the suspect often unknowingly assists the interrogator. Appealing to the bravado, pride, machismo, the need for understanding, or insecurity the suspect exhibits is often effective in overcoming a reluctance to talk.

If interrogators should be good questioners, they must be even better listeners. Interrogators avoid questions that produce nothing more than a yes or no. Instead, they ask open-ended questions that keep the conversation going.

> **Sworn Statement**
>
> The five basic rules of interrogation are:
>
> 1. Be an active listener.
> 2. Ask relevant questions.
> 3. Do not interrupt.
> 4. Maintain eye contact.
> 5. Be attentive.

Look Me in the Eye

Interrogators use many methods to assess the truthfulness of a suspect. Kinesics is one effective method all experienced investigators use, whether they call it by that name or not. Kinesics is the formal study of nonverbal communication, what is familiarly called "body language." There is a lot to be learned from the suspect's movements, expressions, and gestures in response to questions or what psychologists call other "stressors." The suspect may touch his nose, touch his mouth, grab his neck. He may cross his arms over his chest, or may laugh inappropriately. He may avoid eye contact or chew on his lip when being spoken to. Various protective and evasive movements are innate human responses to stressors. They are hardly proof of guilt, but they are indicators of a lack of truthfulness.

In jurisdictions that encompass culturally diverse populations, the interrogator must also be aware of how culture and tradition may influence gestures. For example, in some cultural traditions, it is considered impolite to look someone in the eye. The interrogator needs to be certain that a suspect who appears evasive is not merely acting as a result of upbringing and background.

Search Me

In criminal investigation, a search is a quest for information. As defined in the landmark Supreme Court case of *Elliot* v. *State*, a search is "an examination of a person's house or other buildings or premises or of the person for the purpose of discovering contraband, illicit or stolen property, or some evidence of guilt to be used in prosecuting a criminal action with which the person is charged."

There is usually little glamour in searching a person's body, private drawer, closet, garbage can, vehicle, or file cabinet. The hoped-for result is to find probative evidence, seize it, then use it in a trial. If the evidence located is formidable enough, the accused may plead guilty, and a trial may be avoided.

The Fourth Amendment

All search and seizure law in the United States stems from the Fourth Amendment, which guarantees that people shall "be secure in their person, houses, papers and effects, against unreasonable searches and seizures." The framers of the Constitution wanted to ensure that people would be free from governmental interference in their personal liberties except for those instances in which *probable cause* has been established and a judicial officer has issued a warrant ordering that interference.

Talking the Talk

Probable cause is a collection of facts that would lead a reasonable person to believe that a crime has been committed or is about to be committed. This is a standard less than a certainty, but more than a probability.

As a result of the Fourth Amendment, it is assumed that people have a right to a reasonable expectation of privacy. While not unlimited, this right to privacy cannot be violated lightly and must be intruded upon only on the basis of probable cause.

A search of a person may be conducted after an arrest has been made. A search of a premises may be conducted after a judge issues a search warrant. Both of these instances require preexisting probable cause that a crime has been committed. The Bill of Rights permits no general or blanket warrants. The law enforcement officer must swear that the facts are such that they reasonably justify the search in *this* particular case. The judge reviews the affidavit of the applying officer and grants the search warrant if it is deemed that probable cause of the alleged criminal activity exists. It is not legally sufficient to justify a search after the fact. That is, an officer cannot present the judge with a piece of probative evidence found in an illegal search and ask the judge to issue, in effect, a retroactive search warrant. The probable cause must exist prior to the search.

What Investigators Look For

The search warrant lists items or classes of items to be seized. These may include, for example, narcotics, weapons, "fruits of a crime," money, or clothing. In addition, the searching officer may seize contraband, stolen property, or evidence of another crime. Once the object or objects named in the warrant are found, the search is ended. However, items that are in plain view may also be seized, even though they are not specifically named, provided that they fit into the general categories of objects that may be taken.

Investigators must conduct the search in a systematic manner. No rummaging or ransacking is allowed, and the search must be carried out with reasonable care to avoid damage to property. (This is not always possible. If the police have demonstrated probable cause to search for a body buried in the basement, they are authorized to take sledgehammer and jackhammer to the basement floor.) A copy of the search warrant must be served upon the person whose premises are being searched, and an inventory of the items taken must be left with that person. If no one is present during the search, a copy of the search warrant must be left in a conspicuous place, along with an inventory.

How They Look

A systematic search may be done in a circular pattern or a grid pattern. There is no one right way to do it, and the search is typically tailored to the specific layout of the area to be searched.

To keep to a minimum the number of officers that need to be subpoenaed when the case comes to trial, there is usually one "finding officer" assigned when a search is being conducted. All searchers report to that officer, and he or she takes primary responsibility for anything recovered. The idea is to be thorough, but also to keep the search manageable.

Special Searches

Most searches are routine hunts for particular evidence in a residence or place of business. A few are more specialized.

In the Garbage

A *garbage pull* is one of the least pleasant types of search. It is often part of a narcotics investigation, in which suspects discard drug-related paraphernalia and, if cornered, even the drugs themselves.

The most important factor in a garbage pull is to be certain that the garbage searched actually belongs to the subject of the investigation and that the garbage has been legally abandoned by having been placed in a location for pickup by sanitation workers. Searching through abandoned garbage does not require a warrant.

Talking the Talk

A **garbage pull** is police jargon for a search through trash or garbage in an effort to find evidence.

A garbage pull may yield such evidence as drug residue, packaging materials, and many other indicators of illegal drug transactions or manufacture. The work is hard, time-consuming, unpleasant, and often subject to stringent challenge from defense attorneys. Therefore, it is usually conducted as a last resort and bolstered by a good deal of other investigation.

Vehicle Searches

Often, the most useful vehicle search is not a search as defined in legal terms and is therefore not subject to the Fourth Amendment strictures against unreasonable searches and seizure. Vehicles impounded, for whatever reason, are subject to an inventory, an administrative procedure conducted to catalog the contents of vehicles for safekeeping purposes. No search warrant is required; however, anything found during this administrative procedure may be used as evidence.

Suspect Searches

It is legally permissible for a police officer to intrude upon the personal body space of a suspect if the officer has what is called in law "reasonable articulable suspicion" of criminal activity and that suspicion is particularized to an individual. In such a case, the officer may stop the person for a brief period to investigate further. If the officer can justify his or her belief that the person may be armed and therefore poses a threat, the officer may "frisk" the person for weapons.

This situation is known as the *Terry Stop*, named after the case of *Terry* v. *Ohio*. Although frisking a suspect is not a search, it does come under the Fourth Amendment. If, during the "pat-down of the outer clothing for weapons," the officer immediately recognizes an object to be contraband without squeezing, sliding, or otherwise manipulating it, the officer may seize that item and use it as evidence against the person. This is called the "plain feel doctrine," which was allowed after the 1993 U.S. Supreme Court decision in *Minnesota* v. *Dickerson*.

Once a person is taken into custody or arrested, it is assumed that probable cause existed prior to this action and, at this time, a suspect is subject to a "search incident to a lawful arrest." This is a constitutionally unlimited search and may be conducted at the scene or, later, in a more secure location.

Case in Point

In *Terry* v. *Ohio*, the U.S. Supreme Court ruled: "Where a police officer observes unusual conduct which leads him reasonably to conclude in light of his experience that criminal activity may be afoot and that the persons with whom he is dealing may be armed and presently dangerous, where in the course of investigating this behavior he identifies himself as a policeman and makes reasonable inquiries, and where nothing in the initial stages of the encounter serves to dispel his reasonable fear for his own or others' safety, he is entitled for the protection of himself and others in the area to conduct a carefully limited search of the outer clothing of such persons in an attempt to discover weapons which might be used to assault him."

Dead Body Searches

If a garbage pull is unpleasant and arduous, searching a dead body can be downright gruesome, especially if the body is in an advanced state of decomposition.

Like any other search, the dead body search is conducted systematically, usually beginning with the clothing. Obvious targets of a search include the wallet, identification papers, and personal effects. The investigator is also careful to search around and under the body after it is removed. Beyond these searches, most further investigation is carried out by the medical examiner (see Chapter 15).

Release the Hounds!

The bond between human beings and dogs is older than history, and the working relationship between canine (K-9) officers and their "partners" (that's how they invariably think of their dogs) is especially strong. Police use dogs not only to assist in tracking, apprehending, and controlling suspects, but also in conducting specialized searches.

With their keen sense of smell, dogs can be trained to search for very specific items, from human suspects, to narcotics, to explosives. Dogs can search large areas more efficiently than human beings can, and, in the instance of explosives searches, they can do so in a way that minimizes the risks to police officers.

> **By the Numbers**
>
> According to a 1990 study conducted for the Lansing (Michigan) Police Department, a single K-9 team typically completed building searches seven times faster than four officers working together. The dog team found hidden suspects 93 percent of the time, while human officers found them 59 percent of the time.

Savvy criminals have sometimes attempted to foil dog searches by masking narcotics and even explosives with other odors. However, because dogs can distinguish more than one odor simultaneously and to a degree far beyond that of human beings, such masking efforts fail.

Just because a dog isn't human doesn't mean that dog searches are immune from the Fourth Amendment. The courts consider dogs to be agents of the police and, therefore, dog searches require probable cause. Unlike human officers, however, no dog has ever been subpoenaed to testify in a criminal trial.

The Least You Need to Know

♦ Carefully, accurately, and concisely recording the crime scene, in pictures and words, is not only an aid to solving the crime, but essential to prosecuting suspects.

♦ Investigators must take careful notes, which become part of the record of the criminal investigation; from the beginning of their training, police officers are admonished: *If it's not in the record, it didn't happen.*

♦ Searches and interrogations must be thorough and efficient, and they must be conducted within the strictures of the Bill of Rights, particularly the Fourth and Fifth Amendments.

♦ The typical search is of a dwelling or other building; special searches range from sifting through garbage, searching on and around dead bodies, and using dogs to track suspects or to sniff out explosives or narcotics.

Chapter 11

Gathering the Evidence

In This Chapter

- ◆ Tools of the investigator's trade
- ◆ A catalog of physical evidence
- ◆ Discovering and collecting physical evidence
- ◆ Importance of the "chain of custody"

Edgar Allan Poe is best remembered for his gothic short stories (such as "The Pit and the Pendulum") and his gothic poetry ("The Raven" comes instantly to mind), but, as the Mystery Writers of America recognized when they named their annual mystery fiction award "The Edgar," Poe is also celebrated as the inventor of the detective story.

In 1841, Poe published in *Graham's Lady's and Gentleman's Magazine* (of which he happened to be editor) "The Murders in the Rue Morgue." In it, he introduced the key elements that would become so very familiar in detective fiction: the exquisitely sensitive, brilliant, eccentric investigator (C. Auguste Dupin) who calmly surveys the scene of a bizarre and utterly baffling crime, homes in on precisely the handful of cryptic clues that have escaped the attention of the ordinary policemen, and rapidly works backward from these clues (with nary a misstep) to discover the process, motive, and perpetrator of the crime.

Real-life criminal investigators do, in fact, embody some of the characteristics of Dupin, or Sherlock Holmes, Hercule Poirot, or any of a number of other fictional detectives. A good investigator needs a sharp mind and a sharp eye, a large helping of intuition, and a flexible imagination. But, most of all, he or she needs a willingness to do the often hard, tedious, and always meticulous work of gathering evidence for analysis—because, in the court room, eccentricity, acute imagination, and keen intuition count for precisely zip.

An Investigator's Toolkit

A crime is committed in a big city. Investigators pull up to the scene, one of them carrying an aluminum case, bigger than an attaché but smaller than a suitcase. Ah, what high-tech investigative wonders must it contain?

Few, if any.

For the most part, investigators bring to the scene cameras, a set of simple tools, and an array of containers.

Chalk, Tweezers, Wrecking Bar ...

The standard investigative toolkit holds tools for gathering evidence, not for analyzing it. Accordingly, the typical kit contains little more than the following:

- **Still camera and film.** Often a video camera is also included, because it can provide a good overall picture of the crime scene, one that clearly shows the layout of an area or a room, the relation of one object to another, the location of doors and windows, and so on. The investigator can also supply a running spoken commentary as he or she pans the camera over the scene. Investigators also take a lot of still pictures. (Well-funded departments send along a trained crime-scene photographer to take the pictures.)

- **Chalk.** Yes, investigators really do draw a chalk or, sometimes, tape outline to mark the position of bodies or other objects before they are removed from the scene. In crime scenes, the position of a body or other objects in relation to the rest of the crime scene tells a story. It is crucially important to note and record this.

Sworn Statement

At present, most police departments use conventional film cameras rather than digital cameras, because a defense attorney may point to the ease with which digital images can be altered.

◆ **Compass.** This piece of equipment is essential for obtaining directions and accurately reporting the orientation of bodies or objects at outdoor crime scenes. At some scenes, especially in rural or semiwilderness settings, it is helpful to have GPS (geographical positioning satellite) directions provided by a portable GPS receiver, which can pinpoint the exact longitude and latitude of the scene or scenes involved in a crime.

◆ **Containers and envelopes.** Much of the investigator's toolkit consists of nothing more than bags, boxes, bottles, envelopes, and other scrupulously clean, sealable containers to carry evidence away from the scene.

◆ **Crayon, markers, pencils, pens.** All evidence containers must be clearly and completely labeled. Most police departments provide printed labels with spaces for the required information.

◆ **Fingerprint kit.** This includes the various developing powders, chemicals, and lifting tapes discussed in Chapter 12. Some investigators are equipped with a special fingerprint camera, usually a Polaroid-type camera designed to work at close range, to record prints developed at the scene.

◆ **Flashlights.** These light sources will do for a start. Investigating and recording some crime scenes requires setting up portable lighting equipment or the use of forensic light sources, which will be discussed in a moment.

◆ **Knife.** An ordinary jack knife or Swiss army knife can be used for many investigative tasks.

◆ **Magnifier.** Sherlock Holmes wasn't the last detective to make use of a magnifying glass. Some investigators use handheld magnifiers, some employ hands-free magnifiers that fit like goggles or glasses for locating minute or trace evidence, such as hairs and fibers.

◆ **Measuring tape, rulers, protractors.** Recording precise distances and dimensions is crucial in crime scene investigation. Evidence that is recorded at the scene is often photographed with the inclusion of a ruler in the picture. A protractor is necessary for measuring angles.

◆ **Angle mirror, with collapsible handle.** This device is handy for looking into difficult-to-get-at places and for getting a quick look at the underside of vehicles.

◆ **Picks.** The investigator may need lock picks to gain access to locked rooms or cabinets. He or she may use dental picks to collect (scrape and pry) certain kinds of evidence.

◆ **Plaster.** Plaster of Paris and other molding substances are commonly used to obtain casts of footprints, tire tracks, and the like.

◆ **Pliers.** Gathering some evidence requires prying and twisting.

◆ **Rope or tape.** Fluorescent rope or bright yellow crime-scene tape are required to mark off and protect the crime scene.

◆ **Scissors.** A basic investigative tool.

◆ **Screwdrivers.** These are often necessary to access evidence.

◆ **Sketching supplies.** Paper, graph paper, pencils, and so on are used to make a quick sketch of the scene, mainly for purposes of orientation and layout.

◆ **Spatula.** This tool may be used to dig, scoop, or otherwise gather evidence.

◆ **Tweezers (forceps).** Indispensable for picking up small evidence items without contaminating them.

◆ **Wrecking bar.** This may be used to pry open doors, windows, and so on.

Forensic Light Sources

If the notable absence of high-tech equipment disappoints you, take heart. Most investigative kits also include a very cool *forensic light source* or two.

A forensic light source is a powerful portable lamp that contains ultraviolet (UV), visible, and infrared components of light. Using optical filters, the investigator can select (tune) individual color bands (wavelengths) to enhance the visualization of evidence by means of fluorescence (making the evidence glow), absorption (making the evidence appear darker), and oblique lighting (making small-particle evidence more apparent).

Talking the Talk

A forensic light source is a powerful portable lamp whose spectrum contains ultraviolet (UV), visible, and infrared light components, which can be selectively filtered (tuned) to provide narrow portions of the spectral band for investigative purposes.

Forensic lighting is especially useful in detecting latent fingerprints (see Chapter 12), especially on surfaces that are difficult to dust and lift, such as thin plastic bags, rigid duct tape, thin aluminum foil, heavily grained wood, concrete walls, and brick walls. Investigators lightly dust such surfaces with a special fluorescent powder, which glows under ultraviolet light to reveal the fingerprint.

Such body fluids as semen, saliva, and vaginal fluid are naturally fluorescent under ultraviolet light. Precisely filtered forensic light sources can reveal the presence of these dried fluids on carpeting, mattresses, clothing, and so on.

In its natural state, blood does not fluoresce under UV light, but, using the appropriate filter on the forensic light source, blood traces appear to darken, making it much easier to detect and photograph them. (See Chapter 14 for a discussion of how investigators detect blood traces and analyze blood spatter evidence.)

Strong oblique lighting of a surface tends to reveal small particles such as hair and fibers, which may then be collected as evidence. Some hair and fibers also glow under ultraviolet light.

By adjusting the filters on a forensic light source, bruises and wound patterns, invisible under normal white light, may be revealed. Bite marks, shoe marks, and other distinctive wound evidence may also become visible or more clearly defined. Exposing a suspect's palm may reveal a bruise pattern that links him to a bludgeon-type weapon.

What *Is* Evidence, Anyway?

Evidence is anything that helps to establish the facts of the crime under investigation. As discussed in Chapter 10, some evidence is more valuable in a legal sense (more probative) than others. In addition to witness, victim, and suspect testimony (all promising sources of probative evidence), investigators gather physical evidence, especially of the following types.

Shoe and Tire Impressions

Shoe soles and heels leave characteristic prints and impressions, as do tire treads. If a pattern found at the scene can be linked to shoes worn by the suspect or a vehicle driven by him, a strong connection to the scene is made. If the prints are on smooth surfaces, they are photographed. They may also be lifted, using special transparent adhesive tape.

On soft surfaces, such as earth, shoes and tires make an impression rather than a print. These are photographed at the scene. An investigator will also usually make a plaster cast of such prints. Some investigators use dental casting material, some use plaster of Paris.

> **Sworn Statement**
>
> Many a poorly trained sleuth has been unable to resist the urge to measure a shoe print by attempting to fit his or her own shoe into the suspect's print. The result? A ruined piece of evidence.

Tools and Tool Marks

Tools are commonly used to force entry into buildings or rooms. Any tools found at a crime scene—pry bars, screwdrivers, and the like—need to be collected as evidence and, certainly, dusted for fingerprints. Pieces of broken tools are also important and are collected by investigators. Sometimes it is possible to match a broken tool piece to the rest of a tool found in the suspect's possession.

Tools leave characteristic marks on anything they are applied to. A screwdriver used to pry open a window, for instance, will leave an impression in both the window and sill. These marks need to be noted, photographed, and, perhaps, even cast. They may be matched to a tool found in the suspect's possession.

Sometimes it is possible to match marks on a tool with marks left on the object to which the tool was applied. For example, the sledgehammer used to open a strongbox or safe will leave an impression on the metal of the safe, which may be matched to the surface of the hammer head. If that safe was painted, it may be possible to find traces of the paint on a hammer known to be owned by the suspect.

Broken Glass

Broken glass is nasty stuff. It adheres to shoes and clothing. Finding shattered glass at a crime scene and tiny glass fragments embedded in the sneaker soles of a suspect can provide a strong evidentiary link between crime and suspect. Large fragments of glass are routinely dusted for fingerprints.

The pattern created by broken glass says much about how the glass was broken and from what direction it was hit. Was it broken from the inside of the building or the outside? Was it hit from above or below?

The size and shape of bullet holes in glass indicate the direction of the bullet's travel and the angle of fire. If the bullet does not shatter the glass, it leaves a conical hole, the smaller hole at the point of entry, the larger at the point of exit. It is even possible to estimate the velocity of the bullet from the appearance of the hole. The faster the bullet, the smaller the cracks will be and the tighter the hole at the point of entry. This information, in turn, enables an investigator to estimate from how far away the shot came.

Soils and Minerals

Fans of Sir Arthur Conan Doyle will remember that Sherlock Holmes was always interested in mud and soil tracked into a crime scene. Holmes was an expert on soils and could tell at a glance where, geographically, a particular sample came from. No one expects a criminal investigator to possess Holmes's encyclopedic knowledge of soils and minerals, but investigators are careful to collect any soil or mineral deposits they find at a crime scene. These can be submitted to a forensic geologist for identification, which may ultimately serve to link a suspect to the scene.

Not all soil or mineral samples are natural. They may be traces of cement, plaster, or even building insulation. All of this is typically collected and analyzed.

Cigarette Butts

Sherlock Holmes was also an expert on rare tobaccos, and he carefully analyzed the butts of certain exotic cigarettes left at a crime scene. Today, cigarette butts provide evidence Holmes never dreamed of. Saliva deposits on the cigarette are a rich source of DNA evidence. Many people involved in a crime are nervous, and many people smoke when they're nervous. Investigators eagerly collect and carefully bag any cigarette butts found at the crime scene.

Sworn Statement

I get to the scene. I look at an ashtray—how they put out a cigarette butt. Which one is still warm? The way each of us puts out a cigarette butt shows certain habits. Then we look for whether there's lipstick or grease on it. You sort it out before you send it to the laboratory. If you do the work, you already know how many people sat in there and smoked, and whether or not there were females or auto mechanics. Then if I go to a suspect's home, I look at the way he or she puts out a cigarette to see if there are similarities with what we found. You make an interpretation of existing patterns.

—Dr. Henry C. Lee, forensic scientist

Rope and Tape

Rope and tape are often used to bind the hands and feet of a victim. Burglars may use tape to hold back a door latch. Tape must be dusted for fingerprints, of course, but tape as well as rope evidence are always carefully collected because it may be possible to match the type of tape or rope found at the scene with materials in a suspect's possession or known to have been purchased by him. Tear patterns in tape or fraying patterns on rope found at the scene may be matched with material associated with the suspect.

Drugs

Drugs associated with a crime scene are always important, whether the drug in question is an illicit substance or a prescription product. This material is carefully collected and sent to the lab for analysis.

Weapons and Ammo

Most violent crimes involve firearms. Ballistics, the forensic analysis of firearm-related evidence, can often match a bullet to a gun (see "Firearms Identification" in Chapter 13), but, first, the evidence must be collected.

Investigators look for any weapons left at the crime scene. These may be dusted for fingerprints at the scene, but they must be handled carefully, so that they can be examined further by ballistics experts. The investigator also typically notes at the scene the make, caliber, model, type, and serial number of any weapons found.

Investigators carefully comb the crime scene for bullet holes, bullets lodged in holes, and spent cartridge casings. The position of all bullets and cartridge casings found must be carefully marked and photographed before this evidence is collected and sent to the lab for analysis.

Clothing and Laundry Marks

Clothing may provide a wealth of evidence. Clothing fibers may connect a suspect and victim. A piece of torn clothing—even a thread or two—left at the scene may point to a suspect.

Many professional laundries and dry cleaners use readily identifiable marking systems. The standard systems are on file with the Laundry and Dry Cleaning National Association, and the FBI and other police laboratories also maintain files of marking systems. Such markings can help identify clothed unknown human remains. It should be noted that many laundry marks are visible only under ultraviolet light.

Hair and Fibers

Hair and fibers can provide much valuable evidence because they are often shed ("transferred") by a perpetrator during a struggle or even in casual contact with the victim or with objects at the crime scene (see the section "Hairs and Fibers" in Chapter 13). However, this kind of trace evidence requires a keen eye to locate and great care in collecting. Often, the best thing to do is to collect any objects that may be expected to harbor hair and fiber evidence and carefully bag the entire object for later laboratory analysis.

Hairs and fibers that are definitely located at the scene are collected with a tweezers and put in appropriate envelopes or other containers.

Blood and Body Fluids

The analysis of blood and other body fluid evidence is discussed in Part 5. On the scene, the principal task is to identify the presence of body fluids, which can be collected for analysis.

Blood makes obvious stains—so obvious that perpetrators often try to wash away any blood evidence. Investigators use forensic light sources and chemical agents (Luminol is the best known) to reveal the presence of blood traces. Even with a cleaning so thorough that the visible stains have been entirely eradicated, hemoglobin in the blood leaves traces that fluoresce when treated with Luminol or that turn color when treated with other substances, such as Ortho-tolidine.

These days, blood and body fluid evidence is more important than ever, because DNA analysis can often provide positive identification of the human source of the evidence.

Case in Point

Famed forensic investigator Dr. Henry C. Lee was called in on a murder case that lacked a body. (Without a corpse, it is difficult to obtain a conviction.) A 16-year-old girl who worked at a massage parlor was called out on a job. When she failed to return, the police were summoned. Officers found nothing at her client's house. Frustrated, detectives called Lee. "When I got to the basement, I said it was just too clean. It had a wall-to-wall carpet that had recently been shampooed. It was kind of wet." Lee tested the carpet with Ortho-tolidine, which turned blue, indicating blood traces. Investigators cut the carpet and discovered a pool of blood beneath it. The amount of blood, 2,000 cc, was ample trial evidence of murder. A person who lost that volume of blood *had* to be dead.

Fingerprints

Finding fingerprints is almost always a prime focus of evidence gathering. The process of lifting and analyzing fingerprints is discussed in the next chapter. But before fingerprints can be lifted and analyzed, they must be found. This can require a long and exhausting search. Think of all the fingerprints that accumulate in an average room. Investigators rarely attempt to cover an entire room, but, instead, focus on areas and objects most likely to be associated with the crime. Even so, identifying the pertinent prints and eliminating the prints of others—say, the homeowner and family—can be a massive chore.

And this assumes investigators are lucky enough to find *any* usable prints. Most fingerprints on most surfaces are fragmentary smudges, not neat, full-finger patterns.

An Unbroken Chain

Finding and analyzing evidence is only half of the investigative process. Correctly handling and presenting evidence is vital to the probative value of the material. If a defense attorney can create in the mind of the jury a reasonable doubt that evidence was handled properly, the value of that evidence shrinks—perhaps to zero. A significant portion of the successful defense in the infamous O.J. Simpson murder trial was based on the questionable handling of physical evidence.

> **By the Numbers**
>
> A 1996 survey by criminal investigation specialist Lois Pilant revealed, shockingly, that only 51 percent of police departments have written policies and procedures governing the property and evidence storage room. Fifty-three percent did not know how much money was stored in the property room, 59 percent did not know how many guns were stored there, 62 percent did not know how much evidence came in during the previous year, and 70 percent had no regular evidence inventory process in place.

Evidence, from discovery to courtroom presentation, is supposed to be subject to a flawless chain of custody—a complete record of precisely who had custody of the evidence item at each stage of handling. Any weak, let alone broken, link in this chain admits the possibility of accidental contamination or deliberate tampering and provides the basis for a defense argument of reasonable doubt.

Examining Evidence

As soon as an item of evidence is discovered, the investigator, after initially examining it, labels it, preferably with a department-standard card or label. Typically, the label includes the investigator's signature, certifying the authenticity of the evidence and making him or her the first link in the chain of custody. A label or card accompanies the evidence wherever it goes. Each person who subsequently examines the evidence item, including other investigators, forensics experts, and lab technicians, signs the evidence card, noting the date and time the item came into his or her possession.

City of Decatur Police
Decatur, Georgia

EVIDENCE   Case No. _____

Evidence Description _____
_____

Place Evidence found _____
_____

Date & time of recovery _____
Suspect _____ Offense _____
Victim _____
Evidence recovered by _____
                                Signature, rank
            CHAIN OF POSSESSION ON REVERSE SIDE

CHAIN OF POSSESSION OF EVIDENCE
Signatures required

From   to   date   time

_____

_____

_____

_____

_____

_____

RELEASED TO: _____

Standard two-sided evidence tag.

(Image courtesy City of Decatur [Georgia] Police Department)

Preserving and Storing Evidence

Contrary to what some defense attorneys might claim, evidence is rarely subject to deliberate tampering. However, too often, delicate evidence suffers from poor or careless handling.

Guy Antinozzi logging evidence. Notice the telephone, radio, camera, narcotics test kit, and two-hole punch, all essential investigative tools.

(Photo by Sgt. Connie Rembert, Agnes Scott College Police Department)

Medical and some narcotics evidence is perishable and must be carefully preserved in storage. Investigations may consume days, weeks, months, or years. It may take many months for a case to come to trial, then the trial itself may be subject to multiple delays. Even after conviction, the appeals process can span years. Through all of this, evidence must be preserved under proper conditions.

Labels fall off. Ink on labels smudges, fades, becomes illegible. Improperly sealed containers allow liquids (body fluids, for example) to evaporate. Envelopes containing trace evidence become unsealed. In everyday life, these things happen all the time. In police work, they can destroy evidence—and thereby wreck a case.

Many police departments have adopted the kind of modern methods of inventory control retailers use, logging in each piece of evidence into a computer database and printing out a unique, machine-readable barcode label for the item. Centralizing the evidence inventory in this manner helps ensure an unbroken chain of custody.

Presenting Evidence

At trial, physical evidence is *discussed* by the attorneys for the prosecution and the defense, but it is usually first *presented* by the police officer who discovered the evidence.

When an officer presents physical evidence, he or she is asked to identify the item. The officer examines the object, making certain that it is authentic and unaltered. The officer is then usually asked to describe exactly where the evidence was found. He or she may be asked to establish the chain of custody from discovery to the present.

It is not the officer's job to analyze the evidence or to draw conclusions from it in testimony. The officer establishes the context of the item within the crime scene and the item's authenticity. After this, it is up to various forensic witnesses to persuade the jury of the meaning or significance of the evidence. Then, in the end, it is the jury, not the evidence, not the investigator, not the forensic expert, that convicts or acquits the defendant.

The Least You Need to Know

- Before physical evidence can be analyzed, it must be found and collected. This requires a few simple tools in the hands of diligent, sharp-eyed, experienced, nd patient investigators.

- The potential range of physical evidence is huge, encompassing anything the victim and perpetrator used or came into contact with.

- Equal in importance to collecting and analyzing physical evidence properly is handling and storing it in ways that preserve an unbroken chain of custody.

- The police investigator usually presents the physical evidence in court, saying how, when, and where it was recovered and establishing its authenticity; a forensic expert is then usually responsible for conveying to the jury the analytical significance of the evidence item.

The Fingerprint Story

In This Chapter

- Early criminal identification and the Bertillon System
- A brief history of fingerprinting
- Detecting fingerprint evidence
- Classifying prints
- Role of the computer in fingerprint identification
- DNA "fingerprinting"

Hear the words "criminal investigation" and chances are, fingerprints leap to mind. As the layperson (or civilian, as cops call someone who isn't a cop) sees it, investigating a crime and identifying fingerprints, like salt and pepper at the dinner table, go together.

The association seems so natural that it's hard to imagine a time when fingerprinting was a novel idea, let alone a revolutionary one. After all, archaeologists have discovered evidence suggesting that interest in fingerprints dates to prehistory. On a Nova Scotia cliff face, for example, there is a petroglyph (stone drawing) showing a hand with exaggerated fingerprints—whorls and loops—presumably the work of prehistoric

Native Americans. In ancient China and Babylon, fingerprints were routinely impressed on clay tablets, perhaps for purposes of authenticating (or perhaps out of superstition). Inked fingerprints are present on Chinese documents of the Tang Dynasty.

In this chapter we'll look at the history of fingerprint identification and the role it plays in criminal investigation.

Early Criminal Identification

There is ample archaeological and historical evidence of an age-old belief that each human fingerprint is unique. In the fourteenth century, a Persian physician and government official put the belief in writing, observing that no two persons have identical fingerprints.

As we shall see later in this chapter, the seventeenth-century Italian anatomy professor Marcello Malpighi made careful observations concerning fingerprints and even described their features with terms very much like those fingerprint experts use today, calling them "loops and spirals."

More recently, in 1858, the chief administrative officer of the Hooghly district of British India, frustrated by the natives' habit of voiding contracts and other legal instruments simply by denying the authenticity of their signatures, required businessmen to place their fingerprints on contracts in addition to their signatures. This, the official declared, would surely "frighten [the signer] out of all thought of repudiating his signature."

Yet, well into the nineteenth century, there seems to have been little interest in using fingerprints to help identify the perpetrators of crimes. This does not mean there was a lack of concern about identifying criminals. More than 2,000 years ago, the Roman legions tattooed mercenary soldiers as a means of discouraging desertion—the tattoo would unmistakably identify the runaway as a deserter.

This was, in effect, preemptive criminal identification—a way of discouraging an act *before* it was committed. But many early societies used mutilation (amputating the hand of a thief, for example) or branding as a way to stigmatize offenders. The purpose was not only to punish wrongdoing, but to discourage repeat offenses, to put the public on guard in the presence of the offender, and, in the event of a repeat offense, to make identification easier.

As civilization progressed beyond the brutality of mutilation and branding as punishments for crime, career criminals found it easy to disguise their identity and blend in with the law-abiding crowd. Even when a *recidivist* was apprehended, there was no guarantee that officials would connect him with his past criminal record. Thus, many repeat offenders were treated with the leniency accorded first timers.

Talking the Talk

A **recidivist** is a repeat criminal offender.

The "Father of Scientific Detection"

Alphonse Bertillon (1853–1914), a Frenchman, the son of a physician whose hobby was statistics and anthropology, decided to find a way of identifying known criminals. In 1878, shortly after he became a clerk in the Paris Prefecture of Police, Bertillon undertook the monumental task of rationalizing the police department's chaotic records and slipshod methods of identifying prisoners. After seven years on this job, he formulated the identification method that earned him the title of "Father of Scientific Detection."

The *Bertillon System*, or *bertillonage*, had nothing to do with fingerprinting. Instead, it relied on anthropometry, a carefully formulated combination of physical measurements made by procedures Bertillon standardized. These included (for example) measuring the width of the skull, the length of the foot, the length of the forearm from the elbow to the tip of the middle finger (the biblical "cubit"), the length and girth of the trunk, and the length of the left middle finger. Along with hair color, eye color, and front- and side-view full-length and head-and-shoulder photographs, these key measurements were recorded on standardized cards. Bertillon divided each of the measurements into small, medium, and large groupings, thereby placing the dimensions of any person into one of 243 distinct categories.

The Bertillon System accomplished several important things. It ensured that a good description of each prisoner would be obtained, it focused on features that could not be readily disguised or altered, and it introduced a significant degree of objectivity into criminal identification. While any number of people might be of similar height and build, it was believed highly unlikely (maybe even impossible) that any two people would exhibit the same *relationship* among all of the features Bertillon measured.

Talking the Talk

The **Bertillon System,** also called **bertillonage,** was a systematic method of measuring certain key features of the human body and classifying them rationally as a means of positive identification.

One of the facial features Bertillon focused on was the nose. He recognized 15 distinct types, as illustrated here.

(Image from the authors' collection)

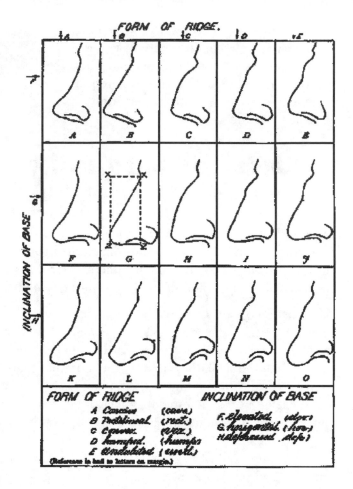

Perhaps most important of all, the Bertillon System made it relatively easy to identify repeat offenders. Once arrested, a suspect was measured, described, and photographed. The completed Bertillon card was indexed and placed in the appropriate category. Statistically, in a file of, say, 5,000 criminal records, each primary Bertillon category would hold only about 20 cards. Police officials had to compare the description and photos of the present prisoner not to 5,000 others, but to about 20.

Not only did the Paris prefecture adopt the Bertillon System (in 1882), but much of the world quickly followed suit. It was introduced into the United States in 1887 by Major R. W. McClaughry, warden of the Illinois State Penitentiary, and it rapidly caught on.

At first, the universal acceptance of the Bertillon System discouraged the development of alternative systems of identification, including fingerprinting. But, after some years, the Bertillon System began to prove increasingly unwieldy. In large jurisdictions, criminal identification still consumed inordinate amounts of time as clerks searched for matching cards. There was also the ever-present problem of the accuracy of the measurements. The Bertillon System required exact training, which was often imperfect or simply unavailable. The result was flawed measurements and inaccurate data.

Then came the real bombshell: Although the likelihood of any two individuals possessing identical relationships among the various features Bertillon measured was remote, it was not impossible. Bertillon measurements were not absolutely unique. Instances of mistaken identity were rare, but they did happen.

Case in Point

In the United States, the beginning of the end of reliance on the Bertillon System came in 1903. A man named Will West was sent to the Federal Penitentiary at Leavenworth, Kansas. He denied that he had ever been incarcerated there before, but his Bertillon measurements matched those on file for a William West. Moreover, the photographs of the new prisoner looked very much like those on file for William West. About to call Will West a liar, the clerk flipped over the card for William West. It noted that he was currently in custody at Leavenworth Federal Penitentiary. The case of the two Wests simultaneously demolished the certainty of Bertillon measurements and encouraged adoption of fingerprint identification.

Fingerprinting: A Short History

Fingerprinting for criminal identification began to catch on in England and the United States at the beginning of the twentieth century, and in 1924, the United States Congress enacted legislation creating the Identification Division of the FBI, a central repository of fingerprint files. How did law enforcement finally catch up with the long history of general interest in fingerprints?

Malpighi's Treatise

Marcello Malpighi was an Italian anatomy professor at the University of Bologna who made a number of important medical discoveries, including observations relating to the structure of the skin (the "Malpighi layer," a deep layer of the epidermis, is named after him) and the existence of capillaries, a key to understanding the human circulatory system.

In a treatise of 1686, he published another discovery, which, at the time, must have seemed rather minor: The human fingertips, he wrote, were characterized by distinctive patterns of spirals and loops and whorls.

Purkinji and Herschel: Fingerprinting Becomes an Identification Tool

Malpighi suggested no practical application for his observations on fingerprints, and it wasn't until 137 years later, in 1823, that John Evangelist Purkinji, a professor of anatomy at the University of Breslau, published a thesis in which he identified nine distinct fingerprint patterns. Even prior to Malpighi, the uniqueness of each human fingerprint was theorized. What Purkinji showed was that, while fingerprints were indeed unique from person to person, they formed recognizable patterns. Most modern fingerprint classification systems are based on Malpighi's patterns (see "The Nine Basic Patterns" later in this chapter).

Yet even this insight seems to have gone nowhere. Certainly, it did not lead Purkinji or any of his contemporaries to suggest that fingerprints, unique but capable of categorization, could be used for personal identification.

Thirty-three years later, it was Sir William Herschel, the British administrator in colonial India, who first deliberately used fingerprints for the purpose of positive identification. He was unfamiliar with Purkinji, and his idea of asking an Indian businessman, Rajyadhar Konai, to put his inked palm (not just his fingers) on the back of a contract so that he couldn't later repudiate it, was something of a whim. But when Herschel saw that Konai was so impressed that he swore he would never repudiate the contract, Herschel made it a rule that all contracts he witnessed had to be signed *and* printed—although he decided that the print of the right index and middle fingers, not the whole palm, would be sufficient (and a lot less messy).

Over his years of public service in India, Herschel accumulated a sizable fingerprint collection, which he offered as empirical proof of what had often been asserted in theory: that each fingerprint was unique as well as permanent to the individual.

Faulds and Galton: The Classification of Fingerprints

Purkinji had demonstrated recognizable pattern types in fingerprints, and Herschel had empirically proved that each fingerprint was unique and, therefore, uniquely useful for purposes of identification. In the 1870s, Dr. Henry Faulds, British surgeon-superintendent of Tsukiji Hospital in Tokyo, Japan, put these two concepts together.

After studying finger marks left on certain examples of prehistoric pottery, Faulds not only recognized the importance of fingerprints as a means of identification, but set out to devise a method of classifying them.

In 1880, he proposed in a scientific journal that printer's ink could be employed to make fingerprints usable for identification. He may also have been the first person to actually determine identity on the basis of a fingerprint clue when he matched to its owner a greasy fingerprint left on an alcohol bottle.

In the same year that he published his early work on fingerprinting, he sent an explanation of his system of fingerprint classification to no less a figure than Sir Charles Darwin, creator of the theory of evolution. Old and ailing, Darwin apologized to Faulds that he was unable to devote time and attention to his ideas on fingerprinting, but he promised to pass the information to his cousin, Sir Francis Galton.

Galton was a prominent anthropologist, and he was quite excited by Faulds's work. Building on it and on his own observations, he published in 1892 a book simply titled *Fingerprints*, in which he clearly identified the characteristics by which fingerprints could be identified. He called these characteristics *minutiae*, but today they are referred to as *Galton's Details*, some of which remain the basis on which fingerprints are classified.

Talking the Talk

Galton's Details, named for the nineteenth-century fingerprinting pioneer, Sir Francis Galton, are distinctive features of fingerprint patterns that can be used to compare and match sets of fingerprints for identification purposes. Galton's Details are also called **minutiae**.

FBI on the Case, 1924

Britain's famed Scotland Yard began systematically using fingerprint identification early in the twentieth century, and various police and correctional agencies in the United States began to follow suit. In 1924, Congress funded the creation of the FBI Identification Division, which immediately took custody of 810,188 fingerprint files, mostly from the Leavenworth Penitentiary.

As the automobile became a fixture of American life, more criminals crossed state lines in the commission of crimes, and the centralized, federalized fingerprint collection became increasingly important in law enforcement. Investigators not only concentrated on obtaining and classifying prints, but began developing techniques for finding fingerprints on weapons and on other features of crime scenes.

By the Numbers

Currently, FBI files bulge with more than 250 million sets of fingerprint records, including criminal and civil prints (prints of government employees and applicants for federal jobs). The FBI receives more than 34,000 fingerprint cards from various federal, state, and local agencies *every* workday. Pile up all of the fingerprint cards on file with the FBI, and you'd have 133 stacks, each as tall as the Empire State Building! The increasingly widespread adoption of electronic scanning of fingerprints promises to put an end to inked cards.

Finding the Prints

Few criminals are either sufficiently stupid or obliging to go about their business with ink on their fingers (although bloodstained or dirty finger and palm prints are sometimes clearly visible at crime scenes). The unfortunate fact is that, at many crime scenes, no fingerprints are found at all and, even when they are, they may not be clear enough to use. Even assuming that good prints can be found, they are of limited use if matching prints are not on file. (While such prints can't be used immediately to identify a known perpetrator, they can be filed and compared to fingerprints taken from suspects who are subsequently apprehended.)

Visible, Invisible, and Plastic

Latent fingerprints are what criminal investigators seek as evidence. These are fingerprint impressions transferred to a surface, either by the natural oils and sweat on the ridges of the fingertips or by dirt, blood, or other substances on the fingers. Latent prints may be visible, invisible, or plastic:

◆ **Visible fingerprints** are made by stained or dirty fingers. They are usually found on smooth, glossy, or light-colored surfaces.

◆ **Invisible fingerprints,** made by natural oils or sweat, are typically found on nonporous surfaces and must be rendered visible either by dusting or chemical processing.

◆ **Plastic fingerprints** are print impressions left in soft materials, such as tar, wax, soap, or even dust.

Dusting for Prints

Special powders are used to "develop" invisible prints left on hard, nonabsorbent surfaces such as glass, tile, mirrors, and painted wood. The powder is carefully dusted onto the surface using a fine brush. It reacts with deposited skin oils, adhering to oils or sweat and thereby revealing an impression of the print.

Fingerprints revealed by dusting are carefully photographed. In addition, they may be lifted, using a special transparent adhesive tape. The tape is applied to the dusted print, lifted off, and the resulting image is immediately transferred to a fingerprint card. The photograph or card is analyzed to determine the classification of the print, and it is then compared to prints that are on file.

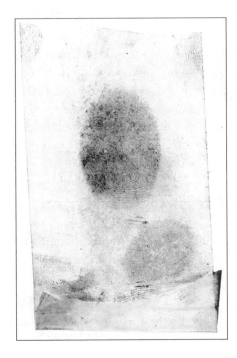

Example of a lifted finger-print.

(Image from the authors' collection)

Chemical Processing

To develop invisible prints that may have been left on soft, porous surfaces such as cardboard, paper, or cloth—substances that don't work well with powders—special chemical agents are used.

Iodine vapors react with skin oils to stain the invisible print brown. For iodine fuming, iodine crystals are loaded into a special fuming cabinet (if the object to be examined is small enough to take to the crime lab and fit into the cabinet) or into a fuming gun (which can be used at the crime scene). The image that results from fuming quickly fades and must therefore be photographed immediately.

Ninhydrin can be sprayed or brushed onto evidence or, if practical, the evidence can be dipped into the ninhydrin. This chemical reacts with amino acids deposited by the fingertips, and an image is produced. At room temperature, development takes as long as two hours, so, typically, heat is applied to hasten the reaction. While the resulting image does not quickly fade, it does lose contrast over time and, as with images produced by iodine fuming, must therefore be photographed.

Silver nitrate develops the sodium chloride (the salt that is in sweat) deposited by the fingers and produces a red-brown print. The evidence may be sprayed with a silver nitrate and alcohol solution or it may be dipped. Exposure to light speeds development. Again, however, the image is ephemeral and must be photographed.

Loops to Whorls: The Classification of Fingerprints

As we've mentioned, fingerprints are a strong means of identification because they are unique to the individual, yet they are readily classifiable into distinct categories that greatly facilitate comparison between any latent prints recovered at a crime scene and prints on file in police agencies.

Fingerprint patterns are divided into three broad groups: loops, arches, and whorls.

Loops

Sixty to 65 percent of fingerprints are loops, a pattern in which one or more ridges enter from one side of the print, curve around, and exit from the same side. Varieties of the loop are the plain loop that enters and exits on the right, the plain loop that enters and exits on the left, the central pocket loop, the lateral pocket loop, and the twinned loop.

Arches

Arches come in two basic varieties, the plain arch and the tented arch. In either case, the pattern begins on one side, rises to a peak or arch, and exits on the other side. Arches account for about 5 percent of fingerprints.

Whorls

A whorl is a circular pattern with no entrance or exit. The two basic whorls are simple and accidental. The simple whorl exhibits only the circular pattern, whereas the accidental whorl contains more than two deltas, which are places where two lines run side by side, then diverge with a significant line that curves around and passes in front of the delta.

Sworn Statement

Fingerprints are of extreme evidentiary value in criminal investigations, because they are the strongest possible evidence of a person's identity.

—Wayne W. Bennett and Kären M. Hess, *Criminal Investigation*

The Nine Basic Patterns

Many fingerprint experts recognize even more varieties of loops, arches, and whorls than the basic patterns just mentioned; however, these basic patterns account for what the FBI calls the nine basic fingerprint patterns: plain arch, tented arch, plain loop (right), plain loop (left), simple whorl, central pocket loop, lateral pocket loop, twinned loop, and accidental whorl.

The basic patterns allow investigators to narrow the search for file prints that may match prints obtained from crime evidence. Once a group of possible matches are obtained, a fingerprint expert compares specific identification points, minute features within the patterns that allow for specific matching of an evidence print with a file print. Common features include islands (small enclosed ridge patterns), dots (isolated dots rather than ridge lines), bifurcations (ridges that diverge or fork in various ways), and ending ridges (ridges that don't connect, but simply dead end). Some experts recognize as many as 100 or more identification points in any given print. In order to declare a match between a file print and an evidence print, a minimum of 12 identical identification points is typically required.

The nine basic fingerprint patterns, used by the FBI and adapted from Purkinji's original classification system.

(Image from the Federal Bureau of Investigation)

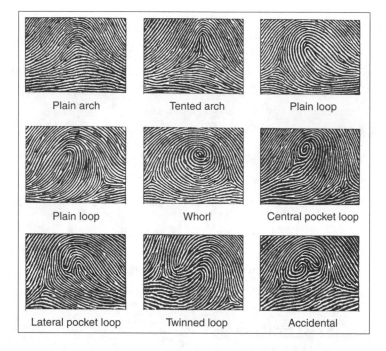

Plain arch	Tented arch	Plain loop
Plain loop	Whorl	Central pocket loop
Lateral pocket loop	Twinned loop	Accidental

AFIS: Automated Fingerprint Identification System

Fingerprint classification and matching takes skill and patience—traditionally, *a lot* of patience. Comparing evidence prints to file prints is essentially an exercise in pattern recognition, an activity in which modern, graphically oriented computer systems excel. Automated Fingerprint Identification Systems are computerized systems that electronically scan evidence prints and compare the scan to a digitized database of file prints, outputting potential matches for a human operator to examine and review.

The investigator runs the evidence print through an optical scanner that is linked to a computer. The computer program analyzes the scan for matching identification points. The computer then outputs a list of file prints that have the closest correlation to whatever criteria the investigator has specified. The computer's "word" is not accepted as law; a trained human expert always examines the prints to verify the match. AFIS technology has greatly accelerated the process of fingerprint identification.

What About DNA "Fingerprinting"?

In recent years, DNA evidence has become increasingly important in criminal investigation, and we often hear about "DNA fingerprinting." This process, which is covered in Chapter 16, should not be confused with conventional fingerprint examination and analysis. It is very different—and yet there are important analogies between the use of DNA and conventional fingerprint evidence in criminal investigation.

DNA, deoxyribonucleic acid, is the principal chemical structure that forms chromosomes, the basis of the various physical traits each of us inherits. The chemical structure of everyone's DNA is identical; the differences come in the order of the chemical substances in the base pairs of the DNA molecules. There are so many millions of base pairs in each person's DNA that every person has a different sequence.

In a sense, then, the sequence of substances in our base pairs is like a fingerprint: unique to each of us. Therefore, it would be possible to identify every person solely by the sequence of his or her base pairs.

But who has the time? There are so many millions of base pairs that the task would be extraordinarily time-consuming, even with the aid of powerful computers.

All is not lost, however. Instead of trying to compare every sequence in every base pair of DNA, scientists identify repeating patterns in the DNA. Focusing on a certain small number of sequences of DNA that are known to vary greatly among individuals, investigators analyze *only* these sequences to obtain a very high probability of a match.

Because most crimes, especially violent crimes, involve the physical manipulation of physical objects, it is likely that conventional fingerprint examination will remain an important part of criminal investigation for a long time to come. But just as fingers leave an imprint, so contact of various sorts leaves the imprint of DNA, and it is certain that DNA evidence will take its place alongside fingerprint evidence as a critically important tool for criminal identification.

The Least You Need to Know

◆ Alphonse Bertillon, a nineteenth-century French police clerk, developed the Bertillon System, the first effective attempt to identify criminals objectively and unambiguously.

◆ Interest in fingerprints dates from prehistory, but it wasn't until the end of the nineteenth century that it became viable as a means of identification.

◆ Flaws in the Bertillon System spurred almost universal adoption of fingerprint identification by the early twentieth century.

◆ Criminal investigators attempt to recover latent fingerprints in order to compare these with fingerprints on file, either locally or at the FBI.

◆ The systematic classification of a relatively small number of basic fingerprint patterns makes fingerprint identification and matching practical.

◆ In the future, DNA evidence will almost certainly play an increasingly important role in criminal investigation, but it is not likely that it will ever supplant fingerprint evidence.

Chapter 13

Crime Lab

In This Chapter

- The field of forensics
- The modern crime lab
- Forensic chemistry
- Ballistics and firearms examination
- Analyzing prints: tools, shoes, and tires
- Special expertise: arson investigators and computer cops

Fans of Sir Arthur Conan Doyle's archetypal sleuth Sherlock Holmes certainly have a vivid picture of a crime lab: Holmes's London parlor at 221b Baker Street, in which flasks, bubbling retorts, and microscope stand cheek by jowl with the detective's Meerschaum pipe and Stradivarius fiddle. Holmes routinely subjected tiny bits of evidence (today these would be called "trace evidence") to microscopic and chemical analysis, and he wrote learned treatises on such arcane subjects as how to determine what type of tobacco an offender smoked by analyzing the ashes left behind.

At one time, of course, all science was a kind of hobby, the leisure pursuit of gentlemen with time on their hands. And, as a Victorian gentleman par excellence, Sherlock Holmes had plenty of time to devote to science in the service of his all-consuming avocation, crime detection.

Twenty-first-century criminal investigation has no patience with amateurs, even those on a par with Sherlock Holmes. As we'll see in this chapter, a high level of professionalism is required when so much rides on the work of the crime lab: the efficient allocation of police resources to apprehend an offender, the thorough and accurate analysis of evidence that will be used to prosecute the accused—or to exonerate the innocent—and the protection of the public safety.

Forensics: What It Is

Forensic science (sometimes simply called forensics) is the application of science—including physical, medical, and behavioral science—as it relates to the law. Scientific methods, procedures, and equipment are used in investigating crimes as well as in proving, in a court of law, the guilt of the accused.

Potentially, any field of scientific inquiry might be applied to forensic work, but it is certain disciplines from the physical and medical sciences that are called on most frequently.

Talking the Talk

Trace evidence is extremely small physical matter (such as a carpet fiber, a hair, a paint chip) that has evidentiary value. **Questioned documents** are any documents that may have relevance to the commission of a crime. The term is often used specifically to refer to suspected forgeries or documents that have been illicitly altered.

Physical Sciences

Chemistry and physics are the two broad fields of physical science that have the most direct application to forensics. Chemical analysis is important in analyzing the nature of *trace evidence*, including questionable substances (such as illicit drugs), hairs and fibers, firearms identification, tool marks, shoe prints, and voice analysis. It is also used to analyze *questioned documents* (documents that may be forged or may have other relevance to the commission of a crime), an area discussed later in the chapter. Specialists often study documents in which ink or paper type might hold clues as to origin, which might, in turn, help uncover the identity of an offender.

Medical Sciences

Homicide leaves in its wake one or more bodies, and other crimes, such as rape, typically leave fluid and tissue traces. The medical sciences have assumed such importance in forensics that they are treated in the three chapters of the next part of this book, Part 5. In this chapter, we focus exclusively on the physical sciences in the crime lab. For a discussion of the forensic application of behavioral science, see Chapter 8.

Work of the Modern Crime Lab

At its best, the modern crime lab is a state-of-the-art research laboratory. Any research laboratory needs up-to-date equipment, highly trained researchers, and a set of orderly procedures scrupulously followed. Good science depends on these things. A laboratory that puts science in the service of criminal investigation must, if anything, adhere to even higher standards. After all, the enforcement of law, the determination of guilt or innocence, and, ultimately, the safety and well-being of the public depend on the work it does.

Chemical Analysis: Trace Evidence

The chemistry section of the crime lab is equipped to subject a variety of trace evidence to analysis, including ...

♦ **The presence and type of dyes and chemicals.** Many banks use specific dyes and chemicals in such security devices as packs of money that are rigged to explode after a certain delay period, spraying a dye marker on whoever is close to the stolen cash. Even after repeated cleaning, traces of the dye remain on skin, hair, clothing, automobile interior, and other items. Also, some cash may be treated with special dye markers, visible or invisible, so that stolen cash can be identified. The chemistry lab can analyze samples of clothing or currency.

♦ **Stained clothing or other items found at a crime scene.** The forensic chemist can analyze the stain to determine what it is. The presence of certain lubricant stains, for example, may provide clues to an offender's occupation as a factory worker, for instance, or an auto mechanic. Often it is possible to analyze stains with great precision, so that the substance found may be associated with a very specific activity or vocation: Motor oil is chemically distinct from lubricants used in various factory processes; silicone lubricants are used in some industries, petroleum lubricants in others. The lab can also compare stains or markings to suspected sources: That stain found on a suspect's clothing may be analyzed and compared to a substance found at the scene of the crime.

- **Unknown substances** found in conjunction with a crime scene; the chemistry lab can run tests to identify them.

- **The composition of inks and papers.** For example, it may be possible to discover the author of a ransom note or a bomb threat when comparing the ink or paper with known samples.

- **Manufacturing or building materials,** many of which have distinctive chemical compositions. A forensic chemist can analyze and compare items found at a crime scene to suspected sources.

- **Plastics** in wire insulation and miscellaneous plastics such as buttons can be compared with known sources.

- **Duct tape,** which is sometimes used to restrain the victim of a violent crime. The lab can analyze tape samples to determine composition, construction, and color, and, from this, determine the manufacturer. The FBI crime lab maintains a National Forensic Tape File, with samples of virtually every known tape. If the manufacturer of the tape is known, it may be possible to identify stores in a given area that sell the tape. Investigators can call on these stores and ask questions concerning suspects.

- **Caulks, sealants, and adhesives,** which may be identified as to color, composition, and maker.

- **Traces of paint.** For example, the color, year, make, and model of an automobile can be determined by comparing a very small sample of paint—rubbed or chipped off, say, when the getaway car sideswiped the side of a building—to a comprehensive file of known sources. Paint on safes, vaults, window sills, and door frames can be transferred to and from burglar tools. Chemical examination of suspicious tools can demonstrate their use in a particular crime.

Sworn Statement

Another important source of automobile-related evidence is found in fragments of trim, which can be compared with plastic remaining on the property (or person) struck in a hit-and-run case.

Chemical Analysis: Drugs

The chemistry section of the crime lab is often called on to analyze substances suspected of being—or known to be—illegal drugs. Even minute traces can be analyzed, and the chemist can usually report on the type of drug, its strength, and, sometimes, its probable origin.

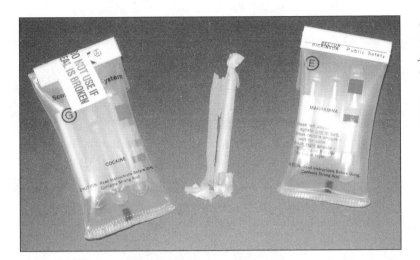

Suspicious substances are tested in the lab or in the field using specially packaged chemical kits.

(Image courtesy of DeKalb County [Georgia] Solicitor-General's Office)

Hairs and Fibers

Like many other items of trace evidence, hairs and fibers can be difficult to locate at a crime scene. Strong lighting and careful searching are required to turn up these items. Often the extra vigilance is worth the effort, because such evidence can place a subject at a crime scene, especially in crimes of violence, in which some interchange of hairs or fibers is likely to occur. It is also possible that the suspect will inadvertently carry hair or fiber away from the scene—for example, if he kneels on a carpet.

Hair has a distinct structure, consisting of an outer cuticle (with overlapping scales that point toward the tip), a cortex (consisting of elongated cells), and the medulla (the center of the hair, consisting of variably shaped cells). Because the appearance of these structures vary, it is often possible, using a microscope, to identify an evidence strand of hair with a known source (such as the victim of a violent crime).

If blood is present on the hair, identification becomes more certain. Hair is also an excellent source of DNA evidence (see Chapter 16).

Under the microscope, it is possible to distinguish between human and animal hair, and between hair from the head, pubic hair, facial hair, and so on. Many drugs and poisons, such as arsenic, accumulate in the hair; analysis of strands is very useful to the toxicologist (see "Death by Poisoning: Forensic Toxicology" in Chapter 15).

Forensic experts refer to hair specimens as "class characteristic" evidence; that is, a hair recovered from a crime scene or suspect may have enough similar properties compared with a known sample to be deemed "consistent with" the sample, but it cannot be said definitively to be a perfect match. Hair samples are very effectively used to *exclude* a suspect; Caucasian hair differs from Negroid hair, so the presence of Caucasian hair on the clothing of a homicide victim may tend to exclude a black suspect.

Nonhair fibers are of many varieties, but they fall into four major groups: mineral, vegetable, animal, and synthetic. Examples of mineral fibers are fiberglass and asbestos; vegetable fibers can include cotton, manila, hemp, and so on; animal fibers can include wool and silk; and the most common synthetics are rayon, nylon, and polyester.

After narrowing down fiber evidence to one of these four groups, the laboratory investigator can begin to compare the questioned fiber with known specimens. In some cases, it is actually possible to identify manufacturers on the basis of synthetic fiber evidence. Suspect A denies ever visiting Victim B's house. Forensic examination has recovered fibers from under Suspect A's fingernails. Analysis reveals that they are from a rug made by Manufacturer C. Victim B's apartment has this carpeting wall to wall.

Case in Point

In 1958, 16-year-old Gaetane Bouchard, a Canadian girl, was murdered. Her ex-boyfriend, John Vollman, who lived across the border in Maine, had been seen with her just before the discovery of the murder. Flakes of paint from the place where they had been seen together were matched to Vollman's car. Also, lipstick stains matching the color Bouchard used were found on candy in the car's glove compartment. But it was strands of hair found clutched in the victim's hand that finally persuaded the jury. Using neutron activation analysis, these were matched to Vollman's hair by demonstrating an identical ratio of sulpher radiation to phosphorus. This ratio differed from the hair of the victim herself.

Neutron activation analysis, developed in the 1950s, is still a high-tech tool sometimes used in the forensic analysis of hair, fiber, and some other trace evidence. The evidence is bombarded with neutrons inside the core of a nuclear reactor. The neutrons collide with the components of the trace elements, exciting them so that they emit gamma radiation of a characteristic energy level. By examining these energy levels, the investigator can measure every part of the sample, no matter how small. A single hair reveals 14 distinct components.

Voice and Image Analysis

The lives we live today are extensively mediated—that is, much of our reality comes to us not directly through our own ears and eyes, but via such media as television, radio, the telephone, and audio- and videotape recording. The one thing criminal investigation must account for above all is reality, and if today's reality includes electronic media, the forensic scientist must figure out ways to examine and analyze it.

Audio and video recordings are very easy to edit and alter. Advanced crime laboratories have the equipment and experts to determine whether recordings are original, continuous, unaltered, and consistent with the stated operation of the tape or video recorder purportedly used.

Evidence recordings are often made under less than ideal circumstances, using hidden microphones in noisy surroundings or hidden cameras in poor lighting conditions. Audio or video recordings may be damaged—as in arson evidence, for instance—or tapes may be deliberately erased. Crime lab experts can sometimes enhance poor-quality or damaged tapes to reduce interfering noise, to increase the readability of an image, and generally to restore and repair damaged media.

Signal analysis is another aspect of examining both audio and video recordings. It is often possible to identify, compare, and interpret such background signals as gunshots or telephone touch tones. From the sound of a gunshot, experts may be able to determine direction and even the type of firearm used. From telephone touch tones picked up on recordings, dialed phone numbers can be recovered.

Most intriguing to the public is so-called voiceprinting, which is the electronic analysis of the human voice as a graphic sound spectrograph. This spectrograph—or voiceprint—is unique to the speaker, as a fingerprint is unique to a particular finger. Any sound, including the human voice, can be represented graphically as a sound spectrograph, a distinctive pattern. As with fingerprints, no two voiceprints are exactly alike—even when a skilled mimic deliberately disguises his or her voice to sound like that of another. By comparing evidence voiceprints with known voice samples—or samples obtained from a suspect in custody—it is often possible to find a match. In this way, offenders such as bomb hoaxers, obscene callers, or others can be identified. Courts generally do not consider voiceprint evidence in and of itself conclusive, but it does provide investigative guidance and can be presented in court as one evidentiary element among others.

Evidence in the form of conventional photography is also often submitted to the crime lab. As with electronic media, photographs can be examined for authenticity and to enhance poor images. The lab can determine if the photograph has been altered or retouched. It can often tell what type of camera was used to produce the picture. Physical examination of film and emulsion types can help determine the date of the photograph.

Voiceprints: The print on top closely matches the lower print, strongly suggesting that the two audio samples were spoken by the same person.

(Image from the authors' collection)

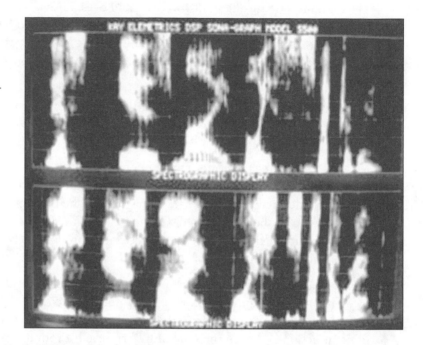

Firearms Identification

Most violent crimes in the United States are committed with firearms. The interiors of gun barrels are rifled (grooved) in order to make the bullet spin and thereby increase its accuracy. The rifling leaves distinctive marks on the bullet that is fired. By examining the markings on bullets recovered from a crime scene or a victim's body, investigators can often determine the make and model of the firearm used. If a suspect firearm is recovered, a ballistics expert—someone skilled in the analysis of all evidence relating to the discharge of firearms—will fire it, recover the discharged round, and compare it microscopically to the bullet from the crime scene. A positive match indicates that the crime-scene bullet was fired from the suspect firearm.

Even if a suspect firearm has not been recovered, bullets and cartridges found at a crime scene can be analyzed using the Integrated Ballistics Identification System (IBIS). Maintained by the U.S. Bureau of Alcohol, Tobacco and Firearms (ATF), IBIS is a comprehensive database of ammunition that is analogous to the FBI's comprehensive fingerprint files.

Firearms, as well as ammunition, are examined in the ballistics lab. The examination begins with an assessment of the general condition of the firearm: Is it functional? A trigger-pull analysis exactly determines the amount of pressure necessary to release the hammer or firing pin of a firearm. A slightly built female defendant claims that she isn't strong enough to pull the trigger of that gun. The results of the trigger-pull analysis may demolish that defense.

Examinations can also determine whether a firearm has been illegally modified to fire in the full-automatic mode. In cases where firearm serial numbers have been filed off by an offender, analysts can sometimes restore them to legibility.

Another important aspect of firearms examination is analysis of how gunshot residue is deposited on such evidence as clothing. The pattern of gunpowder and other blast residue varies with the distance between the muzzle of the firearm and the target. By comparing evidence patterns to patterns obtained in laboratory test firings, such information as muzzle-to-victim distance can be determined, along with the direction (angle) from which the shot was fired.

Firing a weapon also often leaves traces of nitrate (an ingredient in gunpowder) on the skin of the shooter. Applying warm paraffin to a suspect's hand picks up impurities, including nitrate, from the skin and pores. The paraffin is treated with chemicals (diphenylamine or diphenylbenzidine), which turn blue in the presence of nitrate. This tends to indicate that the suspect has recently fired a gun—although the test is by no means foolproof, since the procedure can give both false positives and false negatives. Shooting a gun is not the only way to get nitrate on the skin, and the absence of nitrate does not necessarily mean that the person hasn't fired a weapon recently.

Tool Marks, Shoe Prints, and Tire Prints

Burglars and other intruders often use tools to pry open windows or doors. Just as the barrel of a gun leaves characteristic marks on the round that is fired, tools leave telltale marks on the material they work. Some *tool marks* are easy to identify. A suspected burglar is apprehended carrying a screwdriver with a blade one-half-inch wide and one-eighth-inch thick to pry open a window. Detectives find a one-half-inch-wide, eighth-inch-deep groove on the wooden windowsill of the victim's house.

Talking the Talk

Tool marks are characteristic impressions transferred from any tool to the material it has worked. The impressions left on the material may be matched to marks on the tool.

Other tool-mark evidence is more complex and requires microscopic analysis in the laboratory. A sledgehammer was used to open a safe. The hammer left striated marks on the safe. A sledgehammer is recovered from the suspect. Microscopic examination of the striations on the safe match the striations on the hammer. Conclusion: *That* hammer imprinted *those* marks on the safe.

Shoe and tire prints found at crime scenes can be very important. From the number and direction of shoe prints, the number of offenders may be determined, along with the direction of their approach and exit. By photographing the prints and by carefully making plaster casts of them, it is possible (on the simplest level) to compare the pattern with the pattern of the suspect's shoes. It is also sometimes possible to determine the manufacturer of the shoe and even the approximate weight of the offender (based on the depth of the print in a given material). It is often possible to distinguish between men's and women's shoes and, based on the size of the print, to make a guess about the offender's height and weight.

Large crime laboratories, including the FBI's facility, maintain files of shoe patterns, which can expedite the process of identifying manufacturers.

Tires, like shoes, leave characteristic prints. From the pattern of a tire print, the type of vehicle and the manufacturer (as well as year of manufacture) of the tire can be determined. It is also possible to estimate speed and direction of travel.

Case in Point

The most famous case of shoe-print evidence was introduced in the trial of O.J. Simpson for the murder of his ex-wife, Nicole Brown Simpson, and her friend, Ronald Goldman, on June 12, 1994. Prosecutors showed pictures of bloody footprints leading away from the crime scene. William Bodziack, an FBI expert on shoe prints, testified that the prints were made by expensive and relatively rare Bruno Magli shoes. Just 300 pairs were ever sold in Simpson's size 12. Simpson vehemently denied ever owning a pair of Bruno Maglis, denouncing them as "ugly-ass shoes." But in 1993, he had been photographed wearing them. The jury was apparently unimpressed by the shoe impressions, but Bruno Magli enjoyed a 30-percent increase in sales of its high-end "ugly-ass shoes" during the months following their introduction as evidence.

Questioned Documents

Many crimes and criminals leave a paper trail. Questioned documents, as we've mentioned, are documents suspected of holding evidence to a crime. Some documents are questioned because they are suspected of being forgeries. (Is the signature on that bank draft fake?) And some are questioned because they relate to a crime. (Who is the author of that ransom note?)

The questioned documents section of the crime lab analyzes paper types and watermarks, either of which may identify a manufacturer or even a particular retail supplier, and the composition of inks and pencil or crayon marks. Analysis may reveal erasures and alternations. It may also reveal the age of the document. Treatment with various chemicals and inspection under ultraviolet or black light often resurrect obliterated writing, whether it has been erased, crossed out, or written over. Used carbon paper, discarded in the trash can, may reveal an important message. The top sheet on the scratch pad left on the desk looks blank, but laboratory examination reveals the imprint of something written on a sheet that had been torn off. The impressions can be rendered visible and legible.

Despite some expert claims to the contrary, not all handwriting is identifiable to a specific writer, but the examination of handwriting characteristics can sometimes determine the origin or authenticity of questioned writing. Although a host of dinner club novelty entertainers would disagree, such traits as age, sex, personality, or intent *cannot* be determined from handwriting examinations. However, it may be possible to make inferences concerning the writer's level of education and place of origin—based not only on handwriting, but on such clues as spelling, grammar, and vocabulary—and it can certainly be fruitful to compare a questioned document with known samples, such as writing samples from a suspect.

Sworn Statement

Crudely forged signatures are fairly easy to detect, especially if they have been traced or copied.

In this age of the personal computer, the typewriter has rapidly become an endangered species; however, typewritten documents still sometimes figure in crimes, and skilled examiners can sometimes identify the make and model of a typewriter based on individual characteristics of certain letters.

Modern typewriters use carbon film rather than fabric ribbons, and it is sometimes possible to read the film ribbon. In some cases, it is also possible to study paper fibers picked up by the ribbon and thereby link a particular ribbon (and typewriter, and typist) to a particular document.

Many businesses print checks using checkwriter machines. A checkwriter impression can sometimes be identified with the checkwriter that produced it. The same is true of embossed or seal impressions—these can sometimes be identified with the specific instrument that produced them. Even rubber stamp impressions may, in some cases, be identified with the rubber stamp that produced it.

An offender might well attempt to destroy incriminating documentary evidence by burning it. Even in these cases, all is not necessarily lost. Sometimes it is possible to decipher information on burned or charred documents, and even if this is not possible, the charred remains of the paper may yield useful information upon chemical analysis.

Areas of Special Expertise

Virtually all of the work of a modern crime laboratory requires highly trained technicians with special expertise in specific areas. Two types of crimes very different from one another illustrate the incredibly broad range of expertise forensic analysis may call for. Let's take a closer look at each.

Finding an Arsonist or a Bomber

Arson and explosives-related crimes are notoriously difficult to investigate for the simple reason that the crime, if successful, destroys most of the evidence it creates.

The differences between an accidental explosion and one caused by a bomb are usually fairly self-evident. The differences between an accidental fire and one deliberately set are typically far more difficult to spot. However, trained observers learn to look for certain signs of arson:

- **Alligatoring** is the checkered appearance of charred wood that makes it look like alligator skin. Large, high-relief blisters indicate intense heat. Small, flat alligatoring indicates lower levels of heat. Intense fires are often produced by arsonists, who use accelerants (most commonly gasoline) to set the fire.

- **Crazing** is the formation of irregular cracks in glass. Extensive crazing indicates rapid and intense heat, signs of the use of an accelerant.

- The **depth of charring** tells much about the length of the burn and its origin.

- The presence of a **line of demarcation** between charred and uncharred material may indicate the presence of an accelerant. A puddle-shaped line of demarcation is suspicious.

- **Spalling** is the term for the breaking off of surface pieces of brick or concrete. Intense heat is required to create spalling, and brown stains around the spall area are a strong indication that an accelerant has been used.

- Multiple **points of origin**—a group of fires set in various parts of a room or building—suggest arson.

- The **color of the smoke** the fire produces may indicate the presence of accelerants. Blue smoke is typically associated with alcohol; white smoke with burning vegetable compounds, hay, or phosphorous; yellow or brown-yellow smoke with various chemicals, including sulfur compounds and gunpowder; black smoke is produced by petroleum products.

Charred materials and any suspicious stains or liquid deposits are often sent to the crime lab for analysis. Chemical tests can detect the presence of accelerants and identify what they are.

The lab is also called in to analyze debris and other materials from explosions. Specialists can often determine the materials and methods used in the construction of explosive devices. Serial bombers often build the same type of device from one crime to the next. Analyzing the type of bomb used may yield the signature of the offender.

The FBI maintains an Explosives Reference Search System as well as an extensive Explosives Reference File, which expedite identification of arson and explosive materials.

Computer Cops

Less sensational and certainly quieter than arson and explosives investigation is the work of those who specialize in investigating computer-related crimes and computer evidence in general. Computers are so pervasive in our lives that it is almost inevitable that they would be used to commit crimes.

> **Sworn Statement** _____
>
> Electronic pulses of ones and zeroes sustain our very existence now, nurturing an almost biological dependence upon instantaneous online commerce, coursing like blood through the vessels of our popular culture and our collective consciousness. We are sad to report, however, that these vessels are bleeding from a thousand cuts sustained on the digital battlefield that is the Internet today.
>
> —Joel Scambray, Stuart McClure, and George Kurtz, Introduction to *Hacking Exposed*, 2nd ed. (Osborne/McGraw-Hill, 2001)

Computer crimes include a very wide range of offenses, such as ...

♦ The creation and dissemination of viruses and other destructive programs for malicious purposes.

♦ Hacking into communication and computer systems for kicks (malicious mischief).

♦ Hacking into communication and computer systems for theft of service (illegally using mainframe computer time or long-distance telephone service).

♦ Launching attacks against commercial and other World Wide Web sites in order to disrupt business (denial of service attacks).

♦ Hacking into communication and computer systems for purposes of eavesdropping, blackmailing, or conducting industrial espionage or even espionage against government agencies.

♦ Manipulating computers, software, or data to commit embezzlement or fraud (especially credit card fraud).

♦ Using computers to support criminal enterprises, such as maintaining drug-distribution databases or aiding the laundering of illegal money transactions.

♦ Using computers and the Internet to acquire or disseminate child pornography or to exploit or endanger children.

In addition, computers are used for routine bookkeeping and communication, so they may well play a role in the commission of virtually any crime.

By the Numbers

In a 1995 survey (reported by Wayne W. Bennett and Kären M. Hess in *Criminal Investigation*), 98.7 percent of 150 corporate security directors said that their companies had been victims of computer-related crimes. Of this number, 43.3 percent said they had been victimized at least 25 times. Seventy-five to 80 percent of the crimes were discovered to be the work of company insiders.

Committing computer crime and computer-assisted crime can be quite simple, whereas investigating these crimes is often very difficult and frustrating.

Forensic computer work includes any or all of the following:

♦ Examining computer files for relevant or suspicious data files

♦ Comparing questioned data files to known documents and data files

♦ Examining computer transactions to determine the time and sequence that data files were created

♦ Extracting data files from storage media, including the recovery of deleted files

- Performing data searches using keywords relevant to the crime under investigation

- Decrypting and recovering passwords

- Analyzing computer source code to determine how certain programs work and what they are intended to do

Computer cops or cybercops—law-enforcement officials who specialize in investigating computer crime and crimes in which computers are involved—don't spend all of their time immersed in high technology. Computers are the tools used in certain crimes, but the criminals are people, and human engineering (manipulating suspects to betray themselves and their operations) often plays a major role in tracking down and apprehending offenders. Investigators seeking to break up a child pornography web operation, for instance, might spend days online posing as eager customers and winning the confidence of the offender.

Some people are quick to write off computer crime as victimless crime, because it is generally nonviolent. However, the lifeblood of today's commerce flows through computers, and an assault on this system can be tremendously costly and can deeply affect the lives of hundreds, thousands, even millions.

The Least You Need to Know

- Forensics is the application of science—especially in the physical and medical fields—to the investigation and prosecution of crime.

- Most forensic evidence is not in and of itself conclusive, but it can narrow the field of suspects, guide an investigation, and, as an element in a collection of evidence presented at trial, serve to convict a defendant.

- Modern crime labs use the principles of chemistry and physics to analyze physical evidence. They also use electronics to analyze electronic evidence, such as audio and video recordings.

- Because the vast majority of violent crimes are committed using firearms, ballistics (essentially the identification of firearms from bullet and ammunition evidence) is a key forensic field.

- Tools, shoes, and vehicle tires all leave characteristic marks or imprints, which may be studied to identify origin and association with a suspect.

- Investigation of arson and of computer crime are rapidly growing fields of forensic specialization.

Part 5

The Body in Question

No item of evidence is more revealing than the body of the victim of a violent crime. In this part, we follow the work of the medical examiner from the discovery of the body at the scene, through the forensic autopsy at the morgue, to the chemistry of violent death, and to the cutting edge of forensic medicine, DNA "fingerprinting."

This is the story of how criminal investigators and medical professionals have joined forces to disprove the old pirate saying "Dead men tell no tales." To the forensic specialist, the dead not only speak, they explain, they accuse, and they ask for justice.

Chapter 14

House Call

In This Chapter

- ◆ Is this death a homicide?
- ◆ The victim: preliminary investigation
- ◆ Relationship of murderer and victim
- ◆ Reading the scene
- ◆ Blood evidence
- ◆ Wound evidence

A body has been discovered in a house. A call goes out to 911, and police officers arrive. They find a 60-year-old white female, crumpled at the bottom of a steep, narrow stairway leading to the cellar. Did the woman fall? Did she have a heart attack or stroke and then fall? Did she purposely throw herself down the stairs? Or was she pushed?

The first possibility is an instance of accidental death; the second, natural death; the third, suicide. All are sad events, but only one possibility—the last mentioned—is homicide, a criminal matter. The discovery of a corpse is not sufficient reason to launch a murder investigation. The first step is to determine whether a homicide has been committed and if so, to gather evidence found at the scene. Let's look at how this is done.

The Crime Scene

Much of the investigative work in a case of homicide is performed by the *medical examiner*, some of it on the scene, and even more in the morgue where an autopsy is performed. This is the subject of the next chapter. But the work always begins with the police officers on the scene.

Dying Declaration

Arriving on the scene, the officers do not take death for granted. A dead body may have been reported, but the first responding officer makes certain, by feeling for an arterial pulse, that the victim is indeed dead. If there are any signs of life, emergency aid is rendered and an ambulance summoned. If the victim is conscious, officers attempt to secure a dying declaration, which can be crucial in identifying the victim's assailant and in subsequently prosecuting him. In legal terms, a dying declaration consists of the victim's words identifying the causes or circumstances of his or her impending death. A dying declaration is compelling investigative and courtroom evidence. If equipment is available, it is often audio- or videotaped. To be admissible as evidence, courts require that a dying declaration be made by someone who believed death was imminent. Furthermore, the statement must specifically concern the cause or circumstances of what the victim believed to be his or her impending death.

Talking the Talk

The **medical examiner** is typically an appointed or elected official, almost always a physician specializing in pathology, charged with determining the cause of death in criminal cases or in cases of mysterious death. In larger jurisdiction, the chief medical examiner is in charge of a staff of medical examiners.

Protecting the Scene

The first responders act quickly to protect the crime scene so that evidence is neither disturbed nor destroyed. Because the scene will soon be teeming with investigators, people from the medical examiner's office, and others, the first to arrive determines a path to and from the victim that will least disturb evidence.

Capturing the Scene

If the victim is dead, there is no rush to remove the body from the scene. In many jurisdictions, a medical examiner, typically a pathologist, will perform a preliminary examination at the scene, and only after the examiner has completed work there is the body taken to the morgue for an autopsy.

Before the body is removed, the crime scene is photographed and perhaps videotaped. Investigators usually make simple sketches to indicate the position of the victim relative to other objects in the room or area. In many cases, if the body is lying on the floor or ground, investigators will outline with chalk or tape the victim's exact position, as an aid to investigative work after the body is removed.

Checklist: Gathering Information

The FBI has drawn up a checklist of suggested investigative items to help ensure that police investigators obtain all important preliminary information at the scene of a suspected homicide.

The first priority is to identify the victim. This may be possible with the help of witnesses on the scene and/or identification found on the victim—a driver's license, for example. The victim's address should be determined, as well as marital status and the name, address, and phone number of next of kin.

From the very beginning, investigators carefully note the circumstances under which they were notified of the death, including the date and time of the notification and the identity of the person who made the call. It is especially important to note the relationship, if any, of that person to the deceased.

Signs of Struggle

Investigators also carefully note the date and time the body was found and the exact location of the body. If the body was found inside a place of business or a house or apartment, investigators make particular note of how entry was gained: Was the door forced or a window broken? Or are there no signs of forced entry? The first circumstance suggests that the victim and the perpetrator were strangers or that, in any case, the victim was not expecting the perpetrator to call. The second circumstance suggests that the victim and perpetrator were either acquainted or the perpetrator had presented the victim with a plausible reason for opening the door. Perhaps the perpetrator posed as a delivery person or even a police officer. It is also important to note the type of lock on the door and the condition of other doors and windows.

Exactly where the body was found is important. The basement? The bedroom? The living room? And where was the body found within the room? Sitting at a desk? Lying on a sofa? Or in the middle of the floor? Was the victim discovered face up, face down, or in some other position?

By carefully noting these details, it may be possible to begin putting together a picture of what happened. It is important to look for signs of struggle as well as the absence of such signs, because this information suggests much about the method of the perpetrator and even his attitude toward what he was doing—cool, calm, and professional, or wild, violent, and out of control.

Much can also be inferred about the relationship between the perpetrator and the victim. Signs of forced entry combined with signs of violence suggest the work of an intruder. The absence of forced entry and little evidence of a struggle suggest that the perpetrator was a trusted acquaintance, friend, associate, or even relation.

Condition of the Body

The initial investigators take careful note of the condition of the body. Was it fully clothed? Partially clothed? Naked? Was it carefully undressed, or were the clothes torn and ripped off? If so, what kind and where? Was a ligature (any kind of rope, tape, wire, or article of clothing used to bind or strangle a victim) used?

Although the medical examiner is solely responsible for determining the cause of death, the first investigators on the scene typically take note of five more key items relating to the condition of the body:

1. **Is the body well preserved or decomposed?** This is important to determining the time of death. The presence of maggots, for example, may help fix the approximate time of death (see "The Bug Detectives" in Chapter 15).

2. **How far has rigor mortis progressed?** This information can be important to the medical examiner in assessing the time of death, especially if the examiner arrives on the scene some time after the first officers do. A body is limp after death until the breakdown of certain enzymes within body tissue stiffens the corpse. This is known as rigor mortis—literally, the "stiffness of death."

   Rigor begins in the jaw and head five to six hours after death, and the effect moves downward from there. By 12 hours, the upper body is generally stiff. Within about 18 hours, the entire body becomes rigid. Rigor mortis is not permanent, and it begins to disappear about 36 hours after death, typically in the same sequence in which it appeared.

Related to rigor mortis, but distinct from it, is cadaveric spasm. This is the contraction of specific muscle groups at the time of death—literally, a "death grip"—and it is most frequently found when the hand of the deceased is closed tightly around an object. Unlike rigor mortis, it does not disappear. Nor can cadaveric spasm be counterfeited. Thus, if a victim is found with a gunshot wound to the head, his hand tightly grasping the handle of a revolver, the chances are very good that the victim has committed suicide. If, however, the victim is found with his or her fingers loosely wrapped around the gun's handle, there is a distinct possibility that some other person has attempted to create the appearance of suicide.

3. **What is the appearance and position of postmortem lividity?** When the heart ceases to beat, blood ceases to circulate, and, with the force of gravity, it drains to the body's lowest levels. The result is a dark blue or purple discoloration of the skin known as postmortem lividity. Postmortem lividity begins anywhere from one-half to three hours after death. Its spread slows after four or five hours, because blood congeals within the capillaries by that time, and it reaches its maximum intensity after 10 or 12 hours. Lividity provides an indication of the time of death.

The location of lividity indicates whether a body was moved after death. For example, if a body is discovered on its back, lividity is expected to appear in the lower part of the back and legs. If, however, it appears instead on the face, chest, and stomach, it is likely that the body was originally face down and was moved after death.

The medical examiner will also note the color of the lividity. Cherry red or vivid pink lividity indicates carbon monoxide poisoning, and other poisons also impart a telltale color to the lividity.

4. **Is blood present?** If so, where? Blood evidence points to the cause of death—gunshot, stabbing, beating.

5. **Are wounds present?** What are their location and number? First responders typically take note of gunshot wounds, knife punctures, tears, and lacerations, and *blunt force trauma*. The full extent and number of wounds is not always apparent until close medical examination or autopsy. We'll look further at wound evidence in a moment.

Talking the Talk

Blunt force trauma (BFT) is injury caused by the blow(s) of any blunt instrument, such as a bat, pipe, hammer, or fist.

A Step Back

On the scene of a homicide, it is natural for all investigative eyes to focus on the body. But it is also important for investigators to take a step back and look carefully at the surroundings.

If the room is in disarray, furniture upset, items broken or scattered, it is evident that a struggle has taken place. If, however, the room is orderly, the implication is that the victim did not feel him- or herself to be in danger.

Rooms, apartments, and houses hold other important clues. For example, evidence of the recent preparation of food may provide a clue as to the time of death. The presence of dated material, such as newspapers and mail items, may help fix the date of death in cases where a body is found in some state of decomposition.

Investigators ask themselves if the room or house shows evidence of robbery, or drug or alcohol use. They look, too, for evidence of sexually deviant practices.

Stains and Spatters

Approximately six quarts of blood circulate through the body of an adult. When the body is violently pierced—by bullets, by a knife, by a blunt instrument—some of that blood is spilled. In the case of gunshots or a violent struggle, it is usually spattered.

The spectacle of a blood-stained, blood-spattered crime scene is gruesome, but it is not simply chaotic or meaningless. The location of the stains or the pattern of the spatter have a story to tell. Well-interpreted blood-spatter evidence is often compelling at trial.

From the number and position of stains, it may be possible to determine the movements of the victim relative to his or her assailant. From blood spatter, it is possible to ascertain the direction from which an assault came. The distance between the victim and where the bloodstain came to rest can indicate the type of impact the victim received, the type of object that produced the wounds, the number of blows that were inflicted, and the position of victim and assailant during and after the bloodshed.

This evidence can be compared to statements taken from witnesses and suspects. There have been many cases in which a suspect claims that the victim's death was accidental, but the location and angle of the blood-spatter pattern refutes the claim. When blood drips, it creates round stains. When blood is propelled, as from a blow, the stains are elongated—the more elongated, the harder the blow.

Case in Point

In February 2002, David Camm was tried for the murder of his wife, Kimberly, and his two children, Bradley and Jill, in their Indiana home. Blood-spatter expert Rod Englert testified that blood spatter on Camm's T-shirt was high-velocity, which could only come from firing a gun. In court, Englert used simulated blood to demonstrate to the jury how blood spatter is produced. He testified that Camm's shoes also showed high-velocity spatter, which Camm had tried to wipe off. Lead prosecutor Stan Faith remarked to a reporter: "If you have this kind of blood impact on your T-shirt, there's only one way you can get it. That's in the presence of a gunshot." Camm was convicted and sentenced to 195 years in prison.

Investigators photograph blood stain and blood-spatter evidence and carefully study the patterns. Traditionally, investigators have attempted to evaluate blood-spatter evidence by directional analysis, using strings affixed to certain points in the spatter pattern and extending these back to a probable source of the blood. Recently, a computer software program called BackTrack has been developed to analyze spatter evidence digitally and graphically, using "virtual strings." The investigator enters into the computer the width, length, direction, and position of each blood droplet, and the software calculates an angle of attack for each droplet, then projects a flight path backward from each. Where two or more of the projections intersect, the position of the original wound can be determined.

Given sufficient time, a perpetrator may attempt to remove bloodstains and blood spatter by laundering bed sheets, blankets, and clothing, or by scrubbing walls, floors, and other surfaces. Luminol is a chemical that reacts with even trace amounts of hemoglobin, a constituent of blood, causing it to fluoresce with a bright green color. Faint blood stains—or even invisible stains—can be clearly visualized with Luminol.

Fingernails

The victim's fingernails are often repositories of key evidence. Blood may be visible under the fingernails, indicating that the victim attempted to defend him- or herself by scratching or tearing at the attacker. This blood can be invaluable in identifying a suspect, especially with the availability of DNA testing.

Even when blood evidence is not immediately visible under the fingernails, it or other tissue may be present and can be discovered later by microscopic examination. Typically, the medical examiner or a technician will "bag" the victim's hands—cover them with plastic bags—before transporting the body to the morgue. This avoids contamination and the loss of important trace evidence.

Reading the Wounds

The medical examiner will thoroughly investigate all wounds at autopsy, but, based on the appearance of wounds, an experienced detective can begin to make some important assessments at the scene.

Gunshot

When a gun is fired, the bullet does not simply and neatly exit the barrel. In addition to the emergence of the bullet, gases produced by the explosion of the powder expand, and metal fragments from the cartridge case are propelled out of the barrel, as are burned and unburned gunpowder, along with carbon and soot from the firing of the primer. All of this additional material leaves little trace when shots are fired at a distance from the victim. But if the skin around the wound shows a *powder tattoo* or is stained by soot and carbon, it is likely that the shot was fired from no more than two feet away. By test-firing in the ballistics lab, and comparing the resulting powder pattern and the proportion of burned and unburned powder with the evidence on the body or clothing, it is possible to calculate with reasonable accuracy actual firing distance. If the muzzle of the weapon was in direct contact with the body, a contact wound appears, often along with an impression of the muzzle.

At the scene, investigators can use the gunshot wound evidence to make a preliminary assessment of whether the injury was self-inflicted or a homicide.

A wound indicating that the gun was fired from more than a few inches away or a shot that penetrated clothing tends to rule out suicide. The location of the wound (for example, the back), or the angle of trajectory (as indicated by the shape of the wound or by the relation of the entry wound to the exit wound) may definitively rule out suicide—as does the absence of a weapon at the scene. If, however, the wound shows that the gun was held against the skin, and if the wound is in the mouth or right temple (assuming the victim was right-handed—left temple if left-handed), suicide is likely. Suicides rarely fire through clothing, except in the case of self-inflicted wounds to the chest. The weapon will almost certainly be present at the scene, typically grasped tightly in the hand (cadaveric spasm).

Talking the Talk

A **powder tattoo** is a characteristic pattern created around a gunshot wound by soot or carbon when the shot was fired from no more than two feet away. Presence of tattooing indicates a shot at very close range.

Stab and Cutting Wounds

Wounds inflicted by a knife or other sharp object may be stab wounds, made by thrusting, or cutting wounds. From the angle, location, and number of stab wounds, it may be possible to make inferences about the height and strength of the attacker, and perhaps even something of his state of mind (cool, professional, efficient, panicky, or filled with rage). The presence or absence of defensive wounds—cuts on the hands, arms, and legs resulting from the victim's attempts to ward off the attack—suggest something about the relation of victim to assailant. Absence of defensive wounds may suggest that either the victim was taken completely by surprise and was killed before he or she could offer resistance or that the victim did not expect an attack because the assailant was someone the victim knew and trusted.

Except in the case of certain suicide rituals (the Samurai practice of *sepuku* or *hara-kiri*, for instance), stab wounds are seldom purposely self-inflicted. Cutting wounds, however, are often associated with suicide, especially when the main wounds are accompanied by hesitation wounds—less severe cuts caused by attempts to build up the resolve to inflict the fatal cut.

As with gunshot wounds, the appearance of stabbing and cutting wounds can suggest much, even to those who arrive first on the scene. Knife wounds under (not *through*) clothing, cutting wounds at the throat, wrists, or ankles, and the presence of hesitation wounds all suggest suicide—especially if the weapon is present. Stab wounds through clothing, wounds in vital organs, disfiguring wounds, and the presence of defensive wounds all point to murder. Typically, the weapon is not present, and there are signs that the body has been moved.

As much as the crime scene and the body tell the first investigators who arrive, this information is usually no more than a prologue. It is the task of the medical examiner, as we will see in the next chapter, to read the rest of the story.

> **Sworn Statement**
>
> I didn't want to hurt the man. I thought he was a very nice gentleman. Soft-spoken. I thought so right up to the moment I cut his throat.
>
> —Perry Smith's confession in Truman Capote's *In Cold Blood: A True Account of a Multiple Murder and Its Consequences* (Random House, 1966)

The Least You Need to Know

◆ When a body is discovered, the responsibility for determining the cause of death ultimately rests with the medical examiner, but the first police investigators to arrive on the scene open up the investigation and make the initial determination that the death is or is not a homicide.

◆ Investigators examine the body as well as its surroundings for clues indicating the time and cause of death and, in the case of homicide, the relationship of the victim and the assailant.

◆ Rigor mortis and post-mortem lividity provide important indications of the time of death and whether or not the body was moved after death.

◆ The number and location of blood stains and the size, location, and shape of blood-spatter patterns provide clues to the position of the assailant relative to the victim.

◆ The appearance of both gunshot and knife wounds suggest much about how the victim was killed, providing (among other things) clues that either suggest or rule out suicide and that imply the assailant was either known or unknown to the victim.

Body of Evidence

In This Chapter

- ◆ The role of the medical examiner
- ◆ Preparing a body for autopsy
- ◆ Autopsy procedures
- ◆ Determining the time and cause of death
- ◆ Forensic toxicology
- ◆ Identifying the victim

Even though he or she is a cop, not a doctor, an experienced criminal investigator picks up a lot of forensic medicine on the job and can, as we saw in the preceding chapter, tell a great deal from a fairly quick examination of a victim's body.

But all unexplained deaths must be given more than a once-over. In virtually all jurisdictions, the medical examiner is called in and an autopsy is performed. You learned a bit about what the medical examiner does in the previous chapter; now let's explore that role in more detail.

Meet the ME

The medical examiner (ME) is a physician who specializes in pathology and, in most cases, has received additional training in forensic pathology. This means that a qualified medical examiner is an M.D. who has completed medical school as well as at least four years of postgraduate training in pathology and related disciplines *before* entering a year-long forensic pathology residency program. Such programs are usually offered by large urban medical examiner offices, which are affiliated with a medical school. In the entire United States, there are only about 40 such programs.

The extensive knowledge, skill, and training are only part of what it takes to be a medical examiner. Also required is an insatiable curiosity, acute powers of observation, and the emotional stamina to work with human tragedy and the results of human behavior at its most terribly violent and profoundly disturbing.

Dead Men and the Tales They Tell

The motto of the seagoing pirates of old was "dead men tell no tales," and, driven by this sentiment, they seldom left any living victims behind to betray them. Doubtless many of today's murderers believe much the same thing. They are, however, mistaken. To the medical examiner, the dead speak volumes.

Preparing for Autopsy

Both at the crime scene and in the morgue, the medical examiner searches the body for trace evidence. The ME records any available particulars concerning the circumstances of death, along with any available information identifying the deceased. The ME also notes physical characteristics, such as height and weight.

By the Numbers

In a typical year, the New York City Medical Examiner's Office uses 8,000 body bags for the transportation of remains to and from autopsy.

The body is handled carefully, in the knowledge that careless lifting or carrying may compromise important evidence, such as the trajectory path of a bullet. At this preliminary stage, the ME also remains alert for anything unusual. For instance, certain poisons leave telltale odors. (As any reader of old-fashioned murder mysteries knows, cyanide smells like bitter almonds.)

Once the body arrives at the morgue, a toe tag—an identification card with the victim's name (if known) and other basic information—is attached with a loop of string or wire around the toe of the cadaver. The body is then photographed. If it has been found fully or partially clothed, the body is photographed that way first. Then it is undressed and photographed again.

After photography, the body is x-rayed from head to foot. It is also weighed and measured. All distinguishing marks, such as birthmarks, tattoos, scars, and other evidence of injuries new and old, are carefully recorded. Another examination is performed to recover trace evidence. Hair, fibers, and dirt are collected from the body and from under the fingernails. Usually, the nails are clipped and the parings collected for analysis. The victim is also fingerprinted, and, if suicide by gunshot is suspected, the hands are chemically swabbed to detect the presence of nitrate (gunpowder residue). In cases of suspected rape, the genital area is swabbed for evidence.

Any clothing associated with the body—or, if the body was found naked, the wrapping sheet used by the ME office—is sent to the laboratory for examination.

The Cutting

The *autopsy* proper is an examination of the internal organs. The body is rinsed clean, then laid out on its back on a stainless steel table. A stabilizing block is placed under the head.

The ME begins with a "Y" incision, cutting into the body from each shoulder and meeting at the breast bone (sternum), then continuing down the abdomen and into the pelvis. This efficiently exposes all of the internal organs.

Next, the ME uses a saw to cut through the ribs and collarbone, so that the rib cage can be lifted away from the organs in one piece.

Talking the Talk

An **autopsy** is a medical examination of the internal organs, including the brain, of the deceased in order to determine the cause of death and other circumstances relating to the death.

In the case of death by gunshot, the ME uses the x-rays that have been taken to help locate bullets and trace the bullet trajectory. The ME also wants to avoid cutting into—and thereby compromising or destroying—any wound evidence.

Using the x-ray information for guidance, the ME begins to remove the individual organs and weighs them. Blood samples, tissue samples, and other fluid samples are taken from the organs. The stomach and intestines are opened to examine the contents. This can provide information as to when, what, and perhaps even where the victim last ate before he or she was killed.

After examining the viscera, the ME begins examining the head. First, the whites of the eyes are probed for minute hemorrhages known as petichae, which indicate death by strangulation. Of course, the head is also thoroughly examined for contusions and other wounds.

When the external examination of the head is complete, an incision is made in the scalp at the back of the head, and the skin is peeled forward, over the face, exposing the skull. The ME opens the skull with a high-speed oscillating power saw, then applies a chisel to pry off the skullcap. This exposes the brain so that it can be lifted out, weighed, and examined.

Brain tissue and other organ tissue samples are sent to the lab for additional analysis (see "Death by Poisoning: Forensic Toxicology" later in this chapter). Any organs the ME believes should be investigated further are preserved. The rest are returned to the body cavity.

Death: How?

In the best case, the work of the ME provides clues to the identity of the victim's assailant and produces evidence that helps secure a conviction. At the very least, however, the ME can usually determine, with precision, the cause of death.

Natural or Unnatural

In many instances, determining whether the cause of death was natural, the result of an accident, or a homicide is straightforward. Sometimes, however, the cause becomes apparent only after careful postmortem examination, including an autopsy and, perhaps, toxicological studies.

However simple or difficult, it is crucially important to determine whether or not a crime has been committed.

Shooting

The analysis of gunshot wounds is discussed in some detail in Chapter 14. The ME is in a position to confirm, amplify, or correct many of the observations a police investigator has made at the scene.

The analysis of entrance wounds and exit wounds is typically very important, because the trajectory of the bullet can be calculated using this relationship. With trajectory information, it becomes possible to infer the location of the assailant in relation to the victim. This information may support or refute statements from the suspect. For example, a suspect may claim that he shot the victim in self-defense, whereas wound analysis reveals that the victim was shot at close range, in the back of the head, execution style. The information is also frequently valuable for ruling in or out suicide or an accidental shooting.

Stabbing

As with gunshot wounds, stab and cutting wounds are discussed in Chapter 14; however, a full autopsy can reveal much more about stab wounds than an on-the-scene examination can. The extent of the injuries can be more precisely assessed, as can the angle at which the blade entered the victim. In the autopsy room, a suspect weapon can be more accurately matched to a wound than it can be in the field.

Beating

The extent of injury caused by blows with a blunt object is often apparent only upon autopsy. With autopsy, it is usually possible to demonstrate that certain injuries are consistent with a suspect weapon by showing how the size and shape of the weapon compares with the size, shape, and extent of the injury or injuries inflicted.

Investigation of child battery is greatly aided by autopsy, which can often reveal prior broken bones and internal injuries, thereby demonstrating a history of abuse.

Sworn Statement

We had a patient [at Bellevue Hospital] who was a heroin addict who had an infection of the heart. ... We treated him and he survived, which was a real triumph. Then when I came down that weekend, there he was, dead on the autopsy table. ... We'd treated his infection but not his addiction. That made me think I could contribute more to society by looking at people on the autopsy table and feeding back the findings so that lots of people could benefit, rather than just treating patients one at a time. So I stayed in pathology.

—Dr. Michael Baden, famed former New York City medical examiner, quoted in Katherine Ramsland's, "Crime Investigation Through Autopsy: Dr. Michael Baden," at www.crimelibrary.com/forensics2/autopsy/

Asphyxia

Asphyxiation is common as a method of homicide as well as suicide and as a cause of accidental death. It occurs when the brain and other body tissues receive insufficient oxygen to support the oxygen-carrying red blood cells. It is caused by anything that seriously interferes with breathing or the respiration process.

In cases of suspected asphyxiation, the ME looks for a blue or purple coloration around the lips, fingernails, and toenails. Then the ME looks beyond this sign in an effort to determine the cause of asphyxiation.

Did the victim choke? The presence of a foreign body in the trachea indicates this. Choking is almost always accidental.

Did the victim drown? The circumstances of how and where the body was found provide the most important clue. Most drownings are accidental; however, the ME's examination will reveal if an already dead person had been placed in water to make it appear as if the victim had drowned.

Was the victim smothered? Despite what mystery movies and crime novels portray, few murderers smother their victims, and most deaths by smothering are, in fact, accidental. The ME's examination can sometimes determine if a struggle was associated with the smothering, which would indicate foul play.

> **By the Numbers**
>
> A bizarre form of unintentional suicide by hanging is known as autoerotic asphyxiation, in which sexual gratification is sought by placing a rope around the neck and tightening it, often by hanging, in order to induce semi-consciousness. If this extremely hazardous sexual experimentation goes too far, asphyxiation and death can result. Five hundred to 1,000 people die from autoerotic asphyxiation each year.

Hanging is almost always a means of suicide, not murder, but for that very reason, murderers have used hanging in an attempt to disguise their crime. The ME's examination reveals whether hanging was the cause of death or whether the victim was hanged after death.

Death by strangulation is almost always homicide. The ME looks for evenly grooved, horizontal ligature marks on the victim's neck, in contrast to the type of ligature marks found on the neck of a victim of hanging. In hanging, the ligature marks are not horizontal, but start from below the chin and travel *up* to a point just below the ears. Manual strangulation—choking with the hands—often leaves signs of hand pressure, even long after death.

A number of chemicals, including chloroform and ammonia, can induce asphyxiation, as can an overdose of sleeping pills or the combination of narcotic and alcohol use. In cases of chemically induced and drug-induced asphyxia, there are signs of paralysis of the air passages. Depending on the chemical involved, death may be interpreted as an accident, suicide, or homicide.

Death: When?

In Chapter 14 we discussed how rigor mortis and postmortem lividity serve as important indicators of time of death. The ME also uses four additional factors to help determine how long the victim has been dead.

Temperature

In and of itself, body temperature is a very crude indicator of time of death, but it can be helpful when considered along with other indicators. Body temperature declines 2 to 3 degrees in the first hour after death, then 1 to 1.5 degrees for each subsequent hour, up to 18 hours.

Eyes

After death, there is a dramatic reduction and eventual disappearance of tone in the eye muscles, so that the pupils dilate. After about seven hours, the pupil begins partially to contract. After 12 hours, the cornea clouds over.

In addition to examining the appearance of the eyes, the ME may withdraw fluid from the eyeball to determine the level of potassium present. This level rises after death at a predictable rate, so that, based on the potassium level, an estimate of the time of death can be made.

Stomach

If investigators on the scene can determine when the victim last ate, an examination of the stomach contents at autopsy can serve as a gauge to the time of death. Digestion proceeds at a reasonably uniform rate. Since digestion ceases at death, it is possible to estimate the time of death based on the degree of digestion evident in the stomach contents. It is also true that food remains in the stomach for one to two hours after eating, and then is emptied into the small intestine. A full stomach places the time of death within one or two hours after eating. If the stomach is relatively empty and the small intestine full, death most likely occurred four to six hours after eating. After four hours, the contents of the small intestine begin to pass into the large intestine. If the large intestine is empty, at least 12 hours have passed between the victim's last meal and the time of death.

Decomposition

Few sights are as inherently repulsive as the decomposing body of what had once been a living, breathing, sentient human being. Yet, to the ME, decomposition is not a source of disgust, but evidence to be studied. Based on the state of decomposition, it is possible to estimate the time of death.

Talking the Talk

Adipocere is a postmortem hardening of fatty body tissue, which creates a soapy appearance that develops if the corpse is in a relatively hot and moist location. **Mummification** is the complete dehydration of all body parts; it develops months or years after death.

The first signs of decomposition are a distended stomach and abdomen, the result of internal gases created by the decomposition process. *Adipocere*, hardening of fatty tissue, creates a soapy appearance that develops if the body is in a relatively hot and moist location. It may take as long as three months for this condition to develop extensively. After about a year, if the body has been in a warm, dry area, *mummification*, the complete dehydration of all body parts, will be apparent.

Typically, decomposing bodies are attacked by insects (and, often, other animals as well). In this case, the ME may call in a forensic entomologist, whose work is discussed later in this chapter.

Bodies recovered from water typically undergo changes that are strongly indicative of the time of death. In warm water, a dead body sinks, remains underwater for 8 to 10 days, and then, because of the buoyancy of gases formed during decomposition, rises. In cold water, a body may remain immersed for two to three weeks before rising.

The ME carefully examines the skin of any body that has been recovered from water. Outer skin loosens after five or six days of immersion, and the nails separate in two to three weeks.

By looking for the presence of water in the lungs, the ME can determine whether the person drowned or was killed and then thrown into the water to dispose of the body or to make the death look like accidental drowning.

Death by Poisoning: Forensic Toxicology

Poisoning is a sufficiently common cause of death that the medical examiner's office of most large jurisdictions employs a full-time forensic toxicologist—a specialist trained in the study of poisons, their detection, their use in homicide, and their effect on the human body—to determine if poisoning occurred and what substance or substances caused death. Accidental poisoning is distressingly common, especially among children, but poisoning is also one of the oldest methods of murder.

The forensic toxicologist runs chemical tests on body fluids, blood, and some organs to identify the presence of poisons. Some agents, such as arsenic, accumulate over time in the hair and fingernails. In cases of suspected arsenic poisoning, these are always tested. Traces of arsenic remain in hair and fingernails indefinitely, and, if necessary, a body can be exhumed for examination many years after death.

The forensic toxicologist can test for blood alcohol level, to determine if the victim had been intoxicated at the time of death and perhaps sufficiently so to cause death. The toxicologist also has the ability to test for the presence of a wide variety of illicit drugs that are often abused, including amphetamines, barbiturates, powdered cocaine and crack cocaine, marijuana, and such opiates as codeine and morphine.

Legitimate therapeutic drugs are sometimes taken in deliberate or accidental overdose. The toxicologist tests for the presence of acetaminophen, anticonvulsants, tranquilizers, and aspirin products.

Beyond drugs both legal and illegal, many common substances are highly toxic and can cause accidental poisoning or be used to commit murder. Tests have been developed for most of these, including arsenic, benzene, bromide, butyl nitrite, cyanide, strychnine, and warfarin (a common rat poison).

Identification

Most people carry with them some form of identification, usually a driver's license. Identifying a corpse is frequently as simple as examining the contents of a wallet. In other cases, neighbors or witnesses can provide identification.

But, not infrequently, a body is found without any identification at all and is associated with no friends, neighbors, or witnesses. In these cases, the ME and other forensics experts work from the evidence at hand to make an identification.

They begin with the obvious: the overall appearance of the individual. This information is compared to missing persons reports that are on file. If a match is found, relatives are contacted to make a positive identification.

Fingerprinting

The next obvious step is to compare fingerprints taken from the body with local and federal fingerprint files. If a match is found, the body has an identity.

Forensic Odontology

Forensic odontology is a highly specialized field of dentistry that uses dental evidence to determine identity. Teeth are among the very last parts of a body to decompose. Mummified remains thousands of years old often retain teeth. From the size, condition, and number of teeth, odontologists can tell much about the age and even the sex of fully decomposed remains or partial remains.

Most of us make or have made fairly regular visits to the dentist. The forensic odontologist notes the presence of any dental work (fillings, crowns, and so on), as well as missing or broken teeth, and compares this data to the files in the dental offices of a particular area.

Sworn Statement

The work of forensic odontologists is especially valuable in instances of mass disaster, as in the terrorist attacks on the World Trade Center in New York and the Pentagon in Washington, D.C., on September 11, 2001. In such cases, human remains are often fragmentary, and the numerous victims are separated from any form of identification (such as driver's licenses). Under these chaotic circumstances, dental evidence may be the only reliable means to obtain a positive identification.

The forensic odontologist is also an expert examiner of bite mark evidence. Some murderers bite their victims, perhaps in the course of a struggle, perhaps from sadistic or sexually deviant motives. To the odontologist, the bite mark is nothing less than an impression of the perpetrator's teeth. From this evidence, the odontologist may be able to advise police as to whether they should look for a large or small person. Even more important, it is often possible to match a suspect's teeth to a bite mark found on the victim.

Forensic Anthropology

Most physical anthropologists study ancient mummified or fossilized human remains to learn about the evolution of our species, *Homo sapiens*. Forensic anthropology applies physical anthropology to the legal process. Specialists in this field examine skeletal or badly decomposed human remains for the purpose of making an identification. Frequently, forensic anthropologists work in conjunction with forensic pathologists, odontologists, and homicide investigators.

From even partial and fragmentary skeletal remains, the forensic anthropologist is able to suggest the age, sex, ancestry, stature, and other unique features of a decedent. This specialist can also distinguish between a skeleton that may be decades old or even older and one that is of more recent origin. Skeletal remains often reveal the results of injury, and the forensic anthropologist can help other investigators determine if the injury was likely the result of homicide.

The Bug Detectives

Insects occupy a key niche in any ecosystem because they thrive on decay and decomposition. Sooner or later, a dead body attracts insects. To some extent, this destroys evidence, but the presence of insects, larvae, and eggs also provides clues to time and place of death. Locating and evaluating this evidence requires the expertise of the forensic entomologist (FE)—a biologist who specializes in the study of insect evidence as it relates to criminal investigation and the legal process.

From the presence of insect eggs or of insects at various stages of development (larva, nymph, adult), the FE can often estimate the time of death. Moreover, the FE can use the type of insect or insect eggs found on the body to tie that body to a specific geographical area—which is especially useful if it is suspected that a body has been transported a considerable distance.

To the ME and his colleagues, the dead are hardly mute, and, in recent years, the opening of the vast new field of DNA study has greatly added to their eloquence. The recovery, examination, and analysis of DNA evidence is the subject of the next chapter.

Case in Point
In one case, a body was discovered in a coastal area, about 100 miles from where the chief suspect lived. The suspect denied ever having been in the remote area where the body was found. An FE was called in to examine insects found on the suspect's car. Among these he identified a species of mayfly that is found only in the area from which the body was recovered. Moreover, this species of mayfly was known to be active at a particular stage of its development only during a limited time. The ME determined that the time of death was consistent with the period in which the mayflies were active. This fact, coupled with the presence of the insects on the suspect's car, was sufficient to warrant an indictment.

The Least You Need to Know

- ◆ Forensic autopsies are performed by a medical examiner, a physician who has specialized in pathology and who has additional specific training in forensic pathology.

- ◆ After all possible information has been gathered from external observation of the body, the internal organs, including the brain, are examined by surgical removal. This is the main part of the autopsy.

- ◆ The purpose of the autopsy is to determine, at minimum, the cause and time of death; in addition, the ME looks for clues as to the circumstances of death (including the identity of the perpetrator) and, if unknown, the identity of the body.

- ◆ Other specialists who may be called on to collaborate with the ME include a forensic toxicologist (an expert on poisons), a forensic anthropologist (who principally analyzes skeletal evidence), and a forensic entomologist (an expert on insects).

DNA Evidence: The "Smoking Gun"?

In This Chapter

- ◆ What is DNA?
- ◆ Using DNA "fingerprinting"
- ◆ Obtaining and analyzing DNA evidence
- ◆ Reliability and validity of DNA evidence
- ◆ Using DNA evidence to exonerate the innocent
- ◆ The DNA database controversy

Investigators and, in the end, juries evaluate evidence. Such evaluation determines, step by step, the further course of the investigation or the final verdict in a criminal case. Ideally, the evidence presented is straightforward and clear cut, the proverbial "smoking gun" that pretty much proves guilt or innocence.

But crime is a human activity, and evidence, the product of human activity, is usually far from straightforward and clear cut. Often, the prosecution has only a few pieces of physical evidence—a fragment of fiber, a few strands of hair, a trace of blood—to link the accused to a crime. Analyzed properly and presented persuasively, such evidence may point to the defendant, but, traditionally, material like this has rarely been sufficient to secure a conviction—a verdict, beyond a reasonable doubt, of guilty.

What if there were a way to link such trace evidence, beyond any reasonable doubt, to a particular person? Until recently, this was idle speculation, nothing more. But with the discovery of the role DNA plays in heredity and the development of methods to extract and to analyze the DNA in most tissue and tissue traces, it has become reality. A very short time ago, DNA evidence represented the extreme cutting edge of forensic science. Today, while still technologically advanced and demanding, it has entered the mainstream of criminal investigation, as we'll see in this chapter.

The Double Helix

The field of genetics was revolutionized beginning in 1953, when two biochemists, James D. Watson and Francis H.C. Crick, described the structure of the deoxyribonucleic acid (*DNA*) molecule, which is found in the cells of all living things (and in some viruses, too). DNA was discovered back in 1869, but Watson and Crick demonstrated that, structurally, the DNA molecule consists of two nucleotide chains that twist around one another to form a double helix, rather like a spirally twisted ladder. The curved sides of this ladder consist of alternate phosphate-sugar groups, while the rungs of the ladder are protein bases joined by weak hydrogen bonds.

Talking the Talk

DNA, or deoxyribonucleic acid, carries the genetic information of the cell and is uniquely capable of replicating itself and synthesizing RNA (ribonucleic acid), which, like a chemical messenger, transmits the genetic information.

This unique structure enables DNA to replicate itself—something it does prior to cellular reproduction. When a cell divides to form two new cells, the double-stranded helix unwinds, and each "unzipped" strand picks up complementary nucleotides, which, incorporated into the unzipped strands, create two new DNA molecules that are identical to each other and to the original molecule. The DNA molecule carries chemically coded genetic information for the transmission of inherited traits. When the double helix "unzips," the coded information is passed on.

Biological Barcode

The function of DNA is double-edged. The process of replication during reproduction ensures that a baby born to a human mother and a human father will be a human being, as opposed to, say, a kumquat. The genetic information coded in the DNA signals the pattern for human development. It also ensures that the baby will inherit certain genetic traits from the mother and father. That is, thanks to DNA, the newborn will be neither a new species nor totally different from its parents. Yet even as DNA transmits characteristics in common with one's species and one's parents, it also ensures that each individual is unique. Except for identical twins, each person, at the molecular level of the DNA contained in the nuclei of each cell, is completely unique.

Human beings have 23 pairs of chromosomes containing the full DNA code that serves as the blueprint for everything needed to build the individual and the molecular instructions for how to run him or her once he or she has been built. One member of each chromosomal pair is inherited from the mother, and one from the father. The unique DNA pattern that results is copied in each and every cell of the body.

DNA Fingerprinting

Most of the structure of DNA doesn't differ much from one person to another. That makes sense, if you consider that, viewed as organisms, human beings have more in common with one another than differences: two legs, two arms, two eyes, the ability to walk upright, the capacity to learn and use speech, and so on. In fact, only about 0.10 percent of the base pairs of human DNA differs from person to person. This is a very small percentage of difference, but it represents differences in about three million base pairs of DNA. That is, there are some three million molecular elements in each of us that can be mixed and matched in different ways to produce a unique human being.

The range of possible combinations is virtually infinite. Therefore, if we focus on the DNA in chromosomal regions that do differ, we can identify a unique *DNA fingerprint* for each individual in the human population.

How can criminal investigators make use of this kind of "fingerprint"? The key to using DNA evidence is to identify the unique features of DNA taken from a suspect's tissue with DNA left at the scene of a crime.

Talking the Talk

Some professionals and laypersons alike speak of the **DNA fingerprint,** which refers to how the structure of certain parts of the DNA molecule uniquely marks and identifies each individual, much as an actual fingerprint is unique to each person.

Step by Step

Obtaining and analyzing DNA evidence is a complex, time-consuming, and exacting procedure, which must be carried out step by step, with scrupulous care to ensure scientific accuracy that will produce valid probative evidence. While the principles of DNA profiling are extremely reliable and well established, the practices of individual investigators, technicians, and laboratories must be closely monitored and questioned, because they can produce misleading results.

Obtaining the Specimen

The first step is obtaining the specimen. Getting DNA from a suspect is easy. A sample can be obtained from saliva by means of a simple, quick, and painless swab of the mouth.

> **Sworn Statement**
>
> Every year since 1989, in about 25 percent of the sexual assault cases referred to the FBI where [DNA] results could be obtained … the primary suspect has been excluded by forensic DNA testing.
>
> —Barry C. Scheck, attorney and professor of law and director of clinical education, Benjamin N. Cardozo School of Law New York, New York

Isolating DNA from material at a crime scene can be much trickier. DNA is found in blood, saliva, semen, hair, and other body fluids and tissues. Whichever of these substances are available, investigators collect.

Often, laboratory specialists not only must isolate the DNA, they have to clean it up, because, at the crime scene, it is typically contaminated by dirt and other debris. Very frequently, DNA must be isolated from substances that are little more than stains— for example, dried blood on a carpet or article of clothing. The process of extracting the sample safely from the fabric is painstaking and sometimes risky. If the sample is very small, a botched attempt at extraction can end up destroying the evidence altogether.

Getting at the Good Stuff

As hard as it can be to obtain the DNA sample, it is only after it's been isolated that things get *really* complicated.

There are two kinds of "polymorphic regions"—areas where there is a lot of DNA diversity—in the genome, or genetic material, of a person: sequence polymorphisms and length polymorphisms.

Sequence polymorphisms are simple substitutions of one or two bases in the genes themselves. These aren't very useful for DNA fingerprinting in criminal cases.

Length polymorphisms are nothing more than variations in the length of the DNA molecule. It is a special kind of length polymorphism that is used in DNA evidence. Investigators look for special variations that come from series of short, identical repeat sequences of DNA molecules. A given sequence may be repeated from 1 to 30 times in a row. For this reason, these DNA regions are called variable number tandem repeats, or *VNTRs*.

Now, the number of tandem repeats at specific places—called loci—on chromosomes varies between individuals. For any given VNTR locus in an individual's DNA, there is a certain number of identifiable repeats. Each individual inherits one copy of each chromosome from his or her mother and father. Therefore, each individual has two copies of each VNTR locus (just as each person has two copies of real genes).

Talking the Talk

VNTRs (variable number tandem repeats) are short, identical repeat sequences of DNA molecules in length polymorphisms that may be readily compared. If the VNTRs of one DNA sample match those of another, it is highly likely that both samples came from the same individual.

To arrive at an individual's unique DNA profile, the investigator determines the number of VNTRs at several distinctive loci. This procedure is called restriction fragment length polymorphism (RFLP) analysis, and it is the heart of DNA fingerprinting. It is the process by which the DNA analyst identifies the specific features that mark the individual's DNA as distinctive to that individual.

Just as the analyst of actual fingerprints focuses on a limited catalog of specific features to identify the uniqueness of a fingerprint (see Chapter 12), so the DNA investigator, through RFLP analysis, identifies only the specific features that mark the individual's DNA as distinctive to that individual. This makes comparing a sample from a suspect with a sample from the crime scene manageable. To compare hundreds of millions of molecular features would consume many lifetimes and require an army of analysts. To compare a relatively small number of nevertheless unique markers can be done in a far more timely and practical fashion.

Let It Gel

After the DNA is isolated, special enzymes are used to cut it up into fragments containing known VNTR loci. The next step in the analysis is to sort these DNA fragments by size. This is done by gel electrophoresis, a process in which the DNA sample is loaded into a slab of a gel called agarose. An electric current is passed through the agarose. Because the DNA is negatively charged, it is pulled through the gel toward the positively charged electrode. Larger fragments move more slowly than smaller ones, so that it is possible to determine the relative size of each fragment based on how far it has moved.

Preserving the DNA

At this point, the DNA fragments in the gel are quite unstable and will disintegrate within a day or two. To preserve the evidence permanently, it is transferred by an electrochemical process to a nylon membrane, which not only keeps the evidence from simply vanishing, but prepares it for the next step.

Conducting the Probe

This next step actually determines which fragments of DNA contain a particular VNTR locus and then marks them so that the fragments of the sample from the suspect can be compared to the corresponding fragments from the crime scene.

As Watson and Crick demonstrated in 1953, DNA occurs as a double-stranded molecule, a structure held together by weak chemical bonding between nucleotides (the basic constituents of DNA) on opposing strands. Only certain pairs of nucleotides form bonds with each other; these are called complementary. To locate a specific VNTR sequence on a single-stranded DNA fragment, the analyst employs a "DNA probe" using a DNA sequence complementary to that of a VNTR locus. This probe is tagged with a radioactive compound and allowed to bind with the sample DNA.

> **Sworn Statement**
>
> One thing is very clear, DNA works. DNA is perhaps our most powerful tool in law enforcement to come along since the fingerprint.
>
> —Christopher H. Asplen, Executive Director, National Commission on the Future of DNA Evidence

Next, the sample—preserved in its nylon membrane and now having been probed and radioactively tagged—is placed on a sheet of special x-ray film. The radioactive tag reacts with the film just as visible light reacts with ordinary photographic film. That is, it produces an image. In this case, it is an image of the places on the membrane where the probe has bound to DNA containing the VNTR sequence. The image appears as a pattern of darkened bands. The pattern produced by the DNA sample from the suspect may easily be compared to the sample taken from the crime scene.

In the following example of VNTR sequence analysis, the three columns marked "L" are markers (called allele ladders), which are used as a scale to show the position of the DNA evidence samples. The column marked "E" is from the DNA of a murder victim. The column marked "F" is from the DNA obtained from under the fingernails of the victim; presumably, this material contains skin cells from the murderer, because the victim scratched at her assailant in self-defense. The column marked "G" is from DNA taken from Suspect #1, "H" is from Suspect #2, and "I" from Suspect #3. The analyst concluded that columns "F" and "G" match, indicating that Suspect #1 is the possible donor of the skin cells beneath the victim's fingernails. (More VNTR sequences would need to be examined in order to make a definitive match.)

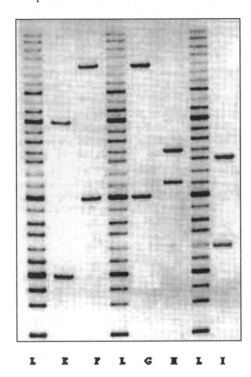

An example of VNTR sequence analysis.

(Image from crimescene.com)

Playing the Numbers and Making the ID

When a fingerprint found at a crime scene is compared to a print taken from a suspect, it is hardly sufficient to compare just one or two features of each print. Analysts look for a pattern of matching features at specifically defined points. Similarly, it is not sufficient to compare the results from one VNTR locus. The key to identifying a DNA match beyond a reasonable doubt is combined analysis of several VNTR loci on different chromosomes. In practice, the forensic DNA profile is built up from the results of four or five probes, each of which targets a different VNTR locus.

Consider what happens when four probes are used. Immediately, you get eight pieces of information about the individual in question, since each person has two separate copies of each VNTR region (two times four is eight). Moreover, each VNTR locus has about 30 different length variants (called alleles). Each allele occurs at a certain known frequency in a population. To arrive at the probability that a given eight-band profile will occur, it is necessary to multiply together the eight different allele frequencies, each of which, remember, presents about 30 possibilities. Thus, using just four loci, the probability of finding any given allele combination in the general population is about 1 in 5,000,000.

> **By the Numbers**
>
> Using FBI analytical standards, you are 2,000 times more likely to win the Publisher's Clearinghouse sweepstakes (odds are 1 in 50,000,000) than to emerge with a DNA profile that matches anyone who is not your identical twin.

If two DNA samples match at four loci, there is only 1 in 5,000,000 chance that the match is a coincidence, an error. However, the FBI insists on using not 4, but 13 loci to build its profiles. This means that not 8, but 26 different bands are studied, making the chance of an erroneous match (that is, finding two unrelated individuals with the same DNA profile) 1 in 100 billion.

DNA Evidence in the Courts

DNA evidence was first admitted into a United States courtroom in 1985. In 1988, a person was convicted in large part on the evidence of a DNA profile. Today, DNA evidence is generally accepted by the law enforcement community, judges, juries, and lawyers—at least in principle. As with any other form of evidence and analysis, however, validity of principle is not enough. The procedure and process by which the evidence is actually collected, handled, analyzed, and interpreted is critical and always open to close scrutiny in a court of law.

In *principle*, DNA evidence can be used to establish identity to an extraordinarily high degree of certainty. In *practice*, however, much can go wrong.

A marvelous feature of DNA evidence is that while it can be used to identify and convict the guilty, it can also serve to defend the innocent and exonerate the wrongfully convicted. In recent years, dozens of persons jailed or even slated for execution for violent crimes, including murder and rape, have been freed because analysis of DNA evidence, using techniques unavailable at the time of the original trial and conviction, ruled out the prisoner as perpetrator.

Case in Point

On the evening of April 27, 1990, a woman was attacked in her home by a man who came at her from behind, placed a pillow over her head, sexually assaulted her, then fled. Even though the victim could not meaningfully describe the man, she picked out Gilbert Alejandro from a photograph in a police mug book. Alejandro was convicted and sentenced to 12 years in prison. The prosecution based its case on the victim's identification of Alejandro, but the smoking gun was the testimony of a DNA expert. A subsequent investigation revealed that the expert, Fred Zain, had falsified results and lied about his credentials. As part of an appeal, a new DNA analyst testified that at least one other DNA test performed had excluded Alejandro. He also said that the test to which Zain had testified was inconclusive. Alejandro's conviction was overturned.

The Future of DNA Identification

DNA analysis is likely to figure more and more prominently in criminal prosecutions, both as inculpatory (guilt-proving) and exculpatory (innocence-proving) evidence. Laboratory methods are continually being streamlined and refined. There is a trend toward developing the ability to analyze smaller and smaller samples, so that even the most minute trace of blood, semen, or saliva may be made to yield sufficient DNA for accurate analysis.

Most controversial are proposals to maintain DNA profile databases, either of convicted criminals or even of large segments of the general population. The idea is to make it possible to match, rapidly and with a very high degree of certainty, DNA evidence recovered from crime scenes with individuals represented in the database.

As thrilling as this prospect is for criminal investigators, many believe such databases challenge one of the most basic rights of our democracy: the legal presumption of innocence. The technology to create and effectively use such databases exists today. The moral and political questions they raise have yet to be resolved.

The Least You Need to Know

- ◆ DNA contains features unique to each individual; therefore, properly analyzed, DNA evidence can be used as a molecular "fingerprint," to identify individuals to an extremely high degree of certainty.

- ◆ The basic procedure for linking a suspect to a crime using DNA is to collect DNA evidence from the crime scene or victim, collect DNA from the suspect, and, through laboratory analysis, compare the two.

◆ Matching the DNA recovered from a crime scene or crime victim to a DNA sample taken from a suspect requires identifying specific features that may be meaningfully compared and that yield unambiguous conclusions.

◆ DNA evidence can be inculpatory, pointing to the guilt of a suspect, or exculpatory, excluding a suspect from having committed the crime in question.

◆ Technically, it is now feasible to create a national database of DNA information for the general U.S. population. Legally, however, this may constitute a violation of the presumption of innocence.

Part 6

The Long Arm

This is the report from the trenches—the streets and the highways, the big cities and the remote villages—that are the front lines of society's struggle with crime: everyday police work.

We begin with the origin of professional policing in classical Rome and in eighteenth-century London, and we survey the development of policing in Europe and the United States. Then we look at the typical police force of today and how cops gather and manage information and harness technology to get at the facts of a case. We end with a look at the fringes of police work, the use of "truth serum," hypnosis, and even "psychic detectives."

Policing: The Way It Was

In This Chapter

- Origins of policing
- The police of ancient Rome
- London: evolution of the modern police force
- The birth of Scotland Yard
- Terrorism and Jack the Ripper
- London police innovations

Police have been a part of civilization for a very long time, at least since the days of Babylon under the lawgiver Hammurabi, nearly 4,000 years ago.

The modern police force, a civil agency answerable, ultimately, to the people, was a long time in coming, however. This chapter covers a portion of the evolution of the police forces familiar to us today, with particular focus on the first modern force, London's Metropolitan Police.

The First Cops

The first cops were specially designated members of religious, military, or political forces who were given the responsibility of enforcing religious, military, or political law and order. The earliest identifiable police forces developed from the corps of personal bodyguards and palace guards maintained by kings and warlords. Their responsibilities expanded from providing immediate protection of the ruler to extending the ruler's reach into the general population by executing and enforcing the laws he imposed.

Sworn Statement

Policemen are soldiers who act alone; soldiers are policemen who act together.

—Herbert Spencer, *Social Statics* (1851)

Some early forces were highly organized. In Rome, the emperor Caesar Augustus (63 B.C.E.–14 C.E.) saw a need to bring order to the often violent and anarchic streets of a capital populated by nearly a million. Using personnel from the Roman legions, Augustus decreed three distinct orders of police. These units were removed from military command and placed directly under the urban prefect. At the discretion of the commanders of this police force, assistance could be secured immediately from the Praetorian Guard, the emperor's personal bodyguard.

The organization and discipline of the great military legions demonstrated the administrative skill with which Rome built its military. Augustus applied similar acumen in deploying his urban police force. He divided the city of Rome into 14 wards, or *regiones*, then subdivided the wards into precincts (*vici*). To each precinct, Augustus assigned a corps of *vigilies*—"vigilant ones"—each corps consisting of seven squads. Each squad mustered 1,000 freedmen, who reported to a precinct captain, or *vicimagistor*.

By day, the squads stood ready to respond to crime, to quell civil disturbances, and to fight fires—which were frequent and very hazardous occurrences in the old city. By night, they took a more proactive approach and ventured out to patrol the city streets.

Through much of history, quasi-military, quasi-civil police forces were active in many parts of the world. The shoguns (hereditary military rulers) of renaissance Japan created elaborate police forces with specially designated samurai warriors, called *yoriki* and *doshin*, who patrolled the streets and reported to a samurai magistrate.

Elsewhere, the police took on a more sinister role, developing into enforcers of tyranny and terror. In prerevolutionary France, the Paris police were agents of the king and had almost unlimited power to regulate the day-to-day activities of the common people of the capital. In early twentieth-century Russia, the Bolshevik Revolution brought with it *secret police*, the Okhrana and Cheka, which evolved into the Soviet NKVD and later the KGB. Japan, under the military dictatorship that prevailed during the first half of the twentieth century, had the Thought Police, and, during the 1950s into the 1970s, the shah of Iran maintained his power by means of the much-hated SAVAK.

Such agencies, associated with totalitarian governments in many parts of the world and at many times in history, represent the extreme of the police as a force of oppression and control. In modern democracies, such as the United States, the sworn function of the police is to "serve and protect" the citizens, but most police officers are well aware that, while those citizens gratefully welcome them in times of danger, they are also wary of the potential for abuses of police power. It is easy to be a cop in a dictatorship, quite difficult and demanding to occupy the same office in a democracy.

Talking the Talk

Secret police is a general term for political police forces whose power derives directly from a dictator or monarch and who have almost unlimited authority to monitor and regulate the day-to-day activities of the common people. Examples include the Soviet NKVD and KGB, the Thought Police of World War II-era Japan, and the SAVAK operating under the former shah of Iran.

Case Study: London

"The man who is tired of London," the great eighteenth-century English man of letters Samuel Johnson declared, "is tired of life." By the 1700s, the bustling metropolis was one of the greatest cities in the world, brimming with life, with civilization, with opportunity—and with crime. The problem was how to cope with the crime without sacrificing the benefits of a free and vigorous society.

From Mr. Fielding's People to the Bow Street Runners

Lovers of British literature remember Sir Henry Fielding as the author of the sprawling and uproarious novel *Tom Jones*, but, from 1748 until his death in 1754, Fielding worked as a magistrate for the City of Westminster, one of London's great boroughs.

At the time of Fielding's appointment to this post, it was no great honor to serve as magistrate. The office was in deep disrepute, and Fielding's predecessors had been little more than racketeers who sheltered and fostered the city's flourishing criminal element. Fielding took charge, determined to rid Bow Street (as the magistrate's headquarters was called) of corruption.

Instead of coddling crime, Fielding looked for ways to fight it. In 1752, he commenced publication of *The Covent-Garden Journal*, which publicized thefts and descriptions of criminals and generally sought to raise public awareness of crime. The following year, securing a modest grant from the government, Fielding recruited a force of a dozen men to investigate a series of murders in London. Dubbed "Mr. Fielding's People," they are considered the first designated police force in London.

On his death in 1754, Henry Fielding was succeeded in the magistrate's office by his half brother, Sir John Fielding. He transformed Mr. Fielding's People into the Bow Street Runners and the Bow Street magistrate's office into a genuine police headquarters. Within that headquarters, Bow Street Runners were continually on call. A pair of horses was kept at the ready just outside, so that Runners could answer the call to pursue robbers and bandits.

Case in Point

Sir John Fielding transformed the city magistrate's office into something resembling a police department, a designated body of officers explicitly dedicated to fighting crime. He wanted to go even further, however, and repeatedly lobbied Parliament to finance a sufficiently large force to deploy on continuous routine patrol, so that the police would not merely chase wrongdoers, but actually discourage and even prevent crime. Fielding's plans for an expanded, full-time force would not be implemented for another 50 years, but Fielding himself was a relentless crime fighter. It was said that he could recognize and identify some 3,000 known criminals by nothing more than the sound of their voices. This founder of the first professional police force for London had developed a keen sense of hearing. He was totally blind.

The Peelers, 1829

Sir Robert Peel had a distinguished career in British politics. The founder of the Conservative Party, he served three terms as prime minister; before assuming this office, however, he was home secretary, the cabinet official responsible for the conduct of domestic affairs.

As home secretary, one of Peel's main goals was to reform the British judicial system, including the police. His great ambition was to create a single national force, but this proposal was met with the objection that it smacked of tyranny. He scaled down his ambition to creating a local force for London and environs. Crime had thoroughly overwhelmed the 350 to 400 "watchmen" (including the original Bow Street Runners) who constituted the city's only police agency.

Peel secured passage of the Metropolitan Police Act of June 19, 1829, creating a unified 1,000-man Metropolitan Police force for most of London, except for the central district (known as "The City"), which remained under the jurisdiction of the Bow Street Runners. The new officers were familiarly called "peelers" or "bobbies." Both nicknames are tributes to the father of the modern London police force, Sir Robert (Bobby) Peel.

Peel introduced a number of policing principles that laid the foundation for modern police forces throughout Europe as well as America. He put the police firmly under government control, not subject to the whim of some individual magistrate. He defined the mission of the police as, first and foremost, crime *prevention*, then, only secondarily, the pursuit of criminals and the investigation of crime. He established the principle that the success of a police force is directly dependent on the goodwill of the people served; accordingly, he instructed his police officers to be courteous, civil, helpful, and trustworthy.

Peel established the value of discipline, and he organized the police force along quasi-military lines, although the force was to be clearly distinct from the actual military. Peel saw the necessity of creating a force of professionals, who were specially trained and who were subject to an initial probationary period before being given full policing authority.

Under Sir Robert Peel's direction, police officers were deployed strategically in high-traffic and high-crime areas, where they were needed most. He instructed officers to prosecute their duties energetically, yet always with the minimum force necessary.

Sir Charles Rowan and Richard Mayne were appointed justices of the peace, charged with the day-to-day administration of the new force.

Sworn Statement

The primary object of an efficient police is the prevention of crime: the next that of detection and punishment of offenders if crime is committed. To these ends all the efforts of police must be directed. The protection of life and property, the preservation of public tranquillity, and the absence of crime, will alone prove whether those efforts have been successful and whether the objects for which the police were appointed have been attained.

—Sir Richard Mayne, 1829

Officer Down, 1830

It was not long before the Metropolitan Police suffered its first casualty. In a riot at Somers Town, Euston, Police Constable Joseph Grantham became the first officer to be killed in the line of duty. His death shocked Londoners, and Parliament immediately voted to increase the ranks of the Metropolitan Police more than three-fold, to 3,300 men.

Metropolitan Police Expand

In 1836, the Metropolitan Police began a further expansion as the organization absorbed the Bow Street Horse Patrol. The next year, a Select Committee proposed that the City of London (central London) be placed under the control of the Metropolitan Police, and in 1838, the committee further recommended that the Marine Police (the department charged with patrolling the Thames River and the docks) and the Bow Street Runners be incorporated into the Metropolitan Police. These measures were carried out, and, by the Metropolitan Police Act of 1839, Rowan and Mayne were officially redesignated commissioners of the newly enlarged jurisdiction.

By the Numbers

In 1847, the Metropolitan Police of London recorded 14,091 robberies and took into custody 62,181 persons. Of this number, 24,689 were summarily dealt with by the police, 5,920 were remanded for trial, and 4,551 were convicted and sentenced; 31,572 people were discharged by the magistrates. The population in London at this time was 2,473,758.

The First Detectives

Until 1842, all police constables were uniformed officers, charged primarily with preventing crimes and apprehending wrongdoers. In 1842, a Detective Department was established within the Metropolitan Police, and in 1846, the duties of plain-clothes officers—detectives who wear no distinguishing uniform—were explicitly laid out. Two officers per division were to be employed on detective duty, and it was firmly established that police constables working in plain clothes must announce themselves as officers when making an arrest or otherwise intervening to restore order.

Headquarters: Scotland Yard

Despite its name, Great Scotland Yard was a tiny London street that ran east from the northern end of Whitehall, parallel with Whitehall Place. The office of the Metropolitan Police Commissioner, at No. 4 Whitehall Place, backed on to it, and in 1875, a new building on the street was acquired to house the Detective and Public Carriage Departments. From this point on, the growing detective division of the Metropolitan Police was referred to simply as "Scotland Yard."

The origin of the name remains a mystery. Some believe the location was once the site of a residence owned by the kings of Scotland before the political union of England and Scotland; the residence was occupied by the kings when they were visiting London. Others say the street name was derived from the name of the man who owned the property during the Middle Ages, a Mr. Scott.

Terrorism 1884: A New Police Challenge

We tend to think of terrorism as a plague of recent times, but Europe had known it far earlier. In the nineteenth century, the Fenians, militant Irish nationalists, staged periodic terror attacks against British targets, including the London neighborhood of Clerkenwell, where a Fenian bomb killed 12 and injured 126 in 1867.

Between 1883 and 1885, the Fenians conducted a veritable bombing campaign. In 1883, Scotland Yard received an anonymous letter threatening to "blow [Police] Superintendent Williamson off his stool" and to dynamite all the public buildings in London on May 30, 1884. True to its word, the Fenians detonated two bombs shortly before nine o'clock on the threatened night. Both targets were police facilities in Scotland Yard, including the superintendent's office, which was completely destroyed—but since the explosions came after hours, only one person was injured, a cabman who was hit by flying glass.

Elsewhere that night, bombs went off in two other locations, and an unexploded bomb was found at the foot of Nelson's Column in Trafalgar Square.

The failure of Scotland Yard to protect its own offices caused a great public crisis in confidence. This was intensified by subsequent detonations under London Bridge, in the Tower of London, and in the House of Commons, all in 1885.

In response to the Fenian bombings, the Metropolitan Police created the Special Branch, and thus police jurisdiction was expanded to combating the political crime of terrorism.

Jack the Ripper and After

As shocking as the police failure was in the Fenian cases, even more scandalous was the inability of London detectives to solve what is surely among the most famous crime sprees in history.

Shortly before 4 A.M., Friday, August 31, 1888, Charles Cross walked through Buck's Row in the London slum of Whitechapel. Through the foggy morning gloom he saw what he thought was a tarpaulin on the ground in front of a stable yard. He approached it and discovered that it was a woman, lying on her back, skirts lifted almost to her waist.

When Cross saw another man, he called to him: "Come and look over here." Assuming she was a drunk or the victim of an assault—typical Whitechapel scenarios—the two passers-by pulled her aside, adjusted her skirt for the sake of modesty, and went to fetch a policeman. They didn't even notice three important things: the woman was horribly lacerated, she had been nearly decapitated, and she was quite dead.

Sworn Statement

I am down on whores and I shant quit ripping them till I do get buckled ....

—Letter, signed "Jack the Ripper," sent to London's Central News Agency, September 25, 1888

Even before Cross and the other man could find a bobby, Police Constable John Neil discovered the body while he was walking his beat. An ambulance was summoned, the victim was transported to a morgue, and an autopsy revealed that her neck had been slashed twice, which had cut through her windpipe and esophagus; her left jaw was bruised; and her abdomen had sustained a long, deep jagged knife wound, along with several other cuts. She was later identified as Mary Ann Nichols, age 42, an alcoholic prostitute.

The horrific slaying of Nichols is generally considered the first of five murders committed by a man who would become known as Jack the Ripper because that's how he signed a taunting letter, dated September 25, 1888, received by the Central News Agency, and forwarded to the Metropolitan Police.

Case in Point

Victorian London was often a violent place. During 1888 through 1891, there were a total of 11 horrific, slashing-style murders of women in Whitechapel, only 5 of which were attributed to Jack the Ripper. The most notorious of these "non-Ripper" slayings occurred on Monday, August 6, 1888, several weeks before Mary Ann Nichols's murder. Martha Tabram, a 39-year-old prostitute, was found dead in George Yard, stabbed 39 times on "body, neck and private parts with a knife or dagger" or, perhaps, a "bayonet." In addition, many other wounds had been inflicted with a penknife. The other five non-Ripper murders were similarly brutal, yet less attention was paid to these crimes, because they weren't attached to the much-publicized name of Jack the Ripper. Like the Ripper murders, none of these was ever solved.

Each Ripper murder was covered by the press in lurid detail, and although the Metropolitan Police assigned a 25-year veteran inspector to the case, Frederick George Abberline, the identity of Jack the Ripper was never discovered, and confidence in the Metropolitan Police was badly shaken. The final Ripper murder, of Mary Jane Kelly, occurred on November 9, 1888.

Policing for a New Century, 1900

In the aftermath of the Ripper murders, the Metropolitan Police were subjected to intense public scrutiny, and the department adopted and adhered to an increasingly stringent code of ethics and professionalism. It also put greater emphasis on the systematic and scientific investigation of crime, so that, by the beginning of the twentieth century, Scotland Yard would set the investigative standard for police forces throughout the world.

Wireless Police Work: The Infamous Crippen Case

Among the many detectives who had participated in the failed investigation of the Jack the Ripper murders was Walter Dew, who became chief inspector of Scotland Yard's Criminal Investigation Department (CID) at the turn of the century. In 1910, Dew headed up a manhunt that was as successful as the Ripper case had been frustrating.

At two o'clock in the afternoon of June 30, 1910, John Edward Nash and his actress wife, Lil, reported to the police the disappearance of their friend Cora Crippen, a marginally successful singer whose stage name was Belle Elmore. The wife of a Dr. Peter Hawley Harvey Crippen, of 29 Hilldrop Crescent, Camden Town, London, she had been missing since February. Nash and his wife had become suspicious when Crippen reported to them that his wife had died while abroad.

Where had she died? the Nashes asked. "Some little town near San Francisco, with a Spanish name, I think," Crippen replied. The doctor's evasiveness aroused their suspicions and sent them to the police.

Subsequent investigation at the Hilldrop Crescent house turned up a body buried in the cellar. It was headless and, even stranger, was missing its skeleton. Detectives described the remains as having been "filleted." Based on an old surgical scar and some hair, a pathologist was able to identify the remains as those of Cora Crippen.

As for Dr. Crippen, he and his secretary, Ethel Clara LeNeve, had disappeared. Apparently, the doctor had "filleted" the corpse in order to facilitate incineration in the cellar grate. With the police closing in, however, he panicked, hastily buried the body, and made his escape.

Chief Inspector Dew launched a spectacular manhunt, using newspapers worldwide to publicize a description and photographs of Crippen and LeNeve. The captain of the SS *Montrose*, bound for Canada, recognized the couple from a published photograph (even though LeNeve had disguised herself as a boy) and used the ship's radiotele-graph to alert Scotland Yard.

Dew took personal charge. He boarded a faster vessel and, all the while maintaining radio-telegraph contact with the *Montrose*'s skipper, overtook that ship at Father Point, off the Canadian coast. Boarding the vessel, he approached his man and calmly greeted him: "Good morning, Dr. Crippen. I am Chief Inspector Dew of Scotland Yard. I believe you know me."

For the first time in history, the mass media and the "wireless telegraph" had been used to extend the reach of the proverbial "long arm of the law." Crippen was returned to London, tried, and convicted of murder. He was hanged. LeNeve was cleared of complicity in the murder.

Women Join the Force, 1914

Four years after the technological triumph of the Crippen manhunt, the Metropolitan Police made an advance on the sociopolitical front by inaugurating the Women Police Service (WPS), primarily to deter pimps and to discourage girls and women from tak-ing up lives as prostitutes. Within a year, the duties of the WPS were expanded to working with women and juvenile suspects and victims, and the female constables were given full arrest authority.

The "Police Box" Experiment, 1928

Since the early days of the Bow Street Runners, police leaders had appreciated the effectiveness of putting officers on routine street patrol, but the persistent problem was how to establish continuous, reliable communication between the patrol officer and headquarters.

In 1928, local police in the towns of Richmond and Barnes installed experimental police boxes. These were large blue kiosks topped by electric lights. Inside was a tele-phone wired directly to the local subdivisional police station. Officers on patrol could report their whereabouts, and the flashing light signaled a patrolling officer to make immediate contact with the station. Civilians could also use the boxes to make emer-gency calls to the police.

Installation of the boxes began in London in 1929, and by 1937, the city was thoroughly networked.

Dial 999, 1937

Deployment of police boxes began a revolution in communication, which greatly increased the effectiveness of the police. The revolution was completed in 1937 with the introduction of the 999 system. A precursor of the 911 system familiar in the United States, the 999 system gave any telephone user instant emergency access to the police. With this innovation, the presence of the police was intimately woven into the fabric of daily life, establishing a relationship between law enforcement and the public so enduring that most of us today take it for granted.

The Least You Need to Know

- The idea of policing is probably as old as civilization, and the first police agencies were extensions of the political or religious ruler's personal bodyguard or palace guard forces.

- Rome's great emperor Caesar Augustus created the first thoroughly organized, formal police force, for the bustling city of Rome, at the start of the first century.

- Dictators and tyrants have little trouble creating a police force; establishing and maintaining a force in a free society, however, is far more complicated, since administrators and officers must enforce the law without compromising the principles of liberty.

- The evolution of a police force for London served as a model for police forces throughout Europe and, by the mid-nineteenth century, the United States.

Policing America

In This Chapter

- ◆ The first American police force
- ◆ Policing old New York
- ◆ Teddy Roosevelt's police reforms
- ◆ A nation of lawbreakers: Prohibition and organized crime
- ◆ Policing goes national: the FBI

Like the British, nineteenth-century Americans had a strong aversion to creating a standing police force—probably an even stronger aversion than that of their trans-Atlantic cousins. After all, one of the causes of the American Revolution was outrage over the maintenance of a large standing army, which functioned chiefly to police the unruly colonists.

But by the early 1800s, American cities, like British ones, were burgeoning—and so were crime and disorder. New York was typical of American cities that, however reluctantly, grew police forces during the nineteenth century.

New York City Before 1895

In 1658, the Dutch settlers of New Amsterdam—as New York City was called before the English took it over on September 7, 1664—paid a band of eight night watchmen to look out for fires and Indian raids. This "Burgher Guard" was the city's first police force.

The English had been running the city for 67 years before they set up a watch service in 1731. The Montgomerie Charter not only established a night watch as a permanent policing body, but gave each constable the right to draft eight citizens for watch duty every night. In the eighteenth century, however, New York was not quite ready to be called the "city that never sleeps," and popular resistance to compulsory night watch duty prompted, in 1734, the replacement of the citizens' watch with a paid force of 3 to 12 men, expected to stand guard over a city of about 10,000. Just a year later, the citizens' watch was reinstated, and it wasn't replaced with another paid force until 1774, when 24 watchmen were hired.

> **By the Numbers**
>
> Both the New York night watch and the constables were kept very busy. By the 1780s, New York had a population of 25,000. The night watch consisted of 28 patrolman and one captain. It wasn't until 1800 that the constables and night watch were supplemented by 16 day patrolmen and some 40 marshals.

Constable System

Only after the American Revolution had been fought and won did New Yorkers introduce an element of real professionalism into their police force by establishing, in 1784, a formal constabulary to supplement the night watch. While the night watch was paid a salary, the constables were compensated on a per-job basis. They were paid a set fee for serving a warrant, issuing a fine, making an arrest, and even detaining prisoners.

Following the London Model

Beginning in 1801, John Hayes was appointed High Constable for New York, and for the next 50 years he single-handedly ran the city's small force.

New York eyes were turned toward London, however. There, the Metropolitan Police was building a reputation for efficiency and effectiveness. In 1845, under New York Mayor William Havermayer, a Municipal Police Act was passed, creating the first full-time professional force in the nation.

Small, poorly trained, badly led, and ill equipped, the New York City police force was hardly equal to the task of maintaining order in a bustling, rough-edged American metropolis. By 1850, the murder rate in New York City exceeded that of London.

Case in Point

The most stunning demonstration of the inadequacy of the department came with the Astor Place Riot, May 10, 1849. About 15,000 demonstrators swarmed outside the Astor Place Opera House to protest the appearance of the British Shakespearean actor, William Charles Macready. Macready was unapologetic in his snobbish advocacy of the British aristocracy and his criticism of Americans as uncultured boors. Meaning to give Macready his comeuppance, the crowd shouted their support of Edwin Forrest, a great *American* Shakespearean. They hurled paving stones and construction debris. The police, unarmed, were summoned, but the crowd overwhelmed them, injuring several. At last, the militia were called in. When it was over, 23 people lay dead or dying. More than 100 were wounded.

Rival Forces

Efforts were made to improve the police force, such as giving them uniforms in 1853. At last, in 1857, the state legislature created the Metropolitan Police for the city of New York, for Brooklyn (at the time independent from New York), and Westchester County.

During this period, the state legislature was controlled by Republicans, whereas the mayor of New York was a colorful—indeed, thoroughly corrupt—Democrat, Fernando Wood. Although the Metropolitan Police were intended to replace the city's Municipal Police, Wood resisted and continued to back "his" force. For nearly a year, two rival police departments existed in New York, the officers fighting with each other more often and with greater enthusiasm than they fought crime. Little wonder that, by 1860, one New Yorker in ten had a criminal record!

Politics as Usual

By 1858, the state-mandated Metropolitan Police had finally supplanted and replaced Mayor Wood's Municipal Police force; however, the state exercised little direct control over the officers who actually patrolled the city's neighborhoods. Patrolmen tended to serve the local political machine, the neighborhood bosses. These men encouraged the police to pursue some criminals—the casual burglar, the occasional street ruffian—and to overlook others: Irish gang members in an Irish neighborhood or the enforcers who provided the muscle for the local loan shark (especially if he also happened to be a precinct captain).

The City's Utility Men

From the decade before the Civil War until nearly the end of the nineteenth century, the police were more often political hacks than public servants. Nevertheless, while they enforced the law selectively, at the whim and behest of local bosses, many of them did make a sincere effort to prevent crime and intervene when a crime occurred.

Sworn Statement

Gentlemen, get the thing straight for once and for all. The policeman isn't there to create disorder; the policeman is there to preserve disorder.

—Chicago Mayor Richard M. Daley, 1968

But they received precious little respect in return. And it was no wonder. The police were not perceived as gallant crime fighters, but as the utility men of the city, the guys who did the jobs no one else wanted to do. Yes, they tried to prevent crime. Yes, they chased after the bad guys. But they also hauled garbage, swept the streets, and ran menial errands for ward heelers and anyone else with a little political clout.

The Precinct: Sanctuary and Dungeon

If the neighborhood cop was there to do whatever had to be done, dirty work a specialty, the building he operated out of, the local precinct house—often simply called "the precinct"—was itself a kind of urban catchall. The precinct is the officially designated city district or subdivision assigned to a specific police unit. The word is also often applied to the police station house within the precinct.

The precinct was not only the place where officers got their marching orders, it was also headquarters for the local powers that be, the neighborhood politicos. And, in bad weather, on frigid winter nights, some of the neighborhood homeless took refuge in the precinct. It was, therefore, a crowded and often disorderly place.

The central feature of the precinct was the holding facility for those arrested. Cells typically ranged from Spartan to filthy, and somewhere in the back of the precinct was a room reserved for interrogation. It was a place where police might beat answers out of a suspect by applying the third degree, which involved using intimidation and even torture. It was also a place where police sometimes administered a shorthand version of justice. Officers might decide that a legal trial for a habitual neighborhood troublemaker was just a waste of time. A summary sentence executed at the business end of a billy club might be just the thing to keep the neighborhood safe, orderly, and as the local precinct captain saw it, decent.

Enter Commissioner Roosevelt

Theodore Roosevelt was born in 1858 into a New York family whose money and pedigree were so old that they disdained the Vanderbilts and Rockefellers as rank upstarts. A frail and sickly child, Roosevelt grew into young manhood determined to strengthen his body, hone his mind, and generally make something very big of himself.

He entered Harvard, graduated in 1880, and went on to get a law degree before achieving election to the state assembly at the precocious age of 23. While serving in the state house in 1884, he headed up a special commission to investigate the long-notorious New York City police department.

Roosevelt was appalled and outraged by what he found: rampant corruption eclipsed only by incompetence and inefficiency. Officers were not only implicated in such fraudulent schemes as rigging elections, they were found to exercise brutality as a matter of casual routine.

Such findings were so much grist for Roosevelt's mill. A progressive reformer, he set about planning how to rebuild and reshape the New York police.

New Zeal, New Discipline

In 1889, Roosevelt was appointed one of four commissioners of the newly created Board of Commissioners, with a mandate to reform the police department.

Roosevelt descended on the department like a whirlwind. With intense vigor, he rooted out corruption and saw to its prosecution. Then, in 1894, the reform-minded William L. Strong was elected mayor of New York. Among his first acts was to appoint Roosevelt president of the Board of Commissioners. With his authority thus augmented, Roosevelt introduced a

By the Numbers

While Roosevelt's reforms deprived some crooked men of power, they also rewarded and elevated the deserving. He saw to the promotion of 130 honest, earnest officers, and he instituted a recruiting program to bring new blood into the organization. During his tenure, 1,700 rookies were inducted into the New York Police Department.

military-style discipline to the department. To loosen the grip of neighborhood political bosses, he consolidated control of operations and policy in a central headquarters, answerable directly to himself.

Thank You, M. Bertillon

While Roosevelt cleared away the cobwebs, he also encouraged the administration to modernize its investigative department. Under his leadership, the detective division became an elite investigative unit to which the most ambitious and able officers aspired.

Roosevelt became highly interested in the innovations Alphonse Bertillon had introduced to the Paris police (see Chapter 12). He ordered the New York department to adopt Bertillon's techniques of suspect identification and classification, and, in 1897, the New York Police Department (NYPD), for the first time, began routinely photographing prisoners while also recording their Bertillon measurements. Soon the department had amassed a thorough file of offenders, which made it far easier to apprehend repeat and career criminals.

The First Bicycle Squad

It is no accident that the inventors of perhaps the greatest single advance in human transportation, the airplane, were bicycle mechanics and manufacturers. At the turn of the century, the bicycle was a cutting-edge vehicle, convenient, efficient, and fast. In 1895, at Roosevelt's direction, the New York Police Department fielded its first bicycle squad. Officers now had an unprecedented degree of mobility.

The fat, lazy denizens of the old-time precincts could not pedal a bicycle; they could hardly survive a few hours walking a beat. Commissioner Roosevelt, the delicate child who had built himself into a powerful man, an all-round advocate of what he liked to call "the strenuous life," introduced tough new standards of physical fitness for officers and officer recruits. He also instituted a carefully planned program of training, with special emphasis—for the first time in the history of any police department—on firearms training.

Honor and Morale

Of all the reforms Roosevelt introduced into the NYPD, none was more important than the sense of honor he revived within the hearts of the officers. By demanding excellence and by giving them his support, he lifted the morale of all policemen.

Thanks in large part to Commissioner Roosevelt, the New York City police officer was transformed from a neighborhood errand boy and sometime bully into a true guardian of the public safety and welfare. Law enforcement became a noble calling—and the rest of the nation watched and learned.

A Nation of Immigrants

Despite his origin in old New York wealth, Theodore Roosevelt was keenly responsive to the everyday world of the ordinary New Yorker. And at the turn of the century, as likely as not, the "ordinary" New Yorker was a recent immigrant.

Many of the monied elite as well as the middle class shunned the immigrants, distrusting, even fearing them. What Roosevelt and other enlightened realists did was to acknowledge them as part and parcel of the new America.

Policing Diverse Populations

Among the 1,700 rookies Roosevelt recruited for the New York Police Department were members of ethnic minorities. Roosevelt met resistance with this policy; however, he believed that it was not only fair, but, even more important, promoted effective policing. He reasoned that ethnic populations would respond more favorably to officers of their own background and heritage.

It was under Roosevelt's administration as well that more women were brought into the force. The number was still small—30 women working in all of the precincts by 1895—but this put New York far ahead of its London model. That city's Metropolitan Police would not take on women until 1914.

Sworn Statement

For the middle class, the police protect property, give directions, and help old ladies. For the urban poor, the police are those who arrest you.

—Michael Harrington, *The Other America: Poverty in the United States* (Macmillan, 1962)

Prejudice and Racism

It was not Roosevelt, but the then-independent city of Brooklyn that hired the first African American officer in 1891. In an era of fully institutionalized racism, it was a bold step—and it failed. Officer Wiley G. Overton was refused a uniform, and he was universally shunned by his fellow cops. Under unremitting pressure, unable to perform his duties because he was prevented at every turn from doing so, Overton resigned after a year on the force.

By 1913, the NYPD had grown to 10,847 officers, one cop for every 463 New Yorkers. It was not until 1914 that Jesse Battle became the first African American hired by the NYPD. In 1920, Lawon R. Bruce became the first African American woman recruited by the department.

A Nation of Lawbreakers

By the turn of the century, the New York Police Department, as shaped by Theodore Roosevelt and other reformers, had clearly emerged as the model for the rest of the nation. But the police force of New York and departments in the rest of the nation were about to face their toughest law-enforcement challenge.

During the nineteenth century, a great national movement developed, mostly in rural America, to combat what was seen as the evil of alcohol. By 1855, this "temperance movement" had succeeded in getting the manufacture, sale, and consumption of liquor banned in 13 of 31 states. The movement boldly soldiered on, and by 1916, 21 states outlawed saloons. In that year, voters sent a "dry" (antialcohol) majority to the United States Congress. Their mandate was clear: Secure a constitutional amendment to prohibit the manufacture, sale, and consumption of alcohol in the United States.

Congress passed the Eighteenth Amendment in December 1917. They did so over the veto of President Woodrow Wilson. A strait-laced minister's son, Wilson was no lover of the bottle, but he believed that federally mandated prohibition would create, in his words, "a nation of lawbreakers."

And so it did.

Talking the Talk

In the Roaring Twenties, **speakeasies,** illicit saloons and clubs that served liquor, were as common as legitimate, teetotaling restaurants and coffee shops.

Prohibition and Policing

Although the required two thirds of the states ratified the Eighteenth Amendment in 1919, and Prohibition went into effect the following year, the people of urban America were never behind it. Immediately, neighborhood folk defied the law, brewing up beer in cellars and making gin in bathtubs.

At first, people made only what they could themselves consume, but, inevitably, they began to share with and sell to their friends and neighbors. Soon, amateur brewers, winemakers, and distillers were marketing their goods to the corner grocer and pharmacist, as well as to local restaurateurs, who opened up *speakeasies.*

As for the cops, it was a hard thing to arrest the otherwise law-abiding people who daily greeted beat officers by name. Most neighborhood police looked the other way, and some did so for a price.

Organized Crime

For some time and in some places, violation of the Volstead Act—the law that enforced the Eighteenth Amendment—was certainly routine, but it was also almost innocent, the work not of hardened criminals, but of thirsty city dwellers.

Before too long, however, it became obvious that big money was to be made by trading in illegal liquor, either making and distributing it or smuggling and distributing it. Bootlegging became the province not of neighborhood entrepreneurs, but organized gangs.

Since at least the mid-nineteenth century, various ethnic immigrant groups, typically discriminated against by mainstream society, formed social and criminal gangs in the neighborhoods dominated by a particular ethnic minority. In New York, the Irish had some of the toughest and most feared gangs.

During the 1920s, the Irish-based White Hand took over bootlegging in some parts of the city and began a fearsome war against the New York Police Department. Also rapidly on the rise were Italian gangs, many of them modeled on or directly related to the Mafia, the traditional criminal organization of Sicily, which, for centuries, had formed a kind of shadow government there.

By the Numbers

During the decade of the Roaring Twenties—the Prohibition era—57 NYPD officers were killed in the line of duty. This stands as the most NYPD officers to die in any decade—although the deaths of 23 NYPD officers in the terrorist attack on the World Trade Center on September 11, 2001, will tragically contribute to the final tally of the first decade of the twenty-first century.

The Evolution of the FBI

With the Roaring Twenties in full swing, it was no longer a question of city police departments turning a blind eye on basement stills and neighborhood bootleggers.

Prohibition had created not merely a nation of lawbreakers, but nothing less than organized crime—a system of gangs that ran their criminal enterprises like big business, pulling in millions of dollars and making big deals, not with a pen applied to a contract, but a machine gun applied to rival gangsters, as well as law-abiding citizens and police officers. Police departments were overwhelmed, and many were also compromised, corrupted by organized crime money.

Tainted Bureau

Since the Eighteenth Amendment was national legislation, the federal government, recognizing that local police forces were inadequate to enforce the Volstead Act, assumed unprecedented policing authority. At first, special agents of the Department of the Treasury, "T-men," were the only federal force detailed to combat violations of the Volstead Act.

Case in Point

The most famous Prohibition-era government agent was Eliot Ness (1903–1957), who was appointed special agent for the Prohibition Bureau of the United States Department of Justice. Surrounded by corrupt colleagues, Ness gained approval of a plan to create a fresh squad of squeaky-clean agents. He wanted to call them the "Secret Six," but the press soon dubbed the incorruptible force "the Untouchables." Over the next six years, the nine-man Untouchables busted up stills and speakeasies, much to the amazement of bootleggers, whose police payoffs were suddenly useless. After repeal of Prohibition, Ness moved to Cleveland, Ohio, to head the Treasury Department's Alcoholic Tax Unit, then, in 1935, became Cleveland's Director of Public Safety. Later, Ness wrote an account of his Chicago gangbusting days, which subsequently provided the basis for a popular television series.

It soon became apparent that more manpower was needed. There was another federal police agency, the Bureau of Investigation. But in the early 1920s, it was something of a bad joke. Created in 1908 by then Attorney General Charles J. Bonaparte, it immediately degenerated into what one congressman called a "bureaucratic bastard." Congress feared that a federal police agency would become a center for the abuse of power, and it was transformed into a dumping ground for political hacks seeking patronage jobs. The Bureau of Investigation was mostly useless and entirely corrupt.

During World War I, a use was at last found for the Bureau of Investigation—chasing draft evaders, suspected spies, and alien "radicals"—but it wasn't until after the war, in

1920, when a zealous young Department of Justice lawyer, John Edgar Hoover, was named assistant director of the Bureau of Investigation, that the agency began seriously to improve its reputation.

The Hoover Era Begins

Under Hoover and his boss, William J. Burns, the Bureau of Investigation continued to pursue individuals suspected of radical subversion until 1924, when Congress decided that prying into the lives and activities of such respected activists as social reformer Jane Addams and future New York Mayor Fiorello LaGuardia constituted an abuse of power.

Congress called for a shake-up in the bureau, and Burns was fired, leaving J. Edgar Hoover director of the agency. It was a post he would hold until his death in 1972.

Building a Rep, Setting a Standard

Hoover transformed the Bureau of Investigation into a high-profile crime-fighting organization. He changed its name to the more impressive *Federal* Bureau of Investigation, and he set about professionalizing the staff, creating a small, elite force of detective-level special agents, who were not only trained in law enforcement and criminal investigation, but came to the FBI with law or accounting degrees.

The climate of organized crime created by Prohibition fostered the growth and enhanced the prestige of Hoover's FBI. Yet strangely enough, Hoover persisted in denying the existence of anything like organized crime in the United States, insisting that this was a fiction created mainly by a sensation-mongering popular press. Thus, during the waning years of Prohibition (the Nineteenth Amendment repealed the Eighteenth in 1933), the FBI dedicated itself to waging war not on organized crime, but on a handful of violent criminals who had become federal felons by virtue of interstate flight or by robbing federally insured banks.

J. Edgar Hoover was as keen on the brilliant use of publicity as he was on acquiring the latest in crime-fighting and investigative technology. While the local police and T-men continued to struggle against Prohibition-related crime, the FBI—*G-men*—tackled the likes of "Ma" Barker, her four career criminal sons and their associate Alvin "Creepy" Karpis, and John Dillinger. Criminals such as these,

Talking the Talk

In 1930s parlance, **G-men** were "government men"; that is, federal law-enforcement officers, especially FBI agents.

who robbed banks, often with great violence, were dangerous to be sure, but Hoover elevated them to the status of "Public Enemies." He created a "Ten Most Wanted" list, which captivated public attention, and he topped this list with such men as Dillinger, identified not just as a public enemy, but as "Public Enemy Number One."

For all his grandstanding, and despite his misdirection of federal law enforcement energy away from organized crime, as well as his elevation of the FBI (and himself) to a status dangerously independent of executive, congressional, and even judicial oversight and supervision, Hoover did set the bar of law enforcement and criminal investigation to a lofty new height. Controversial though it was, the American FBI supplanted the British Scotland Yard as the world's premier crime-fighting and investigative agency.

At its best, the bureau coordinated effective nationwide police efforts, provided much-needed support, instruction, and assistance to local police agencies, developed sophisticated scientific methods of forensic analysis, compiled truly useful databases of crime and criminals, and advocated such proactive investigative approaches as criminal profiling, an attempt to do nothing less than get into the mind of the criminal and even anticipate his next move.

Imperfect as it was, the FBI brought police work to an unprecedented level of sophistication, efficiency, and respect.

The Least You Need to Know

- Until well into the nineteenth century, Americans were resistant to creating professional police departments, which they feared would be abused as instruments of tyranny and intimidation.

- Through most of the nineteenth century, New York's police department, although modeled after the efficient Metropolitan Police of London, was inefficient and corrupt; thanks to the work of Theodore Roosevelt and other reformers, it became a model for the rest of the nation by the turn of the century.

- Prohibition created an opportunity for large-scale organized crime to take root and grow, presenting an overwhelming challenge to local police and prompting the development of federal police agencies, including the FBI.

- J. Edgar Hoover transformed a corrupt and weak agency, the Bureau of Investigation, into the Federal Bureau of Investigation, regarded by many as the premier crime-fighting and investigative organization in the world.

Policing: The Way It Is

In This Chapter

- ◆ To serve and to protect: a police officer's sworn duty
- ◆ Organization of a typical department
- ◆ Police work: the routine risks and the emotional toll
- ◆ The police outgunned
- ◆ Modern police training
- ◆ The deadly force decision

For most of the time they have existed, police agencies have been fairly simple organizations. In the beginning, most had a single role: to chase and apprehend criminals. Later, the mission of preventing crime was added, and police officers were sent out on routine street patrol. Later still, a third element was introduced: criminal investigation.

Even at this point, organization was minimal and tended to follow a military model: There were commanders (often called captains), subordinate commanders (lieutenants), supervisors or managers (sergeants), and the troops (patrol officers).

Today, the typical major-city police department is a complex bureaucracy—but not just for the sake of bureaucracy. If police agencies are complex, it is because the demands society puts on them are complex. Policing is no longer a relatively simple game of cops and robbers. Today's police force is an integral part of a criminal justice system, and officers are often called on to make the kind of judgments about constitutional law and departmental policy that judges and administrators make, yet they must do so not in the comfort of judicial chambers or a cozy corner office, but on the street and in life-and-death situations.

To Serve and to Protect

A police officer must serve many masters, but his or her *sworn* duty is to uphold the Constitution and to protect people and property. The twin missions—to serve and to protect—are emblazoned on the vehicles of most American police agencies. What those words say about the structure of the police department is this: No matter how complex the organization of the police force, ultimately the job comes down to how each officer functions in the field, how the officer relates to the people of the community, and how the officer serves and protects the citizen in peril or need.

> **Sworn Statement**
>
> The Delaware State Police recognizes cultural diversity as a fundamental characteristic of our society and, as a state institution, the Division of State Police is committed to providing effective police services that are appropriate, sensitive and equally responsive to all segments of our diverse society.
>
> —Diversity declaration of the state police of Delaware

Americans are accustomed to big government. They have accepted doing business with agencies many times the size of the typical police department. Yet, when it comes to the police, no citizen can accept an impersonal bureaucracy. Whether the officer dispatched on a frantic 911 call is a rural sheriff or a big-city patrolman, the citizen in trouble expects effective, courageous, and, above all, human aid. In this, police departments are unique among government agencies. They may be the size of a small army, organized to fulfill many requirements and perform many functions, yet they must consistently present to the public a human face and an individual presence.

Typical Organization

There is probably no such thing as a "typical" police department. American cities vary greatly in size and extent. The two biggest, New York and Los Angeles, have comparable populations, but New Yorkers are massed densely together, while Angelinos are broadcast over a vast area. In New York City, the NYPD is by far the most extensive police presence, whereas in Los Angeles, the LAPD routinely coordinates its operations with those of the L.A. County Sheriff, the California Highway Patrol, and other agencies.

Then, of course, there is the great American array of smaller cities, towns, villages, and rural areas. Each has its own needs and its own resources (often limited) to finance those needs. We'll look at a department in a medium-sized Midwestern city, the Cincinnati Police Division.

On the administrative level, a chief presides over an Office of Coordination, Planning, and Budget. On the operational level, that chief commands four bureaus:

> **Talking the Talk**
>
> **SWAT** is an acronym for special weapons and tactics, and a SWAT team is an elite special unit within a police force that uses assault weapons and guerrilla-style assault tactics to resolve such critical crises as hostage situations, mass shootings, and terrorist threats or police facing suspects with superior fire power.

- The **Operations Bureau** is subdivided into five police districts plus the Operational Support Section. The five districts represent geographical divisions within the city and address general criminal activities as well as community relations. These districts handle day-to-day patrol. The Operational Support Section covers the whole city and has units devoted to traffic, crime prevention, youth aid, alarm enforcement (responsible for programs to reduce the number of security-system false alarms that create a substantial drain on police resources), and a *SWAT* Coordination Unit.

- The **Investigative Bureau**—familiarly called the **IB**—is responsible for vice, drug, and criminal investigation. It carries out these missions through a number of sections, units, and squads:

  The IB's **Criminal Investigation Section** (**CIS**) comprises the …

  > **Youth Squad,** which investigates child abuse, child neglect, and other situations involving endangerment of minors.

  > **Homicide Squad,** charged with investigating homicides and all questionable deaths, as well as aggravated assaults where death may occur and rape (when the victim is at least 18 years old); may also investigate kidnapping and abductions, patient-abuse cases, and police-involved shootings.

  > **Robbery Unit,** which investigates robberies of all kinds.

  > **Major Offender Project,** which addresses cases that involve career or repeat offenders.

Criminalistics Squad, which handles crime-scene evidence gathering and processing.

Burglary and Auto Theft Unit, which takes charge of home and business burglaries, as well as "grand theft auto" and auto break-ins.

Pawn Shop Unit, which works with local pawnbrokers to identify stolen property.

Polygraph Unit, which specializes in the administration and interpretation of lie-detector examinations.

Fraud Unit, which is responsible for investigating a wide variety of so-called white-collar crimes.

The IB's **Central Vice Control Section** investigates criminal activity in the areas of prostitution, drugs, gambling, pornography, and liquor law violations.

The IB's **Intelligence Section** focuses on gang activity, cults, and terrorists and terrorist organizations. The section's mission is to develop information on such groups and individuals and, when appropriate, to initiate investigations. This section also conducts special in-service training for police personnel.

The IB's **Narcotics Liaison Section** works with county, state, and federal agencies in a coordinated program that targets illegal narcotics activities.

◆ The **Technical Services Bureau** consists of three sections, including …

Communications, which manages all aspects of police communications, including radio, telephone, 911 dispatch, and computer systems.

Equipment Management, which includes the Impoundment Unit, responsible for impounded vehicles; the Transportation Unit, which manages and maintains police vehicles; the Supply Unit, which manages supplies and equipment.

Court/Records Services, which operates a Court Administration Unit, County Property Unit, Warrant/Identification Unit, and Records Unit.

◆ The **Personnel Resources Bureau** manages the Personnel Section, the Police Academy, the Inspection Section, and the Internal Investigations Section.

Every medium to large police department has an internal investigations section, sometimes called Internal Affairs, which is responsible for investigating police misconduct and corruption. In some departments, this section is independent of the department hierarchy and reports directly to a commissioner or civilian review board.

Community Emphasis

In that quasi-mythical time known only as "the good old days," the cop walking a beat—an old term for the area regularly assigned an officer for routine patrol—was a familiar neighborhood fixture, who was known to the locals by name and who, in turn, knew many of them. As cities grew and police resources grew proportionately thinner, the beat cop disappeared from the scene. It was, after all, much more efficient to put officers in patrol cars.

Then, during the turbulent 1960s, the gulf between the community and the cop widened dramatically. Many identified the police with "the Establishment" and saw them not as public servants and defenders, but as agents of official oppression. In many places, an adversarial relationship developed between the officers and those they were pledged to serve and protect.

But the 1960s also produced a new trend in policing, an approach that put the emphasis back on the community and sought to reestablish a cooperative relationship between the police and the neighborhood.

The trend toward community policing accompanied the rise of restorative justice concepts in criminology (see Chapter 6), an emphasis on law enforcement as a socially healing or restorative process rather than an adversarial one.

Typically, community-based policing embodies some or all of the following principles, approaches, and features:

♦ Community policing programs start with and are maintained by close give-and-take communication between community members and the police.

♦ Community policing employs statistical analysis, so that crime trends and other needs of the community can be quantified and objectively identified as well as monitored.

♦ Community policing makes use of the media, communicating through press releases and public service announcements.

♦ Community policing involves citizens in crime prevention through Neighborhood Watch programs and the establishment of "safe houses" for children walking to and from school.

♦ Community policing often directs special attention to areas surrounding schools, watching for drug dealing, sex crimes, and alcohol-related abuses.

♦ Certain officers are specially trained as community policing officers (CPOs).

◆ CPOs get out of their patrol cars. They initiate contact with locals, especially merchants and school officials. They also establish liaisons with personnel involved in public works, the building department, animal control, the fire department, and area hospitals. These individuals are good sources for targeting community problems.

◆ CPOs may combine automobile, bicycle, and foot patrol. In some cases, they may also ride public transportation.

◆ CPOs monitor and review accident and traffic reports to identify issues that may be referred to public works or the department of transportation.

◆ CPOs don't go it alone; instead, they serve to coordinate the efforts of various police units so those units may better serve the community for which the CPOs are responsible.

Old Dangers, New Pressures

Police work has always been dangerous. After all, it is the business of the police to intervene, very personally, in violent situations. The leading cause of death and injury among police officers is, not surprisingly, gunshots. During the twentieth century, almost 7,000 American police officers were shot to death in the line of duty, an end that accounts for 49 percent of all law enforcement fatalities during that 100-year period.

By the Numbers

Since the first recorded U.S. police death in 1794, more than 14,000 U.S. law enforcement officers have been killed in the line of duty. A total of 1,533 law enforcement officers died in the line of duty during the 1990s, an average of 1 death every 58 hours, or 153 per year. On average, more than 65,000 U.S. law enforcement officers are assaulted each year, and some 23,000 of these sustain serious injury.

Early in the century, from 1910 to 1939, when motorcycles were among the most common police patrol vehicles, 485 officers were killed in motorcycle wrecks, making it the second leading cause of officer death. By the end of the last century, automobile accidents pulled ahead of motorcycle wrecks as the second leading cause of police fatalities; some 2,000 cops were killed in car wrecks during the twentieth century.

Other physical risks to cops include being struck by vehicles (16 officer deaths in 2000), being killed in aircraft—typically helicopter—accidents (7 officer deaths in 2000), falling (3 officer deaths), drowning (3 officer deaths), involvement in a bicycle accident (2 officer deaths), stabbing (2 officer deaths), being killed by bomb detonation (1 officer death), and beating (1 officer death in 2000).

Despite a general increase in violent crime during the second half of the twentieth century and, equally important, an increase in the violence of the individual criminal, officer deaths from gunshots actually declined during the last two decades of the twentieth century. The reason? Better training, the use of soft body armor (such as Kevlar vests or flak jackets), and better police equipment and weaponry. During the 1980s, an average of 187 U.S. officers were shot to death each year; during the 1990s, the annual average fell to 153.

Taking the Point

When a column or patrol of troops advances through hostile territory, one or more soldiers volunteer, or are assigned, to lead the way. As the G.I. says, they "take the point."

Today more than ever, the police officer "takes the point" for society. He or she is at the raw, ragged, and all too often bloody leading edge of modern civilization. The immediate physical dangers are ample, but it has been only in recent years that the emotional and delayed physical dangers of police work have been fully recognized.

Continual exposure to danger, to shocking or traumatic events, and to threats from suspects and prisoners can create tremendous emotional and physical stress. In addition, police officers often face conflicting demands—for example, to be aggressive, but never *too* aggressive, to finely hone one's instincts, but to think carefully before reacting—and they often carry a burdensome workload. Even the stress of testifying in court can take its toll when a successful prosecution may ride on what the arresting officer says and how he or she says it.

In the United States, about 16 of every 100,000 adults commit suicide annually—0.16 suicides per 1,000 adults. During 1984 through 1994, of the 30,000 cops of the NYPD, 63 committed

Sworn Statement

While the Vietnam veteran was at war for a minimum of nine months, police officers alternate between the violence of the street (e.g., shootings, witnessing death and mutilation, dealing with abused children) and the normalcy of civilian life on a daily basis.

—J. Volanti, "Police Trauma: Psychological Impact of Civilian Combat," in *Police Trauma: Psychological Aftermath of Civilian Combat*, Charles C. Thomas, 1999 suicide, making for a rate 31 percent higher than the average. More recent studies suggest that police suicides occur at two to seven times the rate in the general population.

Police units or squads are typically close-knit groups, analogous to a family, and the injury or death of a fellow officer hits everyone very hard. Even compassion for victims can cause burnout, or compassion fatigue—a term some psychologists have used to describe the burnout suffered by police officers and other care givers who are continually exposed to the suffering of others.

Talking the Talk

As defined by the National Institutes of Mental Health, **post-traumatic stress disorder (PTSD)** "is an anxiety disorder that can develop after exposure to a terrifying event or ordeal in which grave physical harm occurred or was threatened."

Stress and burnout are characterized by physical and mental exhaustion. In the worst cases, *post-traumatic stress disorder* (*PTSD*) may occur, bringing flashbacks, nightmares, extreme anxiety, and/or severe depression. Officers may suffer precisely the kind of symptoms that characterize what was called "shell shock" in World War I and "battle fatigue" in World War II and after.

An Armed Camp

The AK-47, also known as the Kalashnikov assault rifle, has long been the workhorse of guerrillas and terrorists worldwide. Invented by a Russian soldier toward the end of World War II and now manufactured chiefly by the Chinese, the AK-47 is rugged, cheap, and powerful, capable of firing 100 rounds per minute in automatic mode or 40 rounds per minute in single-shot mode. Each of these rounds leaves the muzzle at the rate of 2,330 feet per second. Each is a 7.62-millimeter short bullet with a steel core and a hooked nose, which causes tumbling action and solid penetration.

On January 17, 1989, Patrick Edward Purdy carried his AKS rifle, a semiautomatic variant of the standard AK-47, into his childhood elementary school in Stockton, California. In the span of a single minute, Purdy squeezed off 100 rounds. Five children were killed and 30 others wounded before Purdy discharged the final shots into himself.

A shocking story? Perhaps the most shocking thing about it is that this horrific scene is hardly unique. Despite a 1994 federal ban on assault weapons and the presence, in some states, of even more stringent assault-weapon legislation, these deadly machines are still widely available.

Some anti gun-control groups have pointed out that assault weapons account for only a small fraction of police-officer deaths, but the point is that, these days, officers are apt to walk into a situation in which they are woefully outgunned. A police service pistol cannot face down such weapons as the AK-47 assault rifle or the Uzi submachine gun, let alone an RPG, a rocket-propelled grenade launcher. All of these, and more, have been used, in the United States, in the commission of crimes.

Today's police departments must have training and equipment to fight what may amount to full-dress battles with truly formidable weapons. They must also possess the wisdom and restraint to refrain from employing such weapons and tactics except when absolutely necessary.

Police Academy: The Latest Sequel

During the nineteenth and early twentieth centuries, what little training police officers received was on the job. Today, all major departments train recruits in police academies, and smaller departments make use of state-run academies for law-enforcement officers. All states have legal minimum training standards for sworn peace officers in state and local departments. These officers are officially designated, duly authorized law-enforcement officers, who have received legally mandated training and have taken a prescribed oath of office.

Guy Antinozzi demonstrates one of the most important lessons an officer must learn: taking advantage of cover while tactically approaching an offender's vehicle.

(Photo by Sgt. Connie Rembert, Agnes Scott College Police Department)

The typical police academy offers a demanding and extensive educational experience. The St. Louis Police Academy, for example, subjects recruits to a 23-week intensive program, in which classroom instruction is supplemented by practical application exercises, role playing, situational training, and ride-along observation. Eight hundred eighty training hours are committed to a comprehensive curriculum:

Behavioral Studies and Cultural Diversity: 10 hours

Human Behavior: 40 hours

Legal Studies:

>Law I—Constitutional Law: 57 hours
>
>Law II—Missouri Law: 48 hours
>
>Traffic I—Traffic Law: 28 hours
>
>Liability Issues: 2 hours

Skill Development:

>Computer Skills: 18 hours
>
>Defensive Tactics/Physical Training: 139 hours
>
>Driver Training: 16 hours
>
>Firearms: 109 hours
>
>Mobile Field Force: 16 hours
>
>Ride Along: 8 hours

Supplemental Program:

>Administrative Procedures: 18 hours
>
>Community-Oriented Policing: 20 hours
>
>Special Orders: 30 hours

Technical Studies:

>Criminal Investigation: 54 hours
>
>Domestic Violence: 32 hours
>
>First Aid: 42 hours
>
>Hazardous Materials: 8 hours

Juvenile Procedures: 22 hours

Patrol: 56 hours

Report Writing: 64 hours

Traffic II—DWI and Accident: 43 hours

The 2002 graduates of DeKalb County Sheriff's Office SWAT Training Class, including Special Investigator Guy Antinozzi, Sergeant David Aderhold (DeKalb County Sheriff's Office), and law enforcement officers from several agencies. SWAT training is no longer reserved exclusively for SWAT officers. Cross training and joint training are increasingly essential training methods.

(Photo by Rod Huene, DeKalb County [Georgia] Sheriff's Office)

Deadly Force and Gentle Persuasion

In the terrorist attacks of September 11, 2001, police officers from several departments demonstrated heroic and relentless commitment "to serve and protect." Eighty-six officers of the NYPD, Port Authority, and other agencies lost their lives on that day.

The tragic events of 9/11 showed us all just how much we count on our police. It was something victims of accident and crime already knew. And yet, in a nation that fought for its independence in part because of the British crown's oppressive laws and oppressive policies of law enforcement, we have always had a love-hate relationship with our cops. It is, after all, a solemn and profoundly disquieting thing to entrust any group with the authority to use deadly force on our behalf.

As much training as police receive in responding quickly and decisively to crime, they also learn to evaluate each situation, so that they may apply the least force possible that is consistent with their safety and the safety of others. State laws governing the use of force are typically quite broad and leave much to the discretion of the individual officer in a particular situation. Most police departments attempt to provide a clear policy statement on the use of force, and many employ the *Use of Force Continuum*, which prescribes a logical escalation of force.

In many cases, the mere appearance of an officer, in the uniform of authority, will secure cooperation and compliance from a suspect. This is Level 1 on the Use of Force Continuum. If this fails, the officer proceeds to Level 2, verbal communication. From here, Level 3 calls for control holds and restraints, including physically taking control of the suspect using various bare-handed defensive holds and then applying handcuffs. If Level 3 force is ineffective or impractical against a violent or threatening suspect, officers may use nonlethal weapons, such as pepper spray or tear gas. This represents escalation to Level 4.

The next level, Level 5, falls just short of deadly force. Against extremely violent suspects, it may be necessary to use a baton (popularly called a nightstick) or a stun gun, which delivers a disabling electric shock. The object is to temporarily incapacitate the suspect, so that handcuffs or other restraints can be applied. The risk of doing serious injury or even killing the suspect is significant. A stun gun may cause cardiac arrest, and even though officers are trained to use their batons to administer soft-tissue blows, rather than blows to the face or skull, any forceful blow can be lethal. Certain choke holds and martial arts holds that pinch off the carotid artery may incapacitate a suspect, but they may also result in death or permanent injury. Many departments explicitly outlaw such procedures.

The highest escalation in the continuum is Level 6, the use of deadly force. It is applied when the officer has reason to believe the danger of severe injury or death is imminent to him- or herself, or others. If possible, the officer must warn the suspect of the intent to shoot. However, once the officer fires his or her weapon at the suspect, the intent is to shoot to kill.

It is a testament to modern policing that most officers not only strive to resolve confrontations at the lowest possible continuum level, but that they deem it a mark of consummate professionalism to do so. Indeed, most officers look upon having to fire on a suspect as something of a professional failure.

The Least You Need to Know

♦ Large modern police departments are complex bureaucracies that must nevertheless deal directly, immediately, effectively, and compassionately with people in urgent need.

♦ Today's police forces are integral parts of the criminal justice system and often work closely with other social service agencies as well.

♦ The typical modern department is organized into units dedicated to specific categories of crime, yet these units must coordinate their actions with one another and with other public agencies.

♦ In many jurisdictions, modern police face daily urban combat, analogous to warfare, which creates great physical dangers and may take a heavy toll on the emotional health of officers.

♦ Police training today is extensive and comprehensive, as befits agencies whose members are authorized to use deadly force.

Chapter 20

The Ultimate Weapon: Information

In This Chapter

- ◆ Information—and how police get it
- ◆ Problems with information from witnesses and victims
- ◆ Information obtained from suspects
- ◆ Use of confidential informants
- ◆ Undercover assignments: types and hazards
- ◆ How police share information

There are few professions that depend more on the flow of information than law enforcement. This is especially true in criminal investigation. A detective is first and foremost a good communicator. Seasoned, professional, and savvy, a detective above all knows how to tell a story and find good material.

But detectives are not the only police communicators. Dispatchers and 911 operators—as discussed in Chapter 9—as well as the patrol officer all must gather, process, and transmit vital information quickly, clearly, and without possibly life-threatening error.

Sources of Information

Wheels spin and little is accomplished without good information. The criminal investigator needs to know who, what, when, where, and why. Beating the bushes, doing all the legwork required to get vital information, is glamorized on television, but, in reality, it is just plain, hard work, and it is time-consuming work done in situations where time is almost always in short supply. The precinct detective who starts out with a thorough knowledge of the neighborhood has a major advantage over any outside investigator sent from "downtown" or another law enforcement agency.

Reports and Records

All police responses produce some kind of documented record. If any police action is taken, an *incident report* is prepared.

The incident report may be very simple or highly complex, depending on the officer and the incident. Most departments provide officers with some training and guidelines in report writing, but all good reports share certain characteristics:

- ◆ They are written from clear, well-organized notes made at the scene.
- ◆ They are factual, accurate, and objective.
- ◆ They show rather than tell; opinion is excluded.
- ◆ They are complete and thorough, but concise.
- ◆ They contain no internal contradictions.
- ◆ They are written in clear, standard English, without police jargon, street slang, grammatical errors, or misspellings.

Talking the Talk

An **incident report** is the responding officer's written account of the call to which he or she has responded. It is generally the first official record made of a crime or other incident.

Some departments have adopted computerized report-writing systems. These allow police officers to prepare incident reports using special software that provides preformatted screens and questions, which not only speed the report-writing process, but help to ensure that all relevant information is included and presented in a usefully organized form. Preparing reports on a computer also makes them more readily accessible to other investigators and to prosecutors.

Domestic violence incidents require a special domestic violence incident report, which, typically, is a form that asks for information about the physical condition and state of mind of both the victim and the suspect, the nature of the relationship between victim and suspect, what medical treatment the victim received (if any), and what physical evidence has been collected. On-the-spot photographs, showing the victim's injuries, are essential to domestic violence reports. Currently, most police agencies use Polaroid or Polaroid-type cameras for on-the-spot victim photography. Many courts hesitate to accept digital photography as evidence, because it is readily subject to alteration.

Most of the time, at the request of the reporting officer, the dispatcher assigns a unique case number to the incident, so that even if an incident report is not made, there is a record of the officer's actions in the form of a dispatch log.

When an officer is dispatched, the times of dispatch and arrival are recorded, as are the names of the personnel responding. If the response is self-initiated—the officer responded to something he sees, for example—it is protocol to call out the location and type of action over the radio. The dispatcher, monitoring this call, makes a record at this time. Such records can be very important later, when a follow-up investigation is conducted or a case is prosecuted in court.

In contrast to uniformed patrol officers, detectives are not expected to call out on the police radio their every move. Part of being a detective is accepting responsibility for greater independent action.

Victims

Victims would seem a natural and willing source of information, yet, often, this is not the case. In most crimes, the victim and perpetrator are not strangers to one another, and this relationship may prompt the victim to avoid cooperating in the investigation.

The best chance investigators have for obtaining the victim's help is at the scene of the crime, immediately after the incident has occurred. Fear and anger move many to cooperate, whereas the more time that passes, the less urgent the motive for cooperation becomes. Worse, in the many cases in which victim and the perpetrator know one another, the perpetrator often finds a way to intimidate or otherwise influence the victim. Victim and perpetrator may be wife and husband, for instance, or they may even be partners in some criminal enterprise.

Modern criminal investigation—particularly in domestic violence crimes—no longer centers on the cooperation of the victim. Responding officers are still trained to obtain as much information as possible from the victim at the scene of the incident, but the main emphasis is placed on gathering evidence that is separate and apart from anything the victim may say. Witnesses such as neighbors, family members, co-workers, and strangers are interviewed and always questioned independently.

Witnesses

Not surprisingly, witnesses are very important to a criminal investigation. Unfortunately, eyewitness accounts are notoriously unreliable. Police officers quickly become accustomed to the shock and frustration of hearing a dozen eyewitnesses to a crime give a dozen earnest, well-meaning, but entirely different accounts of the incident.

By the Numbers

Incorrect eyewitness identifications account for more convictions of innocent persons than all other causes combined. In a 1996 study by the Institute for Law and Justice, of 28 people released from long prison terms on the basis of DNA tests, 24 had been misidentified by eyewitnesses.

Because it is subject to so much distortion, the coloring of perception, the shading of emotion, the imperfection of memory, eyewitness testimony is not slam-dunk courtroom evidence. It is evidence, but it must be corroborated by other, more objective evidence. Most importantly, all eyewitness evidence must be obtained independently, so that the recollection of one witness does not influence that of another.

Suspects

Willingly or unwillingly, suspects provide information in criminal investigations. Suspects can be tracked, their behavior observed, their patterns analyzed. In some cases, a search warrant may be issued to obtain blood, hair, or other items of evidence from a suspect. This can be analyzed and compared to an unknown sample found at the crime scene.

While the Fifth Amendment guarantees that a suspect cannot be forced to testify against himself, he may be compelled to provide the tissue evidence just described, and he may also be compelled to participate in a lineup, in which the victim or other witnesses (usually shielded behind a one-way mirror) may identify him as he stands next to five other similarly featured men.

Undercover Work

Possibly the most misunderstood job in police work is the undercover investigation. The glamour portrayed on television and in the movies is, for the most part, missing from the real-life assignment.

Some investigators work undercover in a limited capacity and for a limited time. For example, they may pose as construction workers, taxi drivers, medical patients—whatever it takes to get close to people who have outstanding warrants against them and need to be taken into custody.

There are also investigators, typically in narcotics, who work undercover on a much more extended basis. They attempt to fit the image of a narcotics dealer or heavy user, and their goal is to infiltrate the drug world in order to develop a case and bring charges against the dealer or the dealer's suppliers or distributors.

That is a dangerous assignment, but even riskier are "deep undercover" investigations. In these, the investigator virtually assumes a new life and new identity to infiltrate a criminal enterprise so thoroughly as to become all but indistinguishable from those he or she is investigating. The physical risks of this work are obvious. More subtle are the psychological hazards of coming to identify oneself with the criminals under investigation.

Case in Point

Operation Drug Wheels was a major 1990 undercover "sting" operation in which federal undercover agents posing as narcotics dealers offered to purchase a fleet of cars for cash from an automobile dealership, which agreed to disguise the identity of the purchasers. The dealership also introduced the undercover agents to an insurance company, which agreed to furnish insurance on a fraudulent basis. Working undercover, the agents ultimately identified five New York dealerships and two insurance company agencies, which were charged with money laundering and cash reporting and mail fraud violations. Thirty-one new cars valued at $880,700 were seized by agents. Operation Drug Wheels is typical of undercover work on a large scale.

The Information File

Record keeping is essential to effective criminal investigation. The evidence must be kept secure after it is seized; the chain of custody maintained and the integrity of the evidence safeguarded. The narcotics, the bloodstained shirt, the gun, the knife, or other pieces of evidence seized at the crime scene must be the exact same items, in the exact same condition, presented at the trial before the jury.

Cases must be preserved for many years. The trial process is long and the appeals process even longer. The file must be maintained and available. Witnesses need to be contacted and kept track of. All officers involved must ready themselves for trial—and keep themselves ready.

The Rat—a Necessary Evil

Who could be more despicable than someone willing to turn on his or her compatriots for money? Many juries answer this question with a resounding "no one," and they may discount or entirely reject information that has been bought and paid for.

The informant—also called by police a confidential informant (CI) and by the bad guys, a rat—is a special breed. This person's value as a witness increases as his or her value as a member of society decreases. That is, the more an informant is involved in criminal activity, the more valuable his or her testimony becomes.

The use of confidential informants in criminal investigations has become such an integral part of American law enforcement that it would be difficult to conduct an investigation without the use of such unsavory characters. But, even here, there is a Catch-22. For while intimate involvement in criminal enterprises makes the informant a valuable insider, the informant's criminality undercuts his or her credibility. The reliability of an informant is proportional to his or her involvement in criminal activity; as that increases, reliability increases because, in court, the informant can be shown to have adequate and personal knowledge of the criminal activity in question. At the same time, as involvement in crime increases, credibility decreases.

Informant testimony is always a precarious balancing act. The investigator pulls it off by using the totality of circumstances test—a package of facts and circumstances relating to a case and used to evaluate and corroborate informant information. If all the facts and circumstances, taken in their totality, support the informant's information, the information is considered probably reliable. The detective may also build up the credibility of the informant by stating that he or she has used the informant in the past to obtain information that led to arrests, seizures, and convictions.

Sworn Statement

All good police officers develop informants, people living or working in the areas under their responsibility who provide them with information. Some of these informants are citizens who simply want to make their community a better place. Some are criminals interested in ridding their turf of a competitor. The job of managing informants is a delicate and often dangerous one. The fact is this: All information is just that, information, not proof. Whatever the CI supplies must be verified by independent investigation.

A Question of Cash

Informants may be rewarded by being paid for the information they provide or pardoned for petty offenses. There is no general rule as to which type of incentive is better or more likely to produce reliable results. Cash payment does not necessarily compromise the information provided by the informant. Indeed, the informant may be more responsible and truthful because he or she is being "paid for the work." A tangible reward is a powerful motivator, and it is rare for a well-informed criminal to do anything out of a sense of social responsibility.

The Pitfalls

Obviously, there are drawbacks to using informants. If their reliability and credibility cannot be substantiated to a degree that meets judicial scrutiny, then the information they provide is useless. If they are relied on to the exclusion of other evidence or without proper independent investigation, their value is also very limited. Even more serious is the possibility that juries will simply tire of taking the word of one admitted criminal against another.

Police Networking

A well-known maker of computer systems used to employ as its corporate slogan this sentence: "The network is the computer." The message? Individual computers are fine and dandy, but the work of such a computer is made truly meaningful only when it is shared, combined with the work of other computers in a network.

Much the same can be said about the information police obtain. Scribbled in a detective's notebook or stored in a file drawer, information does little. Made accessible to other cops, harvested, winnowed, shared, and compared, information takes on enormous power.

Interpersonal Cooperation

Fighter pilots, alone in the cockpit—one pilot, one plane—are by nature independent sorts. But even the topmost top gun knows better than to try to go it alone. Fighters work in formations of two or more. Doing so multiplies their effectiveness far beyond the numbers involved. A formation of *2* planes is probably *10* times more effective than a solo flier.

Criminal investigators quickly learn much the same lesson. They eagerly take responsibility for a case, but they don't go it alone. They look at the files, they identify the cops who've worked on similar or perhaps related cases, and they talk to them—pump them for information.

Cops talk cases out. They network, both formally and informally. Grandstanders who jealously guard information relating to "their" case because they don't want to share the glory of solving the mystery are not likely to find any glory to share. They won't crack the case.

Like most professionals, cops form relationships with each other. Some find mentors among their colleagues, a veteran who's seen it all and has plenty of time-saving advice. Some find friendly adversaries—people to bounce ideas off of, people who won't pull punches concerning what's wrong with your theory.

Most seasoned investigators network both inside and outside of their department. A city cop may be well aware that his or her department does things a certain way and no other way. When that cop wants a fresh point of view, he or she contacts a friend in the county sheriff's office.

International Accord

Networking can be interpersonal, or it can be international. After World War I, an economically devastated Europe was swept by a great crime wave. In 1923, the head of the Viennese police department, Johann Schober, called for an international meeting of police agencies to create a network for cooperation among law enforcement officials across borders. The result, ultimately, was the International Criminal Police Organization, better known as Interpol.

Today, Interpol, with 125 member nations, is the chief organization by which criminal police forces cooperate worldwide to fight international crime. Each Interpol member maintains a domestic clearinghouse (the National Central Bureau), which acts as liaison between individual police forces and the police of other affiliated countries. Interpol is not an international police agency, but a means of communication and coordination, a worldwide network that makes it much more difficult for criminals to find refuge in a foreign land.

The Least You Need to Know

◆ Information is the most valuable weapon in the police arsenal. Information sources include witnesses, victims, suspects, informants, and the officers themselves.

◆ Undercover work has been glamorized in film and fiction, but, in reality, is hard work that puts officers in physical and, often, psychological peril.

◆ The confidential informant—the "rat"—is the ultimate criminal insider, a criminal who agrees to provide the police with information concerning the criminal enterprises he or she is privy to.

◆ Police officers are inveterate networkers, sharing information both formally (from department to department and even from nation to nation) and informally, developing working relationships with mentors and colleagues.

Chapter 21

Lie Detectors

In This Chapter

- ◆ The polygraph: what it is and how it works
- ◆ Lie detector pioneers
- ◆ The polygraph examination
- ◆ How reliable is the polygraph?
- ◆ The polygraph and the courts
- ◆ Alternatives to the polygraph

At some point in the course of human evolution, hominids (our collective evolutionary precursors) discovered lying. And, shortly after this time, they must have begun thinking up ways to find out who was lying and who wasn't.

At various times in history and among various cultures, methods have been devised and prescribed to test the truth. Some of these have been based on keen observation. For instance, the ancient Chinese understood that a dry mouth accompanies nervousness and nervousness accompanies lying, so they questioned a suspect as he chewed dry rice. After questioning, he was told to spit out the rice. If it came out nice and gooey, he was telling the truth; if dry, the suspect was caught in a lie.

Other methods have been less scientific. In Europe during the Middle Ages, if a woman suspected of witchcraft denied being a witch, her veracity could be tested by binding her hand and foot and tossing her in a pond. If she survived, she was a witch, because witches float; if she drowned, well then, she was—that is, *had been*—telling the truth.

Gooey gobs of rice or drowned innocents? By the twentieth century, law enforcement personnel decided: There has *got* to be a better way.

The Polygraph

The truth (yes, the truth) is that perceptive questioners have always been able to gauge the trustworthiness of a source. Body language speaks loudly to those who can "hear" it. A liar rarely looks you in the eye, he puts his hand to his mouth, he shuffles his feet, he rubs the back of his neck, he shakes his head no while *saying* yes, his voice trembles, he sweats, he blushes.

The anxiety that accompanies lying often produces plainly visible physiological effects, but even when the effects are not clearly visible, they are almost always present—and measurable.

> **Sworn Statement**
>
> Man is the only animal who blushes—or needs to.
> —Mark Twain.

What It Is

The *polygraph*—commonly called a lie detector—is nothing more or less than an instrument that measures and graphically records the effects of several physiological processes.

> **Talking the Talk**
>
> The **polygraph** is an assemblage of instruments (at minimum, a pneumograph, galvanograph, and cardiograph) that measure and record respiration rate and depth, electrical resistance of the skin, and blood pressure and pulse rate, which indicate the status of physiological processes commonly affected by the emotion of anxiety.

Actually, as its name—polygraph, "many writings"—implies, the polygraph is an assemblage of several instruments to measure several distinct processes:

◆ A pneumograph measures the rate of respiration and the depth of breathing.

◆ A galvanograph measures changes in the electrical resistance of the skin. Perspiration increases the skin's electrical conductivity.

◆ A cardiograph measures blood pressure and pulse rate.

Some polygraphs add another instrument, a plethysmograph, which attaches to a finger to measure peripheral blood flow.

How It Works

The premise on which the polygraph operates is simple, sound, and time tested. Socialized human beings lie, but they don't like to lie, because they've been conditioned to believe, deeply, that lying is wrong. Therefore, lying produces nervousness and anxiety. Nervousness and anxiety, in turn, produce distinct—sometimes visible, almost always measurable—physiological effects, including ...

- An increase in the rate of respiration and a decrease in the depth of the breaths taken (shallow breathing). The polygraph's pneumograph module measures these effects.

- An increase in perspiration. The galvanograph does not measure perspiration directly, but it does measure the difference in the electrical resistance of the skin produced when the subject perspires.

- Increases in pulse rate and blood pressure. The cardiograph measures these vital signs.

The polygraph machine records the measurements graphically. For some 50 years, polygraphs have traced out their measurements on moving rolls of chart paper, which is annotated by the polygraph examiner during the examination, then analyzed by the examiner later. In recent years, desktop computers and sophisticated computer programs have been married to the polygraph. These newer systems are paperless, graphing the data on a computer screen—and recording it digitally on disk, so that it is storable and retrievable and, if desired, can be printed out on paper. An important feature of digital polygraph machines is the software, which includes complicated chart analysis formulas designed to aid the examiner in evaluating results.

Sworn Statement

At this time the computerized [polygraph] systems are not well-enough advanced to be called superior to the analog [traditional] systems, although they are admittedly easier to use. A competent and qualified examiner can be equally effective with either system.

—Michael Martin in "Everything You Wanted to Know About Polygraphs," Nationwide Polygraph Network at www. polytest.org/polyfaq.htm

We'll outline the examination procedure in just a moment, but the general idea is that the examiner asks questions, notes the verbal responses, and also notes the physiological response produced on the machine's graphical output. By analyzing variations in the physiological responses, the examiner can render an opinion as to the truthfulness of the verbal responses.

What It's Used For

Polygraphs are used in criminal as well as civil applications. In criminal investigations, polygraph examinations can reduce a large pool of suspects by eliminating people who seem clearly innocent.

During interrogation of a suspect, the polygraph may be used to elicit a confession; however, the suspect must be fully advised of his rights.

Polygraph examination is also used to gauge the veracity of informant information, from a jailhouse snitch or a confidential informant or CI. (A CI is a civilian who is usually paid to provide information to the police regarding criminal activity; on the street, that person is usually called a snitch or a rat.) Key potential witnesses may also be screened by a polygraph examination.

Outside of the law-enforcement community, polygraph examination has been used for preemployment screening—accounting for more than 80 percent of polygraph tests administered in the United States. Employers asked potential employees about past dishonesty and criminal behavior. However, in 1988, Congress passed the Employee Polygraph Protection Act (EPPA), which barred most preemployment polygraph examinations, except in the following cases: government jobs, companies that manufacture or dispense controlled substances (pharmaceutical drugs), and companies engaged in sensitive work on government contracts.

By the Numbers

The FBI administers about 5,000 polygraph examinations annually to persons entering sensitive jobs. Each applicant is given two separate tests with different types of questions.

An employer may ask a *current* employee to take a polygraph examination only if the employer provides clear documentation of specific suspicions; however, the employee cannot be discharged solely on the basis of the polygraph results, nor can the employee be dismissed solely because he or she refused to submit to a polygraph examination.

In the civil arena—for example, in lawsuits involving personal injury, property damage, intentional misconduct, and breaking contracts—polygraphs may be used on witnesses and litigants, as long as rights under the Employee Polygraph Protection Act are not violated.

A Short History of the Lie Detector

Like many others, Boston attorney William M. Marston understood that liars paid a physiological price for their untruths. They blushed, they sweated, they breathed heavily. In 1917, he decided to use these physiological effects to make the detection of falsehood scientific. He designed a machine to continuously monitor systolic blood pressure (the pressure created during the contraction phase of the heartbeat) and claimed that an increase in this pressure accompanied verbal falsehood. (Diastolic pressure, on the other hand, is that created during the relaxation phase.)

Marston's Marvel

Marston's invention created a popular stir and began to be used by some law enforcement officials. In 1923, however, a federal appeals court issued a strong challenge to Marston's marvel.

Convicted of murder, James T. Frye appealed on the basis that the court had not permitted an examiner to testify about the results of a "systolic blood pressure deception test" he had taken and passed. The appellate court denied the appeal, introducing what came to be known as the "Frye Test." The essence of the Frye Test is this: The device or procedure on which any expert testimony is based must be "sufficiently established to have gained general acceptance in the particular field in which it belongs." In 1923, Marston's device was new and little tested, and the legal future of the "lie detector" was thereby put in doubt. The Frye Test or Frye Standard was generally accepted in American courts until it was superseded in 1975 by the Federal Rules of Evidence.

Larson's Refinements

Despite the blow Marston's machine had been dealt, many in the law enforcement community continued to be interested in the great potential of a lie detection device. Working independently of Marston, Dr. John A. Larson, a police officer turned educator and practicing psychiatrist, developed a true *poly*graph device (it measured pulse rate and respiratory changes in addition to blood pressure) in 1921. Unlike Marston, Larson was more cautious in introducing the device and, by the time he did, he had honed the machine and developed more solid procedures for using it.

Larson focused much attention on developing an interviewing technique, which he called the R/I procedure—the "R/I" standing for relevant/irrelevant. It worked like this: In the course of questioning, the examiner was to ask questions relevant to the crime ("Do you own a Glock handgun?") and questions that have nothing to do with the crime ("Do you live at 123 Felony Drive?"). Larson's assumption was that the innocent would exhibit a similar physiological response to both types of questions, whereas the guilty would react more strongly to the crime-relevant questions.

Keeler the Popularizer

There is no doubt that Larson improved the lie detector by inventing the true polygraph, measuring more physiological factors than just blood pressure, and developing better methods of questioning. However, Larson failed to consider that innocent people, under police interrogation and suspected of a crime, might be quite nervous, perhaps even *more* nervous than a hardened criminal who was guilty.

> **Sworn Statement**
>
> During the 1930s and after, the law enforcement community embraced the polygraph, and Leonarde Keeler prospered after he established the first private lie detection agency in 1938. The enthusiasm was not entirely blind, but the fact is that not until 1950 was a series of objective studies done to test the validity and reliability of the polygraph.

Despite this, Larson's protégé, Leonarde Keeler, succeeded in popularizing the polygraph. He introduced refinements to the machine (obtaining a patent in 1931) as well as a greater degree of sophistication in the procedures for questioning, which addressed some of the shortcomings of the R/I approach. He based his work on an extensive study he carried out in the penitentiary at Joliet, Illinois, testing more than 500 inmates to develop reference points and baselines for analysis.

The Lindbergh Kidnapping

The popularity of the polygraph received its single greatest boost by its involvement—or, actually, high-profile noninvolvement—in the "crime of the century."

The time: night, March 1, 1932. The place: near Hopewell, New Jersey, and the home of aviation hero Charles A. Lindbergh and his wife, Anne Morrow Lindbergh. Someone snatches from his second-floor nursery the couple's 20-month-old son. As soon as the abduction is discovered, a network of roadblocks and a massive manhunt are put into place. There are clues: a homemade ladder, footprints, and a ransom note written in broken, German-accented English:

Dear Sir!

Have 50000$ redy with 25 000 $ in 20 $ bills 1.5000 $ in 10$ bills and 10000$ in 5 $ bills. After 2-4 days we will inform you were to deliver the Mony.

We warn you for making anyding public or for notify the Police the child is in gut care.

Indication for all letters are singnature and 3 holes.

A ransom payment with marked bills is prepared and delivered; as promised, directions to the baby are provided. Heartbreakingly, they prove false, and on May 12 a truck driver discovers a child's skull in woods about four miles from the Lindbergh home. Police find a shallow grave—and, in it, the body of the Lindbergh baby.

In the aftermath of the tragedy, leads did emerge, only to result in one dead end after another. Strangest of all was the questioning of Violet Sharpe, a maid who worked for Lindbergh's in-laws. Her stories were inconsistent through several interrogations—until, after one session with the cops, she gulped down silver polish and died minutes later. In desperation, investigators asked Lindbergh's permission to use Keeler's polygraph in questioning his household staff. Flatly refusing to believe that anyone who worked for him could be guilty, Lindbergh withheld permission.

The investigation then stalled until, on September 15, 1934—more than two years after the murder—someone purchased 98 cents' worth of gas with a $10 gold certificate. In the depths of the Great Depression, this was a notable event, and the gas station owner scribbled down the license plate number on the certificate. He had spoken to the driver about the bill. He was a man with a German accent, who boasted that he had a lot more of these gold certificates at home.

The gas-station owner called the police, who traced the license plate to a carpenter, a German immigrant named Bruno Richard Hauptmann. A search of his house revealed more than $14,000 of the ransom money hidden away, and a missing rafter in Hauptmann's attic had clearly been used in the construction of the homemade ladder found at the kidnap scene.

Hauptmann certainly appeared guilty. He claimed that his former business partner had given him the money. The problem with this alibi? That man, Isador Fisch, had returned to Germany—and was now dead.

While in jail awaiting trial, Hauptmann learned about the "lie detector machine" and asked to be given the test. His request was denied. His defense attorney, a self-important incompetent who believed his client guilty, made little attempt to pursue the request, and FBI chief J. Edgar Hoover (it was discovered many years later) had issued a confidential memo: "Under no circumstances will we have anything to do with the [polygraph] test of Hauptmann."

In the "trial of the century" for the "crime of the century," Hauptmann was convicted and sentenced to death. While the public clamored for the speedy execution of a fiend, New Jersey's scrupulous and courageous governor, Harold G. Hoffman, wasn't so sure. He ordered a short reprieve for additional investigation and wanted Keeler to administer a polygraph examination. Keeler agreed to provide his services not only pro bono (at no charge), but in secret from the press.

That was key. Hoffman wanted no sensationalism. But Keeler, burning to promote his invention, broke his word and leaked the news. Instantly, he was off the case—and, instead, his rival, William Marston, equipped with his more simplistic blood-pressure machine, was called in to perform the test. The trial judge, however, would have none of it. He denied Marston access to Hauptmann, Governor Hoffman could not legally override the judge, and no lie detector was ever used in the Lindbergh kidnapping case. Hauptmann was executed, and debate over his guilt or innocence continues to this day.

And yet, the fact that the "lie detector" was *almost* used in this sensational, high-profile case enhanced its reputation probably far beyond what would have resulted had it *actually* been used. After all, experts and public alike were now forever free to speculate on how the machine *might have* solved the case.

The Polygraph in Action

Today, polygraph examinations are conducted systematically by trained, qualified, and certified examiners. Much of the work takes place before a single question is asked. The examiner begins by reviewing all the facts surrounding the case in question. Following this, the examiner reviews the facts with the subject before the test is conducted. Based on the view of the facts and the pretest interview, the examiner prepares specific test questions.

In the next step, the examiner explains the test process to the subject and, again before the test is administered, reads each question to the subject to ensure that all are easily understood. During the examination itself, the subject is not asked any surprise questions about the crime.

The subject is hooked up to the polygraph instrument, and, in a neutral voice—without comment of any kind—the examiner reads the questions several times, noting the questions and answers on the resulting *polygram* (either in digital form or on paper, depending on whether the instrument used is digital or analog). No one other than the examiner and the subject is present at the interrogation (unless a translator is required). Interrogations are typically limited to no more than 90 minutes. If more time is required, additional examinations are scheduled.

After the examination, the examiner analyzes the resulting polygrams and, using prescribed standards, develops a numerical score for the test, which results in a verbal conclusion of either "truthful," "deceptive," or "inconclusive." Results are typically furnished within 24 hours.

> **Talking the Talk**
>
> The graphical readout, or chart, produced by a polygraph examination is called a **polygram**.

Polygraph examiners must design questions that can be answered *yes* or *no*. Nothing else is acceptable. Furthermore, the questions must have definitive, objective answers; they must not elicit mere opinion. Each question must bear on past events of a factual nature, and they must be worded without possibility of ambiguity. Here are some examples:

Unacceptable question: "On April 5, 2002, were you thinking of robbing the convenience store at 234 Guilty Street?"

Acceptable question: "On April 5, 2002, did you rob the convenience store at 234 Guilty Street?"

Unacceptable question: "Have you ever lied to the police?"

Acceptable question: "On April 5, 2002, did you rob the convenience store at 234 Guilty Street?"

Unacceptable question: "Are you a thief?"

Acceptable question: "On April 5, 2002, did you rob the convenience store at 234 Guilty Street?"

Questions asked in the same exam session must be related to one another. The examiner may ask the subject questions relating to the robbery at 234 Guilty Street, but not about (for example) illegal drug use. If the subject is suspected of illegal drug use, this issue must be addressed in a separate examination.

What Can Go Wrong?

Today, some champions of the polygraph claim accuracy rates as high as 99 percent. Critics disagree, arguing that examiners' techniques are based on some questionable psychological assumptions.

By the Numbers

A 1981 study of six polygraph interpreters revealed an error rate varying from 18 percent to 55 percent. Predictably, the most experienced examiners made the fewest errors.

While few question the accuracy of the polygraph instrument in registering the physiological changes it monitors, objective tests have found that many examiners are consistently most likely to label a truthful subject untruthful rather than an untruthful subject truthful. The principles on which the polygraph operates are considered quite sound, but there is significant variation in the quality and accuracy of interpretation.

False Confession

People fear polygraphs. The idea that the machine will absolutely determine the truth sometimes elicits confessions, including false confessions. False confessions, resulting from some deep-seated compulsion in the subject to confess, are not at all uncommon.

Beating the Machine

Certain deceptive subjects can defeat the examination by using cognitive or physiological countermeasures to gain control of their physiological responses. Moreover, people with antisocial personality disorder—a psychological condition that renders the individual incapable of feeling remorse—have reduced autonomic activity. That is, feeling no guilt, they exhibit few of the physiological effects that customarily accompany lying about a crime.

Guilt or Fear?

The polygraph registers heightened physiological responses, period. Such responses may be produced by fear, including the fear of being caught in a lie and punished, but they may also result from just plain fear. Fear is not always about deception. Indeed, an innocent, truthful person may be very fearful.

Inadmissible? The Courts and the Polygraph

The polygraph has traveled a rocky road through the nation's courts. Some courts allow the introduction of polygraph evidence, while others do not. Judges in many jurisdictions worry that polygraph evidence is given greater weight than other evidence and tends to sway a jury unduly. For this reason, in most cases, polygraph evidence is used during the maneuvering and negotiations that take place before a trial, rather than during the trial itself.

In 1993, the U.S. Supreme Court ruled in *Daubert* v. *Merrell Dow Pharmaceuticals, Inc.* (509 U.S. 579) that polygraph evidence does have a reliable scientific foundation and compares favorably with such other scientific evidence as fiber analysis, ballistics comparison, and blood analysis—all of which are routinely accepted by the courts. However, the Supreme Court's 1998 decision in *United States* v. *Scheffer* reduced the effect of the so-called *Daubert standard* by holding that any court can decide to exclude polygraph evidence per se (under any circumstances) or to evaluate it case by case. Thus, the admissibility of polygraph evidence depends on the discretion of the individual court.

Talking the Talk

The **Daubert standard,** based on the 1993 Supreme Court decision in *Daubert* v. *Merrell Dow Pharmaceuticals, Inc.* (509 U.S. 579), is often used to support the legal admissibility of polygraph evidence. The standard holds that courts may admit evidence based on tested, peer-reviewed scientific methods, which are widely accepted as valid in the scientific community.

Alternatives to the Polygraph

While the polygraph remains the most widely used and accepted technology for lie detection, two alternatives have emerged. The first began development in the 1970s as the psychological stress evaluator, or PSE, a device that measured stress in the "microtremors" of the human voice. By the early 1990s, the device was extensively refined as the computer voice stress analyzer (CVSA).

The principle behind the CVSA is that the voice involuntarily, if subtly, registers stress when the speaker is being deceptive. Experience and common sense support this assertion, of course; most people caught in a lie are unable to make themselves sound convincing.

CVSA equipment and training are considerably less expensive than traditional polygraph examination, and advocates claim an extraordinary 98 percent accuracy rate (versus the 45 percent to 85 percent claimed for the polygraph), but while numerous law enforcement agencies use the technology during interrogations and for pretrial negotiation of pleas, many courts do not admit CVSA results as evidence because of insufficient experience with the technology and a shortage of scientific tests.

Critics of the traditional polygraph find that CVSA suffers from the same major flaw that afflicts the polygraph: Both technologies measure emotion rather than knowledge. But, then, what technology could possibly look into a suspect's mind to measure his knowledge of a crime?

In the 1960s, researchers began studying what they called the p300 pattern of electrical activity in the brain, a "bump" in electrical activity that occurs from 300 to 800 milliseconds after a person receives a recognized stimulus—for example, is shown a familiar image. The electrical activity may be monitored via electrodes placed on the head and hooked up to amplifying and graphical recording devices.

In the 1980s and 1990s, a small group of researchers began developing this "brain wave" technology as *brain fingerprinting*, a more refined process for plotting p300 patterns in order to distinguish when a subject possesses or lacks knowledge about an event. In one experiment, Dr. Lawrence A. Farwell was able to identify eleven genuine FBI agents and four imposter agents by measuring brain wave responses to cues that would be familiar only to persons who had been trained in the FBI academy. These cues consisted of specific terms, acronyms, and images. Emotion played no part in the experiment. Simply, those who had the knowledge showed a p300 bump, while those who lacked the knowledge did not show such a pattern.

Talking the Talk

Brain fingerprinting describes a new technology that monitors the brain for p300 electrical patterns, which appear when the subject is exposed to a familiar stimulus. The presence of the p300 pattern indicates the subject's knowledge of the stimulus. Some researchers have begun to apply the technology to lie detection.

Brain fingerprinting is a very new technology, which has yet to be extensively tested in the courts. However, *The New York Times* reported (October 9, 2001,) that in 1998, Missouri police used the technology to generate evidence in support of a confession by James B. Grinder, who admitted to having participated in an unsolved 1984 rape and murder.

The new technology has critics, but even many of these believe that, with further development, brain fingerprinting may play a significant role in criminal investigation and even in prosecution.

The Least You Need to Know

- In most people, lying produces significant physiological effects, some of which may be seen (blushing, sweating) and others measured (elevated blood pressure; rapid, shallow breathing; and decreased electrical resistance of the skin due to increased perspiration).

- William M. Marston created the first physiologically based lie detector in 1917; Dr. John A. Larson substantially improved it in 1921; and his student, Leonarde Keeler, added further refinements as well as improvements to interrogation technique, thereby gaining widespread acceptance of the polygraph.

- The polygraph measures and records the physiological effects associated with anxiety, which, in turn, is associated with telling lies.

- The scientific basis of the polygraph is well established, but practical results depend on the skill and experience of the examiner, factors that introduce a significant element of subjectivity into the examination process.

- The polygraph is used extensively in law enforcement during criminal investigations, but it is often not admitted into evidence by the courts.

- Emerging alternatives to the traditional polygraph are the computer voice stress analyzer (which correlates voice stress with deception) and brain fingerprinting (which monitors the p300 brain wave patterns associated with recognition of a familiar stimulus).

22

Beyond the Fringe

In This Chapter

- The truth about investigative use of "truth serum"
- Hypnosis in police work
- Problems with testimony under hypnosis
- Psychic detectives
- ESP: psychic ability or "cop sense"?

Criminal investigators share with the rest of humanity a basic reality and a common source of frustration. While we travel every which way through the dimension of space, in the dimension of time only one direction, forward, is possible. We cannot go backward to discover, for certain, what happened in the past.

Investigators have developed various means to compensate for the one-way street of time. In sensitive areas—banks, for example, or retail establishments—video cameras and video recorders make a copy of events. But visions of Big Brother notwithstanding, universal surveillance and recording are impossible. Plentiful as they may seem these days, cameras and recording devices are actually in very few places.

Over the years, law enforcement agencies have amassed an arsenal of techniques, each aimed at, in some measure, recovering the past. Fingerprint analysis, for instance, looks for traces of past presence and activity. The forensic autopsy attempts to read a victim's body as a record of past events. Polygraph technology, likewise, tries to resurrect elapsed events.

All of these techniques and technologies are conventional and widely used. Sometimes, however, the quest for bygone truth has led to unconventional, unusual, and even desperate avenues to the past.

"Truth Serum"

Of the many perils Agent 007 and his fictional ilk face—stretching on the rack, a searing slice up the midline with a laser beam—none is more dreaded than exposure to "truth serum." Why? The name says it all. *Truth serum.* Who can resist it? Get a dose of this, and you spill your guts. You can't help it. You have no choice. Or so goes the popular myth.

What Is It?

Actually, there is nothing miraculous—or irresistible—about truth serum. Its chemical name is thiopental sodium, but it is better known as Sodium Pentothal, the name trademarked by its manufacturer, Abbott Laboratories.

Talking the Talk

Truth serum is the colloquial term for a class of sedatives that reduce inhibition and therefore tend to elicit verbal communication that might otherwise be self-censored or suppressed. The most common truth serum is thiopental sodium, but it is better known by its brand name, Sodium Pentothal.

Physically, Sodium Pentothal is a yellow crystal, which can be dissolved in water or alcohol. It has an alliaceous odor, which means it smells like a cross between onions and garlic.

Sodium Pentothal is a fast-acting barbiturate, producing quick, short-term sedation. It is commonly used as a surgical anesthetic. Within half a minute to a minute of injection into a vein, the patient is unconscious—albeit only for a few minutes. Therefore, the sedative is often used to induce initial unconsciousness to give slower but longer-acting anesthetics time to work. It's also the first drug administered in execution by lethal injection; the Sodium Pentothal is not itself delivered in a lethal dose, but it puts the condemned person into a deep sleep prior to the administration of a paralyzing agent (such as pancuronium bromide) and a toxic agent (potassium chloride, which induces cardiac arrest).

Sodium Pentothal is the most familiar truth serum; however, a related substance, sodium amytol, is also sometimes used. In the past, other sedatives—scopolamine and hyascine—were similarly employed to elicit verbal information.

Does It Work?

In lesser doses than those given to surgical patients, Sodium Pentothal slows the metabolism, minimizes stress, but leaves the subject conscious. In reducing the level of stress, it also reduces the inhibitions that typically act as self-censors in most of us, holding us back from speaking our minds or revealing embarrassing (or potentially incriminating) truths.

There's a very old saying, *In vino veritas*—"In wine there is truth." And most of us are familiar with the bibulous friend who talks out of school when in his cups. Under the influence, many of us have, alas, said things we later regret having let slip. The action of Sodium Pentothal is similar to that of alcohol. A depressant, it acts first to depress the mechanisms of self-censorship and inhibition.

In psychotherapy, psychiatrists use Sodium Pentothal as a narcoanalysis agent, a drug to help elicit recall of events and facilitate the expression of feelings. In a criminal justice setting, just because the subject's inhibitions are neutralized does not mean that he will begin spewing out incriminating truths. Careful, focused questions must be asked—and, even then, there's no guarantee that the information forthcoming will be useful or accurate.

Will the Courts Accept It?

In the end, Sodium Pentothal is just one more investigative tool, and, in fact, it's rarely used in law enforcement, except as a last resort. Indeed, rather than administer Sodium Pentothal to a *suspect*, it's more likely that the *victim* of a violent crime, who may be suffering some form of traumatic amnesia, would be treated with the drug in the hope that it might enable him or her to recall relevant details of the crime and the perpetrator.

Sodium Pentothal is a powerful narcotic, which must be administered by a physician (usually a psychiatrist) and preferably in a hospital setting, so that the subject can be monitored. As with any strong sedative agent, there is danger of an adverse reaction, which may require prompt medical action.

As if this weren't problem enough for law enforcement, no American court officially recognizes the reliability of truth serums, and testimony or confession obtained under the influence of this (or any other) narcotic is inadmissible as evidence.

You Are Getting Sleepy ...

Late in the nineteenth century, Sigmund Freud formulated his theory of the unconscious as the great repository of powerful motives that shape particular actions and even our entire lives, yet keeps these motives secret from our conscious awareness. Freud reasoned that if we could gain conscious access to the realm of the unconscious, we would gain valuable insight into ourselves and, in cases of certain mental illnesses, even help effect a cure.

Eventually, Freud developed psychoanalysis, a method in which a patient, awake and alert, but relaxed, lets his or her mind wander in free association and, sometimes prompted by the therapist, gains access to the unconscious mind. Freud arrived at this method first by way of hypnosis, which he saw used by the French psychiatrist Jean Martin Charcot (1825–1893) in an attempt to discover an organic basis for so-called hysterical illnesses.

Hypnosis may be described as a special psychological state, which outwardly resembles sleep, but is really an altered form of the ordinary conscious state. In hypnosis, the subject shows increased receptiveness and responsiveness, which raise inner perceptions to the same level as perceptions normally created only by external reality. Thus the hypnotized subject can be induced to imagine a reality that is as present and real to the subject as if it existed externally.

Talking the Talk

Hypnotic regression uses hypnosis to elicit recall of "lost" memories, memories typically repressed because the conscious mind finds them painful or traumatic.

Hypnotic Regression

Charcot didn't invent hypnosis, the origin of which is as ancient as sorcery and magic. Scientific interest in hypnosis began toward the end of the eighteenth century with the work of the Viennese physician Franz Mesmer (from whose name the word *mesmerize* comes), but Charcot was the first to use it medically. In his early work, Freud and an associate, Josef Breuer, employed it specifically to help neurotic patients recover childhood memories that, because the memories were painful, had been totally repressed—forgotten by the conscious mind, but still locked in the unconscious, where they caused mental illness, psychosomatic symptoms, or even motivated self-destructive acts.

In the early development of psychoanalysis, then, Freud and others practiced *hypnotic regression*, using hypnosis to, in effect, travel backward in time. More recently, hypnotic regression has appeared to some law enforcement professionals as a promising alternative to truth serum, a way to induce recall of memories that, for some reason—typically because they are intensely painful—have been repressed.

Not an Option for Suspects

Hypnosis is used in law enforcement situations, but, these days, less and less frequently. In contrast to truth serum, hypnosis is never used on suspects. Suspect testimony obtained under hypnosis is completely inadmissible in court and, indeed, may even taint other testimony, if a defense attorney can persuade a jury that his or her client had been unduly influenced by the hypnotist or even by the process of hypnosis itself.

However, hypnosis has been used on crime victims as well as witnesses to attempt to recover repressed memories and details of the crime and perpetrator. These individuals submit to hypnosis on a strictly voluntary basis, and the hypnosis, including the interrogation, is conducted by a medical specialist (usually a psychiatrist) trained in hypnotic technique. The session is usually recorded and videotaped.

Digression: A Story of Alien Abduction

Victims and witnesses have apparently recalled astonishing things under hypnosis, including the details of crimes and even the identity of perpetrators. Many law enforcement professionals and others have hailed hypnosis as a tool of extraordinary, even miraculous, utility.

But, while undergoing hypnotic regression, some people have recalled events far more extraordinary than any crime. And this gives many police and judicial officials pause. Take the case of Betty and Barney Hill.

On the night of September 19, 1961, the Hills were returning to their Portsmouth, New Hampshire, home after a visit to Niagara Falls. They were driving south on Route 3 through the White Mountains, when, at 10 P.M., near Groveton, some 70 miles south of the Canadian border, Betty noticed a bright star or planet just below the moon. An hour later, when the Hills were just south of Lancaster, a companion object appeared near the planet.

The Hills stopped their car and observed the object through binoculars. It had red, amber, green, and blue flashing lights. It appeared to have a fuselage shape, but no wings, and it flew in what Barney Hill described as a "steplike flight pattern, dropping vertically, leveling off, tilting upward again." It was absolutely silent.

The Hills resumed driving, the object keeping pace with their car. South of Indian Head, the object approached closer, and Betty saw a change to a steady white glow in the pattern of flashing multicolored lights. When it stopped to hover about 100 feet above the ground, the Hills stopped their car. Barney got out and approached the object, which now appeared to be a huge glowing disc with a double row of windows curved around its perimeter. Fifty feet from the object, using his binoculars, he could see eight to eleven humanlike creatures through the windows. They stood still at first, then began to scurry about within the ship, apparently manipulating controls on the wall. One of the figures remained at the window, gazing at Barney Hill.

At this point, two finlike projections, a red light on the tip of each, slid out of the sides of the ship as Betty, waiting in the car, heard Barney yell, "I don't believe it ... I don't believe it .... This is ridiculous."

> **By the Numbers**
>
> A number of studies, most recently one conducted at Ohio State University and released in August 2001, suggest that hypnosis cannot help the subject to recover lost memories, but does tend to make the subject more confident in the validity of false memories—including memories that are entirely fabricated by the unconscious mind and bear little or no relation to external events.

Barney ran back to the car, shouting that they were going to be captured. He put the car into gear, stepped on the gas, and took off down the highway. Strange beeping sounds, apparently coming from behind the car, made the vehicle vibrate. Both Betty and Barney Hill were overcome by a peculiar sensation of "tingling drowsiness." A while later, the beeps resumed. Then the Hills continued home without further incident—except that they arrived at 5 A.M., about two hours later than they should have. They had lost two hours out of their lives—two hours of which they had no conscious memory.

In the days, weeks, and months that followed, both of the Hills were plagued by nightmares, unbearable feelings of anxiety, insomnia, and, in Barney's case, the development of duodenal ulcers. They sought psychiatric help and were given regressive hypnosis therapy, during which they apparently recovered the two missing hours.

Under hypnosis, Betty related how a group of humanoid beings approached their stopped car, opened the door of the vehicle, and pointed a small device at her. ("It could have been a pencil," she reported.) Independently, both of the Hills described being taken aboard an alien ship and given quasi-medical physical examinations. Betty recalled:

> Most of the men are my height …. None is as tall as Barney, so I would judge them to be 5' to 5'4". Their chests are larger than ours; their noses were larger than the average size although I have seen people with noses like theirs—like Jimmy Durante. Their complexions were of a gray tone; like gray paint with a black base; their lips were of a bluish tint. Hair and eyes were very dark, possibly black.

> In a sense, they looked like mongoloids …. This sort of round face and broad forehead, along with a certain type of coarseness. The surface of their skin seemed to be a bluish gray, but probably whiter than that. Their eyes moved, and they had pupils. Somehow, I had the feeling they were more like cats' eyes.

Barney Hill's description differed in some significant details, particularly concerning the hair and nose of the extraterrestrials:

> The men had rather odd-shaped heads, with a large cranium, diminishing in size as it got toward the chin. And the eyes continued around to the sides of their heads, so that it appeared that they could see several degrees beyond the lateral extent of our vision. This was startling to me …. [The mouth] was much like when you draw one horizontal line with a short perpendicular line on each end. The horizontal line would represent lips without the muscle we have. And it would part slightly as they made this mumumumummming sound. The texture of the skin, as I remember it from this quick glance, was grayish, almost metallic looking. I didn't notice any hair—or headgear for that matter. I didn't notice any proboscis, there just seemed to be two slits that represented the nostrils.

The beings, according to the Hills, communicated among themselves through audible language ("mumumumumming sound"), yet communicated with the Hills through telepathy in English (according to Betty, "with an accent"). "I did not hear an actual voice," Barney Hill reported. "But in my mind, I knew what he was saying. It wasn't as if he were talking to me with my eyes open, and he was sitting across the room from me. It was more as if the words were there, a part of me, and he was outside the actual creation of the words themselves."

Following six months of this regressive hypnosis therapy, the emotional state of both Betty and Barney Hill improved markedly.

Case in Point

In a 2001 study, Professor Joseph Green of Ohio State University questioned 96 college students about the date of certain historical events. Half of this group answered the questions under hypnosis, while the other half answered after performing a relaxation exercise. After the test, the students were asked to rate their confidence in their answers. Regardless of whether they were right or wrong, all subjects were told they had given at least one wrong answer. They were allowed to change their answers and to rank their confidence in the revised answers. Green found no difference in the accuracy of the hypnotized students versus the other group; however, the hypnotized subjects changed significantly fewer responses. Green concluded: "While hypnosis does not enhance the reliability of memory, there is some evidence that hypnosis leads to increased confidence in memories."

Those who believe the earth is regularly visited by extraterrestrials point to the regressive hypnosis of Betty and Barney Hill as ample evidence. Those who are skeptical about "close encounters of the third kind" suggest that Betty and Barney Hill were victims of the inadequacies of regressive hypnosis. Subjected to it, critics say, people "recall" all sorts of things.

What the Courts Say

Testimony obtained from victims and witnesses under hypnosis was newsworthy but not rare in American courtrooms during the 1970s and, again, during the early to mid 1990s. As it became increasingly apparent, however, that much of this testimony was contradicted by attempts to corroborate it independently, law enforcement and legal professionals began to conclude that hypnotic regression was highly unreliable. Defense attorneys now turn to recent studies, including that conducted at Ohio State in 2001, for powerful ammunition to demolish incriminating victim and witness testimony obtained under hypnosis.

Psychic Hotline

Psychic detectives or PDs are civilians who claim psychic power and who offer to use it to help law enforcement agencies solve crimes. In desperation, police agencies have, from time to time, called in a PD.

When the work of the psychic apparently leads to the solution of a seemingly hopeless case, tabloid magazines and tabloid TV shows rush in with ample coverage. In contrast, the failures and the outright phonies receive little if any media notice. Let's look at a few examples of psychic detectives helping solve a crime.

Dauphine, France, 1662

One day, Jacques Aymar, a "water witch"—a person who claims to be able to locate sources of underground water with a divining rod—finds not water, but the severed head of a woman. The dead woman's face is recognized by a villager, and her head is brought back in a sack to her husband. Approaching the man's house, Aymar feels his divining rod vibrate. As the widower approaches, the rod vibrates so strongly that the man, seeing it, suddenly flees—and is later apprehended, charged, and convicted of his wife's murder. Subsequently, local police call on Aymar to solve other crimes.

Manville, Alberta, 1928

A famed Austrian medium, Maximilien Langsner, is invited by Canadian police to work on an apparently unsolvable multiple murder case. A woman, her son, and two workers are found dead on a Manville farm. Vernon Booher, the remaining son, claims he discovered the bodies after returning home. The murder weapon, a rifle, belongs to a neighbor, Charles Stephenson, who says the weapon had been stolen from his home the week before the murders. Police detain Booher in a holding cell. Langsner sits outside of the cell and claims to read Booher's thoughts. The psychic reports that Booher had slipped out of church and had stolen the rifle. According to Langsner, Booher wanted to marry a girl of whom his mother disapproved. A quarrel ensued over this, and it ended with Booher killing everyone in the house. Confronted with this psychic report, Booher breaks down, confesses, is tried, and hanged.

Williston, Florida, 1997

On March 24, 1994, 76-year-old Norman Lewis goes missing in Williston, Florida, and stays missing for two years. His family asks local police to consult a psychic. Investigator Brian Hewitt is acquainted with Noreen Reiner, a self-proclaimed psychic, who performs a reading in the case. She says that Lewis had traveled in his pickup truck east from his home to a place "where there is ... water in something like a pit." Reiner reports seeing Lewis surrounded by metal. She sees a cliff wall, loose bricks, a railroad track, and a bridge. She also sees the numbers "45" and "21."

After several searches of local bodies of water prove fruitless, police call in U.S. Navy divers to search a flooded limestone quarry. They locate the missing truck and the skeleton of Norman Lewis.

The story of Reiner's "reading" is widely reported and apparently inspires a spate of psychic readings, one of which persuades authorities in Graniteville, Missouri, to drain a three-million-gallon quarry in search of a girl missing for seven years. She is not found.

Intuition on Steroids

The list of apparently psychic solutions to mysteries unsolved by conventional police work goes on and on. Fortunately for the authors, a book on criminology and criminal investigation is not the place to debate the nature and validity of psychic insight or extrasensory perception (ESP) and its possible value in criminal investigation. Those interested in obtaining a quick but balanced assessment of Noreen Reiner, perhaps the best-known recent psychic detective, might look up Gary Posner's article, "A Not-So-Psychic Detective? A Case Study of Noreen Reiner's Latest and Greatest 'Success' Story," in *Skeptic* magazine (1998) and reproduced online at www.parascope.com/en/articles/notSoPsychic.htm.

Doubtless, some so-called psychics are well-meaning but deluded, while others are out-and-out frauds. Yet some do seem to hit the proverbial nail on the head. Are these individuals possessed of a psychic gift or extrasensory power? Or, as some cops believe, are these civilians no more or less psychic than a really good detective? Perhaps the psychic, like the detective, merely combines keen powers of observation, years of experience, a savvy sense of human behavior, and a talent for putting two and two together to identify and track the most productive clues. Perhaps psychic detectives are just very capable detectives, people who, like any veteran criminal investigator, have extensively developed their intuition—have figuratively put their gut instinct on steroids, as it were, pumped them up, and become acutely sensitive and always attentive to what it tells them.

> **Sworn Statement**
>
> Psychics claim their instinctual feelings come from special powers within; detectives say their gut feelings and hunches emanate from years of experience, that they have developed a "cop's sense."
>
> —Harvey Rachlin, "Psychics and Police Work" (*Law and Order* [professional law enforcement journal], June 1995)

The Least You Need to Know

◆ Sodium Pentothal is a narcotic that lowers inhibitions and, therefore, may loosen the tongue; despite its popular name, however, it is far from being an infallible truth serum and is rarely used by law enforcement agencies.

◆ In the 1970s and in the early to mid-1990s, hypnosis (especially hypnotic regression) was occasionally used on victims and witnesses to recover "lost" memories of crime.

◆ Recent studies suggest that hypnosis cannot recover memories and may instead elicit the fabrication of false memories.

◆ Psychic detectives—civilian psychics who offer help to criminal investigators—have received much attention in the popular press.

◆ Veteran cops say all really good detectives are, in a sense, psychic; that is, they have "cop sense"—keenly developed intuition based on the perceptive interpretation of the subtle facts and clues most people miss.

Part 7

Crime in a Crystal Ball

The two chapters in this part look toward the future—the future of crime and the future of the police response to crime. Our outlook is based on current trends in crime, with an emphasis on the explosion of "cyber crimes" and the continued prospect of terrorism. So far as police work is concerned, the emphasis will be on the increasingly efficient acquisition and processing of information—intelligence—and the development of effective alternatives to deadly force.

For some two centuries, criminologists have explored the relationship between crime and society. In the future, police and the society they serve and protect will have to explore, improve, and strengthen their relationship to one another.

Chapter 23

Future Crime

In This Chapter

- Identifying crime trends
- Crime and the economy
- The emerging drug scene
- Data, computer, and identity crime
- Cyber terrorism and Internet child pornography
- Desktop counterfeiting

In the early days of organized police forces, the work of law enforcement was a business of reaction. A crime occurred; the police gave chase. Later, police departments attempted not merely to react to crime, but to prevent it, mainly by maintaining highly visible patrols on the streets. As police agencies grew increasingly sophisticated, they began to keep statistical records in an attempt to anticipate where and when crimes were most likely to occur. This allowed police administrators to deploy their forces more efficiently, putting more cops in high-crime areas and during high-crime periods. The idea was to be proactive rather than merely reactive.

Most recently, police agencies have been applying similar principles to long-term planning in an attempt to anticipate crime trends and the nature of crime in the future.

Based on Current Statistics ...

Predicting the future is a highly seductive occupation. It's exhilarating to exercise the imagination, and no one can prove you wrong—at least not for years or decades to come. Criminal justice professionals try to base their predictions on extrapolation from hard statistical data rather than on unbridled imagination. Crime statistics are valuable as a measure of the current state of society and the current state of law enforcement. They also provide a valuable basis for projecting future trends.

Public Perception Versus the Numbers

As mentioned in the first chapter of this book, crime is very high on the list of our concerns. Ask most people about crime, and they'll tell you that it continually increases.

This is a common popular perception, but, actually, over the past decade, the *crime rate* has declined. For example, in 1999, according to the FBI's *Uniform Crime Reports*, one of the standard digests of crime statistics in the United States, 11,634,378 crimes were reported. The number fell to 11,605,751 in 2000, a drop of 0.2 percent. This translates to a crime rate of 4,266.5 crimes per 100,000 inhabitants of the United States in 1999, and 4,124.0 in 2000.

Nevertheless, if we take the long view, let's say encompassing 50 years or so, crime rates today remain near their all-time highs. And it's no wonder that Americans are concerned about crime. Despite the modest (but significant) declines in the crime rate during recent years, the FBI's most recent "Crime Clock" reveals the following:

◆ One murder every 33.9 minutes

◆ One forcible rape every 5.8 minutes

◆ One robbery every 1.3 minutes

◆ One burglary every 15.4 seconds

◆ One motor vehicle theft every 27.1 seconds

◆ One larceny-theft every 4.5 seconds

In all, one crime is committed every 2.7 seconds in the United States.

Talking the Talk

The **crime rate** is the number of crimes in a given period (usually a month or a year) among a fixed sample number of persons within a given population. The FBI reports the U.S. crime rate in terms of number of crimes per 100,000 persons.

What's Hot

Sixty percent of all crimes committed in 2000 were classified as instances of larceny-theft, which FBI crime statisticians define as "the unlawful taking, carrying, leading, or riding away of property from the possession or constructive possession of another. It includes crimes such as shoplifting, pickpocketing, purse snatching, thefts from motor vehicles, thefts of motor vehicle parts and accessories, bicycle thefts, etc., in which no use of force, violence, or fraud occurs." This is nonviolent, garden-variety theft, and, while the writers of thriller cop fiction will never pay much attention to it, it is by far the most common type of crime. There is no reason to believe that, in the future, it will be any less prevalent.

In fact, most crimes are property crimes: Burglary accounted for 17.7 percent of crimes reported in 2000; motor vehicle theft, 10 percent; robbery, 3.5 percent. Therefore, 91.2 percent of all crimes reported in 2000 were crimes against property.

What's Not

Murder, rape, and other violent crimes constitute a relatively small fraction of crimes reported: Murder, 0.1 percent; forcible rape, 0.8 percent; *aggravated assault*, 7.8 percent.

Yet if these are not statistically America's hottest crimes, they are nevertheless frighteningly prevalent. In a 1996 Scripps syndicated article, "Tracking the Crime Curve into the Future," Paul Akers reported that about 10 million violent victimizations occur annually in the United States. Americans, according to Akers, are twice as likely to be assaulted, robbed at gunpoint, raped, or abducted than they are to be seriously injured in an automobile accident.

Talking the Talk

Also called felonious assault, **aggravated assault** is an unlawful attack by one person against another for the purpose of inflicting severe bodily injury.

Optimists look at the recent decline in crime and attribute it to better policing and stricter law enforcement. Pessimists say that it is merely due to the aging of the Baby Boom generation—older adults commit fewer crimes than youngsters—and they point out that, in the first few years of the twenty-first century, there will be a significant spike in the U.S. male population, ages 14 to 17. It is among this group that violent crime is most prevalent. Disturbingly, while the murder rate has generally declined during the 1990s, it has increased among teens. For example, during 1990 to 1994, the teen murder rate grew by 22 percent.

Statistically dwarfed by property crimes, violent crimes are likely to remain a very serious force in the future, and, if the violent activity among male teens is any indication, we may begin to witness a reversal of the recent decline in violent crime.

Economy and Opportunity

For much of the 1990s, Americans enjoyed economically prosperous times, with unemployment levels at unprecedented lows—near 4 percent nationally, and in some areas even lower. Since most crimes are property crimes, some of the decline in crime during the decade of the 1990s may well be attributable to general prosperity.

Hard Times and Crime

As the twentieth century drew to a close, unemployment rose and the economy retreated. Are we likely to see an increase in crime as a result? Several recent studies suggest that the rate of unemployment directly affects the crime rate. Higher unemployment means more crime.

Case in Point

Economists Steven Raphael (UC, San Diego) and Rudolf Winter-Ebner (University of Linz, Austria), published a report in 1998 indicating the impact of unemployment on crime. Analyzing statistics from 1970 through a portion of the 1990s, the authors noted a correlation between the economy and the crime rate. Especially dramatic was the period from 1992 to 1996, a time of falling unemployment, which saw a decline in crime. The economists argue that a drop of two percentage points in unemployment can be expected to bring a 9 percent decline in burglary, 14 percent decline in rape and robbery, and a 30 percent decline in assault. Raphael and Winter-Ebner claim that had unemployment been 1 percent higher in 1992, there would have been almost half a million more crimes in the United States.

New Opportunities

Economic conditions don't affect the crime rate alone (lower unemployment, less crime; higher unemployment, more crime); they also create new opportunities for criminals.

The FBI *Uniform Crime Reports* does not deal with so-called "white collar" crime—fraud, embezzlement, and the like—yet, over the past decade or so, these areas of criminal enterprise have seen significant growth. Many criminals have moved away from lifting physical merchandise to siphoning off information. This makes sense when you consider that, these days, money is less a physical thing than a set of digital records in a vast computer network. Cash doesn't change *hands*, it merely changes *number*. The typical business transaction isn't between a *you* and a *me*, but between a magnetic stripe on a credit card and a chunk of data stored somewhere in the electronic ether. Techno crime is an intense growth area in criminal enterprise, which we'll discuss in a moment.

New Victims: Elder Crime

The tale of the especially despicable criminal who preys upon the elderly is at least as old as the two wicked daughters of Shakespeare's *King Lear,* but the fact that more people are living into advanced old age these days suggests that financial exploitation of elderly citizens by family members, fiduciaries, care givers, and acquaintances will continue to rise.

The special needs of the elderly also provide various unscrupulous individuals, especially in the medical, legal, and insurance fields, ample opportunity to rip off the federal health care system, as well as private insurers.

By the Numbers

As of 2001, it is estimated that health care fraud amounts to two, perhaps three, *hundred billion dollars* a year.

The Drug Scene

Prior to the 1960s, illicit drug use was a problem confined to "poor neighborhoods" and "the criminal classes." During the 1960s, the use of such substances as marijuana, amphetamines, tranquilizers, cocaine, and hallucinogens (especially LSD) became widespread as drugs were increasingly perceived as "recreational" or even "mind expanding." Clearly, illicit drug use reached epidemic proportions during the 1960s, and it continues to be very serious, a powerful driver of organized crime on a national and international scale.

To gauge trends in illicit drug use, the U.S. Department of Health and Human Services closely monitors drug-related visits to the emergency rooms (emergency departments, or EDs) of U.S. hospitals. From January to June 2001, the department estimated that there were 308,368 drug-related emergency department episodes in the continental United States. This was about the same number as were reported in 2000. In some cities, the rate increased significantly—by 18 percent in Minneapolis,

10 percent in Boston, and 9 percent in Baltimore. In some places, it went down by similar numbers.

New Designs

If, on balance, drug use is not sharply on the rise, recent years have seen an influx of new, so-called "designer drugs"—clandestinely produced drugs that are structurally and pharmacologically similar to controlled substances (federally regulated narcotics), but are not themselves controlled substances. Since 1987, federal statutes have prohibited the manufacture and use of these "controlled substance analogs."

The most important new designer drug is MDMA, popularly called Ecstasy, and also known as XTC, Adam, hug, beans, and the love drug. MDMA has stimulant (amphetamine-like) and hallucinogenic (LSD-like) properties and is chemically similar to methamphetamine, methylenedioxyamphetamine (MDA), and mescaline, all drugs known to cause brain damage. High doses can cause a sharp increase in body temperature (a condition called malignant hyperthermia) leading to muscle breakdown and kidney and cardiovascular system failure.

U.S. Department of Health and Human Services data indicates that while MDMA was once used primarily at dance clubs, youth parties—raves—and what the department describes as "the college scene," it is now even more widely used. In 2001, it was reported as the most prominent stimulant used in Chicago. In Denver, many singles' bars sell it illegally. It has become the drug of choice among white middle class young adults in Washington, D.C. In Miami in 1999, eight MDMA-related deaths were reported. Five were reported in Minneapolis/ St. Paul. In Boston during the first three quarters of 2000, MDMA was the most frequently mentioned drug in telephone calls to the Poison Control Center.

The fact that the United States Drug Enforcement Administration (DEA) seized 13,342 MDMA tablets in 1996 and 949,257 in 2000 suggests that the use of this dangerous drug may well rise. Likely, increased use of MDMA is also an indication that additional synthetic drugs will be developed and abused.

New Users

In recent years, it has become distressingly evident that illicit drugs have new users: the very young. From 1999 to 2000, the use of MDMA increased among eighth, tenth, and twelfth graders. Among eighth graders, MDMA use increased from 1.7 percent in 1999 to 3.1 percent in 2000. Among tenth graders, the increase was from

4.4 percent to 5.4 percent. Among twelfth graders, it rose from 5.6 percent to 8.2 percent. Alarming as these increases are, they seem to have leveled off from 2000 to 2001, and from 2001 to 2002.

What is true of MDMA use is generally true of other commonly abused or illicit drugs as well: Abuse has become prevalent among increasingly younger groups.

Techno Crime

It is a cliché to remark that our lives these days are carried along on the endless stream of zeroes and ones that is cyberspace. Our personal and financial data is, it seems, everywhere. In the case of our homes and places of business, we know where the keys are—in pocket or purse. In the case of our digital lives, well, who knows who has the keys?

Credit Card Crime

It is a rare day that most of us go to the mail box without getting an offer for a credit card. Most Americans carry upward of half a dozen cards, many have far more.

Unfortunately, credit cards are very easy to use fraudulently. All that is required is information—not even the physical card itself, just the number on it. This can be obtained from discarded receipts or from rifling through a person's mail. With more and more purchases being made online, a computer-savvy thief can obtain credit card numbers without having to get anywhere near the victim. An enterprising cyber thief can set up a website advertising some entirely fictitious product, include an online purchasing form, and then collect credit card numbers along with names and mailing addresses. Despite the development of various security countermeasures, this type of crime is likely only to increase.

> **By the Numbers**
>
> In 1977, there were 8.2 million Visa and Master-Cards in use. In 2001, there were 44.1 million. In 1982 (the first year statistics were kept), Visa and Master-Card reported writing off $15.88 million in fraudulent charges. In 2001, the companies reported a write-off of $142.27 million.

ATM Spoofing

A whole generation of Americans may never see the inside of a bank. Automated-teller machines (ATMs) proliferate across the landscape. One obvious risk of using these typically very exposed machines is getting robbed at gunpoint as you withdraw your cash. But no truly enterprising ATM thief uses a gun.

Unlike credit cards, ATM cards require a password—a personal identification number, or PIN—to work. This is an excellent security measure, but hardly unbreakable.

Recently, in a Connecticut mall, thieves set up a fake ATM, which looked and worked just like a real one. The only difference was that, after you fed it your card and typed in your PIN, it reported itself out of order. However, it had recorded both the card information (account number and name of user) and the PIN. Using this information, thieves were able to withdraw funds from the accounts of various victims.

It is also possible to stake out a legitimate ATM, focus a video camera on the keypad, and record keystrokes. When a PIN is successfully recorded, the thief runs to the machine and looks for a discarded receipt—many people throw them down or even leave them in the ATM's dispenser slot. If he finds a receipt, he can put it together with the PIN and make a withdrawal.

Identity Theft

But why stop at fraudulently charging a few items with a credit card number or stealing a few dollars from an ATM? Increasingly, many techno criminals do not, in fact, stop at these.

Just what is *identity theft?* Here's an example. After obtaining someone's personal data, a convicted felon charged some $100,000 on fraudulent credit cards, obtained a federal home loan, and, in the victim's name, bought homes, motorcycles, and handguns. Then he decided, apparently just for fun, to give the digital knife a twist by taunting his victim with phone calls, telling him that he could continue assuming the man's identity for as long as he wanted because identity theft was not a federal crime (as it was not, at that time). Finally, the thief filed for bankruptcy—in the victim's name.

The victim and his wife had to spend some $15,000 and more than four years of their lives restoring their credit and reputation. The criminal, apprehended at last, served nothing more than a brief sentence for making a false statement to procure a firearm. It was this case, and others like it, that moved Congress in 1998 to create a new federal offense: identity theft.

> **Talking the Talk**
>
> **Identity theft,** also called identity fraud, is a federal crime in which someone wrongfully obtains and uses another person's personal data in some way that involves fraud or deception, usually for economic gain.

It does not require a James Bond to steal the identity of another person. Nor does it even require picking the victim's pocket or breaking into his or her home or place of business.

Identity thieves may engage in shoulder surfing—surreptitiously looking over your shoulder as you punch in your telephone calling card number on a public phone or your PIN at an ATM. They may also eavesdrop as you give your credit card number over the telephone to a hotel or rental car company.

An identity thief may also engage in dumpster diving—going through your garbage cans, dumpster, or trash bin, looking for copies of checks, credit card or bank statements, or other records that bear your name, address, telephone number, and various financial account numbers.

Computer-savvy identity thieves obtain personal information of all sorts from the Internet, often setting up phony websites to capture victim information.

Once the identity thief has sufficient identifying information about an individual, the thief can effectively take over that person's identity and use it to make applications for loans and credit cards, withdraw money from bank accounts, use telephone calling cards, and so on. Identity theft is very clearly an alarming growth area in criminal enterprise.

> **Sworn Statement**
>
> Discarded junk mail is a treasure trove for identity thieves, who pore through garbage looking for "preapproved" credit cards, which they may be able to activate. Word to the wise: Cut up—in small pieces—any unwanted or expired credit cards, and consider purchasing a shredder to destroy any discarded junk mail or documents bearing your financial data.

Cyber Crime

As the Model T automobile transformed America's geographical landscape early in the twentieth century, so the development of the personal computer and the related evolution of the Internet have transformed the intellectual, commercial, and communications landscape. Something this sweeping, this pervasive, this important has to have a dark side. Right? Right.

Hacking It

A few years ago, when the Internet was in its infancy and when communication between and among computers was a highly esoteric field, a new kind of criminal came into being: the hacker. Actually, back then, many people did not consider the hacker a criminal, but, rather, a kind of merry prankster, a techno wit who delighted in tweaking the nose of big business and big government by sneaking into computer systems and leaving little calling cards, something in the nature of digital graffiti—nothing more, just a token to show he or she had been there. As the term is used today, a hacker is a person who surreptitiously and illicitly breaks into computer systems to disrupt them or to obtain data, usually, but not always, for financial gain.

Hackers may engage in industrial espionage or even espionage against the government. They may be identity thieves. They may commit credit card fraud. Some may be industrial or commercial saboteurs, disseminating computer viruses, worms, or other malicious programs to disrupt private and corporate computer systems. Or they may find ways to overload a commercial website, effectively bringing it to a halt and preventing any transactions from taking place (this is known as a "denial of service" attack).

Cyber Terror

Hackers may be pranksters, they may be vandals, they may be spies, they may be thieves. They may also be terrorists. The potential harm cyber terrorists might cause is truly terrifying. They could, for example, hack into the computer that controls the mix of ingredients in a pharmaceutical or food-processing plant. They could detonate explosive devices from remote locations. They could cause massive disruption of financial institutions and stock exchanges. They could hack into the computers at the heart of the air traffic control system. They could shut off city water supplies or regional electric service.

So far, the world has seen very little of this, but it is all too apparent that cyber terror offers a vast field for future crime.

Child Porn

The Internet has been compared to the Wild West, a digital Great Plains, free of censorship, free of government regulation, a vast space in which anything and everything goes.

No freedom, of course, comes without a price. The anonymity of the Internet, the ability to plug into the world without being seen or heard or otherwise identified, has led to the proliferation of pornography on the World Wide Web. Some of this material is easy enough to take or leave as one wishes, but a portion of the Internet porn business exploits children, and may lead to abduction, child rape, and even worse.

Who could have anticipated that the miracle of civilization embodied in the Internet would be used for such purposes? The only possible answer is that much of the future consists, precisely, of the unanticipated.

The New Counterfeiters

You've seen those gangster movies, circa 1940: The counterfeiting genius who has managed to engrave near-perfect plates, who has formulated near-perfect paper, who has compounded near-perfect inks. Ah, the counterfeiter! For years, he was the most exalted of criminals, highly skilled, practically a magician, and certainly a genius.

Today, just about anyone with a personal computer, halfway decent desktop publishing software, a modest desktop scanner, and a good color printer can counterfeit checks and currency. At least one government agency has called *desktop counterfeiting* the gravest threat to U.S. currency today.

But, in addition to printing money, desktop counterfeiters have pulled off other feats of digital fakery. For instance: In 1989, an international counterfeiting ring bilked Los Angeles banking giant First Interstate Bancorp out of $750,000 by stealing a legitimate corporate dividend check, scanning it (including the authorized signature) into a computer, then electronically altering the amount and the name of the payee. The fake was then printed out on a laser printer and successfully presented at the bank for payment.

Talking the Talk

Desktop counterfeiting is the use of readily available personal computer equipment, scanners, color copiers, and color printers to produce bogus currency, checks, and other documents.

Or this: In 1993, Ahmed Abdullah al-Ashmouny, a citizen of Egypt, was indicted in the United States for counterfeiting thousands of visas on a color copier and selling them to other Egyptians, including followers of accused terrorist leader Sheik Omar Abdel Rahman, a New Jersey–based Muslim cleric now serving a life sentence in the United States for conspiring to assassinate Egyptian President Hosni Mubarak and blow up five New York City landmarks, including the World Trade Center, which was bombed in 1993. It is not known how many persons have used these visas to enter the United States illegally. Nor is it known how many were—or are—terrorists, the associates, comrades, and colleagues of those who attacked America on September 11, 2001.

The Least You Need to Know

- Police agencies use current statistics to spot crime trends in order to formulate future law enforcement plans.

- The state of the economy appears to be an important predictor of the general crime rate: Low unemployment is associated with lower crime rates, high unemployment with higher crime rates.

- The emergence of "designer drugs" and the widespread use of illicit drugs among younger people are two leading trends in drug-related crime.

- The Internet and the continued evolution of a digital economy offer expanding possibilities for such cyber crimes as credit card fraud, ATM fraud, identity theft, various computer hacking crimes, and even cyber terrorism and the exploitation of children through Internet-based child pornography.

- The universal availability of computer-based desktop publishing hardware and software has led to the development of "desktop counterfeiting," a serious threat to U.S. currency, as well as a challenge to all businesses and government agencies that rely on "authentic" documents.

24

Future Cops

In This Chapter

- ◆ New developments, traditional values
- ◆ Crime prevention vs. the Constitution
- ◆ New emphasis on security
- ◆ Information: the most powerful police weapon
- ◆ Nonlethal weapons of the future
- ◆ Police and the community: a work in progress

Law enforcement planners think about the future, and they think hard. In 1991, they organized the Society of Police Futurists International (head-quartered at Eastern Kentucky University in Richmond, Kentucky) to bring together some of the best thought.

The goals of Police Futurists International reflect the major concerns of law enforcement in the years to come: to encourage partnerships between law enforcement, the academic community, and private industry; to develop, analyze, and interpret long-range forecasts; to promote the use of technology; to research and promote creative, innovative, and proactive policing strategies; and to advance ethical behavior in law enforcement. Future police will be more thoroughly integrated into all aspects of the community, they will emphasize proactive and preventive strategies rather than reaction, they will exploit technology, and they will put increasing emphasis on ethics.

New Technologies and Traditional Values

In 1987, film maker Paul Verhoeven directed a vision of law enforcement in the near future. The city was Detroit, overrun with crime, its police force now managed by a private corporation, which transformed an officer, killed in the line of duty, into an armed and armored cyborg called Robocop. This futuristic vision of a bionic cop proved immensely popular, spinning off more than a few sequels, and it reflected the popular impression that urban crime had become so formidable that only a superhuman robot could fight it.

The fact is that cops really do use robots—right now, today. Well-equipped bomb squads use highly mobile remote-controlled robots, equipped with mechanical arms and capable of real-time video transmission, to investigate and handle potential explosive devices. Such robots can also be used in "urban warfare" scenarios, to seek out hidden gunmen and terrorists without exposing a live officer to gunfire. For that matter, video surveillance cameras, which are proliferating in many public buildings and public areas outdoors, may be seen as robotic extensions of the officers' vision.

But police agencies regard all of these "robots," technical marvels though they are, as nothing more or less than tools to make the human cop's job safer and more effective.

Law enforcement is a social service, like government itself, and can never be automated. Cops are, first and foremost, people aiding other people. This requires and will continue to require human responsiveness and human judgment.

Some Things Just Don't Change

As discussed in the preceding chapter, technology, especially the information technology that has been enabled by the personal computer and the Internet, has opened new fields of techno crime and cyber crime. Yet, while the modality of these crimes is new, the underlying nature of the wrongdoing is older than the Eighth Commandment: *Thou shalt not steal.*

Overwhelmingly, cyber crime or techno crime is property crime, theft of intellectual property, theft of identity, ultimately theft of money. Cops of the future will have to continue to develop the technological sophistication to foil and apprehend cyber criminals, but, like the cops of today and the cops of a hundred years ago, their principal business will be policing property crime. Second to this—in volume, but not importance—will be policing violent crime against persons, most of it associated with property crime.

Not all cutting-edge police work involves advanced technology. Special Investigator Guy Antinozzi and Sergeant David Aderhold demonstrate a blocking defense and elbow strike counterattack using the state-of-the-art law enforcement defensive tactics method known as Krav Maga developed by the Israeli Defense Forces.

(Photo by Rod Huene, DeKalb County [Georgia] Sheriff's Office)

Policing: From Reactive to Proactive

While the modalities of crime may change, the underlying crimes remain the same. Historically, police agencies have found that their greatest challenge has not been coping with new kinds of crime, but dealing more efficiently with the kinds of crime long familiar. From the very beginning of professional policing, the Bow Street Runners of eighteenth-century London (see Chapter 17), the effort has been to get the police force ahead of the crime curve, to transform the police from a reactive agency to a proactive one.

Future cops will most likely accelerate this drive toward anticipating crime and applying law enforcement resources wherever and whenever most needed to combat—and prevent—crime. Technologically, this requires creating

Sworn Statement

By trying to envisage what the crimes of the future may be we are one step closer to preventing them.

—Home Office (United Kingdom) Minister Charles Clarke, quoted by the BBC ever more sophisticated means of gathering and analyzing intelligence. This means developing computer programs that can model reality in great detail, enabling police agencies to construct place- and time-specific pictures of crimes to come and to work through the implications of each scenario.

Nobody is likely to object to a technological wonder like this. However, such computer modeling will have to be built on present-moment, real-time intelligence, and that means increased systems of tracking and surveillance. It is at this point that police technology and the long-cherished rights of free people in a democratic society begin to clash.

An Ounce of Prevention ...

"An ounce of prevention," the old saw goes, "is worth a pound of cure." But unlike so many time-worn sayings, this one still rings with solid truth. In general, preventing a bad thing is more efficient, easier, and cheaper than mopping up the mess that a bad thing makes.

Everyone agrees that crime prevention is a good thing. The disputes arise over methods of prevention. Our Constitution guarantees that we are presumed innocent until proven guilty by due process of law. This legal safeguard alone greatly limits the application of various means of crime prevention:

- ◆ The police cannot stop, search, or detain people without probable cause.

- ◆ Many forms of surveillance constitute an illegal presumption of guilt, invasion of privacy, or illegal search.

- ◆ *Racial profiling*, singling out individuals in the belief that members of their race have a high likelihood of committing or having committed a crime, has been found unconstitutional.

Talking the Talk

Racial profiling occurs when the police target someone for investigation or search on the basis of that person's race, national origin, or ethnicity.

Clearly, the police will always be limited in the type and degree of prevention they can exercise. And, in a free society, we wouldn't want this any other way. In a free society, therefore, other means of crime prevention need to be developed and applied. In the future, society will likely look increasingly to criminologists and other social scientists to provide meaningful data on the causes of crime. Addressing these causes will not be a matter for the police alone, but for society as a whole. Crime prevention will doubtless require a willingness to restructure various aspects of society, to continue to increase economic opportunities for everyone, to make room in our society for everyone, to create, ultimately, a society in which crime is perceived not only as dangerous, costly, and morally wrong, but as simply unnecessary.

Security Horizons

Upholding constitutional rights is, obviously, of vital importance, as is working toward a more just and open society. But what does a people do after the terrorist attacks of September 11, 2001? How can we preserve the Constitution and foster an open society when doing these things, apparently, leaves us that much more vulnerable?

The answer seems to be a compromise of some freedoms in certain, strictly defined settings. That is, we accept searches of our baggage and even our persons in airports. We agree to furnish identification when purchasing airline tickets. We tolerate delay. We try to be understanding and patient when a flight is cancelled because of security concerns. We relinquish the convenience of parking spaces close to the airport terminal. We ask that employees in sensitive areas be subjected to background checks, to uncover any criminal record. We ourselves willingly open our lives to inspection in order to get certain jobs.

In recent years, the most pervasive trend in law enforcement has been in the area of security, and since September 11, the security industry has burgeoned. It is likely that, as the future unrolls, many police duties will be assumed by private security personnel. Even more important, search and surveillance, of a kind and degree constitutionally unacceptable on the street, will be increasingly commonplace in many other public and semipublic places: airports, major events, even bars and restaurants.

Violence and other crimes have become of increasing concern in schools and in the workplace. Doubtless, these venues will experience an increase in the presence of security personnel, in video surveillance, and in the use of personal identification cards to gain access and to track people.

> **Sworn Statement**
>
> We need a national ID card with our photograph and thumbprint digitized and embedded in the ID card.
>
> —Larry Ellison, CEO, Oracle Systems, TV news interview, September 21, 2001

Emphasis on Information

By definition, the future is an uncertain place, but within this unknown, at least one trend in criminal investigation is sure: Information will be regarded as an increasingly valuable commodity, and law enforcement agencies will, increasingly, become information gathering, sharing, and processing agencies.

New Computers, New Networks

Just a few years ago, stand-up comics found much grist for the laugh mill in anecdotes about hopeless arguments with anonymous corporate or government computers—monologue bits about spectacular billing mix-ups with the electric company, grotesque IRS snafus, and the like.

Lately, comedians have been looking for new material. The reason? People are now quite accustomed to communicating with computers, and the computers are much better than they were just a few years ago; more accurately, computer *networks* are better and far more extensive. For the problem never really was one of people talking to computers, but of computers failing to talk to other computers.

Like the electric company, the IRS, and other big businesses, police agencies have also benefited from the quantum leaps in computer technology and computer networking. Today, criminals enjoy unprecedented mobility in geographical space, but they are increasingly hemmed in by cyberspace. Criminal records and suspect information are computerized, not tucked into a jacket stuck in a detective's file drawer. Stored on computer, these records can be shared by virtually any law enforcement agency anywhere.

And not just shared. Computer files can be rapidly searched according to whatever criteria the investigator specifies. Let's say the investigator's looking into a rash of burglaries in which the perp always ensures that the home is empty, always enters through the garage, always strikes at night, always steals jewelry, and never leaves fingerprints. The investigator narrows the search through the computer files by specifying these and whatever other particulars he or she has. The computer returns a short list of suspects.

> **Sworn Statement**
>
> Today, law enforcement computer networks are works "under construction." As extensive as the networks are, some experts have pointed to the absence of adequate computer networking among immigration officers, the FBI, and local law enforcement as one reason the September 11 terrorists were able to operate so easily, even taking flying lessons without raising suspicion.

Communications and Access

Networking computer information is not just a matter of sharing information within and among law enforcement agencies. Look inside a modern police cruiser, and you're likely to see a computer screen and keyboard mounted on the dashboard or elsewhere in the front seat area.

Today's patrol officers do much of their communicating by computer. Files available at the station house may be summoned up in the patrol car. Dispatchers can make available more information, and more specific information, on the computer screen than they could in the space of a radio call, and they can continuously update the information.

For example: The computer inside the car beeps, signaling a call is coming in. The patrol officer glances at the screen. There he or she sees an incident report, which gives the nature of the call—a home burglary—and the address the officer's being dispatched to. The officer strikes a computer key, and a map of the city appears, with the address location pinpointed. The officer types a message to the dispatcher, indicating that he or she is responding to the call.

More information comes across the screen: a description of the suspect, together with the street down which he was seen running. His description corresponds with a known criminal, and headquarters transmits a picture to the cruiser's computer. By the time of arrival at the scene, the officer has been more thoroughly informed en route than if he or she had been extensively briefed at the station.

This technology is appearing in police mobile units now, and it promises to become increasingly sophisticated. The more a patrol officer knows, the safer that officer and the public are.

Artificial Intelligence

While police increasingly depend on computers and computer networks to store, process, and share hard information quickly and accurately, they have also begun to exploit the more speculative side of computing.

Artificial intelligence software is used in many scientific, commercial, industrial, and social-science fields to model certain real-world situations and to predict outcomes of various situations and combinations of factors. For example, an aircraft manufacturer might use artificial intelligence programs to study what happens to a certain wing if it is subjected to a specified set of stresses. How much can this or that design take before the wing fails? Asking a pilot to perform such tests in an actual airplane is expensive and potentially lethal. Computer modeling is cheaper and safer, and it enables designers to test a virtually limitless number of designs under a virtually limitless number of conditions.

Police agencies have also used artificial intelligence to "age" suspects. A murderer has been on the run for 15 years. Police have nothing more than a 15-year-old picture of him. Using an artificial intelligence program, they "age" the picture, creating a reasonable prediction of how he might now appear. On a larger scale, police agencies use artificial intelligence to make long-term plans for deploying police personnel in order to address probable areas of crime as efficiently as possible.

Talking the Talk

Artificial intelligence uses computers and computer programs to emulate and extend human logical reasoning.

In the future, it is likely that artificial intelligence will aid in solving actual crimes by helping investigators reconstruct events and predict the suspect's next moves.

Identification Technologies

The positive identification of suspects and others has always been important in police work (see Chapter 12). With the proliferation of identity theft and desktop counterfeiting (see Chapter 23), positive identification has become an even more urgent matter.

In recent years, several new biometric identification technologies have emerged and will surely play increasingly important roles in identification. These technologies analyze certain features of the human body, such as DNA, retinal patterns, iris patterns, or fingerprints, to provide positive identification of persons for security purposes. They include the following:

- **DNA technology.** This technology continues to undergo refinement and to find wider and wider application in criminal investigation as well as in the judicial process (see Chapter 16).

- **Retinal scanning devices.** Until recently these were the subject of science fiction, but they are now in use, typically in places where positive identification is required for access to sensitive areas. A digital camera images a person's retina, and a computer analyzes the distinctive pattern of retinal blood vessels, then compares it to patterns on file. No one can fake another person's retinal pattern.

- **Iris scan.** This simpler alternative to the retinal scan uses the distinctive patterns of the human iris to identify individuals.

- **Fingerprint readers.** These are also now commonly in use, and many more are likely to appear. An electronic scanner reads the individual's fingerprint pattern, and a computer digitizes and compares it to other patterns on file.

- **Odor detectors.** These are not yet in use, but some experts believe that electronic devices capable of identifying odors unique to an individual will soon be employed as the digital equivalent of that old analog standby, the bloodhound. The electronic devices could be used to track suspects who have fled.

Already, many states have adopted driver's licenses that incorporate a digitally encoded image of the driver's thumb print. In the wake of the September 11 attacks, serious consideration is being given to creating a national identity card, which would probably include some mode or modes of biometric identification.

Big Brother?

Take a drive or go for a walk. Look up and around. Chances are, on lampposts, on building corners, you'll notice any number of long rectangular enclosures. They house video cameras. Five years ago, you'd have seen few outside of military bases and other high-security installations. Today, they are quite common—everywhere. Over the next several years, they will become increasingly so, a fixture of city streets no more unusual, say, than a traffic light.

Video surveillance is here. Often, we welcome it. The sight of a video camera in a cavernous and deserted parking deck is highly reassuring. In some settings, we *should* welcome it. The "eye in the sky" at your local department store reduces losses from shoplifting, which, ultimately, helps keep prices lower for all of us. But in other settings, on city streets, for example, the presence of surveillance is more disturbing and has been subject to debate and court challenges. Nevertheless, the likelihood is that, little by little, more public areas will be deemed suitable for surveillance. In England, today, a number of small cities and portions of larger ones are extensively covered by on-street video surveillance. Freedom-loving

By the Numbers

As of 1999, there were 2,397 hidden video surveillance cameras in use in New York City. Only about 300 of these were monitored by city authorities; the rest were maintained and monitored by private individuals or firms as part of their own security programs.

Brits seem, for the most part, willing to trade some degree of privacy for a feeling of security.

Another emerging technology with "Big Brother" implications is electronic tagging. For years, some persons sentenced to house arrest have been compelled to wear transmitters, usually around the ankle, which alert monitoring authorities if the convict ventures more than a prescribed distance from his home. Now under development are more sophisticated tagging devices, which may be used to track all persons who are on parole. No matter where the parolee goes, officials will be able to pinpoint his whereabouts.

The Arsenal of the Future

As discussed in Chapter 19, the ready availability of military-grade assault weapons sometimes leaves police officers dangerously outgunned. The police arsenal of the future will doubtless include more assault-type weapons, but, even more important will be the addition of an array of nonlethal weapons.

Guns and More Guns

During the 1920s and 1930s, the availability of the Thompson submachine gun—the "Tommy gun"—was a rude awakening for many police forces. Cops armed with revolvers found themselves going up against gangsters with high-powered automatic weapons. Accordingly, police agencies equipped themselves with automatic weapons as well as rifles fitted with sniper scopes, and, ever since, the arms race between the bad guys and the good guys has escalated. In the late 1960s, the high-stakes drug trade and various domestic revolutionary movements (for example, the Black Panthers) resulted in an influx of assault weapons. Over the past 30 years, despite assault weapon restrictions, the number of these high-powered weapons has multiplied dramatically. Police agencies across the country keep SWAT and other special weapons teams in a high state of readiness, anticipating situations in which officers will face formidable hardware.

Non-Lethal Weapons

Even while police departments upgrade their firepower, as well as the training to go along with it, they also look for non-lethal alternatives. According to the U.S. Department of Defense directive, *Policy for Non-Lethal Weapons* (1995), "Non-lethal weapons are weapons systems that are explicitly designed and primarily employed so as to incapacitate personnel or material, while minimizing fatalities, permanent injury to personnel, and undesired damage to property and the environment."

Tear gas, pepper spray, and other incapacitating agents have been around for many years, but they are not fully dependable because their performance—the degree of incapacity they induce—is not uniform against all persons in all situations. The great problem with nonlethal weapons is that, if they fail to incapacitate, they may provoke a suspect to respond with desperate and deadly force. Police agencies continue to look for effective, reliable, and consistent non-lethal weapons.

> **Sworn Statement**
>
> So-called non-lethal weapons are still powerful and dangerous. They do not guarantee a zero probability of producing fatalities or permanent injuries, but they are designed to reduce that probability while incapacitating a suspect.

Non-lethal weapons in use or under development include …

- **Acoustics.** A noise generator emits very low-frequency sounds that can incapacitate people by making them dizzy, vomit, or lose control of their bowels. Another acoustic weapon system uses high-frequency "acoustic beams" to produce what experts describe as "blunt-object trauma like being hit by a baseball."

- **Chemicals.** Weapons experts are experimenting with sticky foam fired from a shoulder-slung dispenser. Strings of the foam expand on contact, stopping a person in his tracks. Another kind of weapon uses aqueous foam, a soapy substance that expands up to 500 times its original volume and prevents people from seeing, hearing, or moving. Police are even considering polymer agents that act like super glue to immobilize a suspect.

- **Electromagnetic devices.** The Taser is a low-powered hand-held device that can operate up to 15 feet away from a suspect. It fires a pair of dartlike electrodes into the suspect, which deliver 50,000 volts, inducing spasms and immobilization. Tasers are in use by some agencies, as is the stun gun, a two-pronged, handheld device that delivers a controlled charge of electricity to temporarily incapacitate a person. Unlike the Taser, which can operate from a distance, the stun gun requires close contact with the target.

- **Mechanical devices.** Rear air bag restraints were developed at the request of law enforcement agencies to subdue agitated assailants while they are being transported in the back seat of a police car. An officer can inflate the bag, thereby immobilizing the prisoner. Unlike the air bag that deploys in a front-end collision, the rear air bag inflates slowly and remains inflated. It is air permeable, so that there is no danger of suffocation. Another nonlethal mechanical device under development is a snare net launched from a canister attached to a rifle barrel. The net opens up over a fleeing suspect, entangling and immobilizing him.

◆ **Optical weapons.** Low-energy lasers can be used to blind people temporarily; an infrared laser can heat the skin sufficiently to cause incapacitating pain but not an actual burn. A newly developed argon laser beam can be aimed at a window or windshield and will turn the glass opaque green, thereby preventing a sniper from seeing his target or a driver from speeding away. High-energy pulsing strobe lights can be employed to disorient suspects, and optical hand grenades, like giant flash bulbs, can be used to create a flash that will blind a person for about 30 seconds.

A special class of non-lethal weapons is designed to be used against things—especially vehicles—rather than people. Police departments currently use various spike strips laid across a roadway to blow out car tires. On the horizon are "supercaustic" chemicals designed to "eat" vehicle tires, hoses, shoe soles, rooftops, and even road surfaces. Sticky foams are being developed to penetrate mechanical parts of vehicles or weapons, rendering them inoperative. At the other end of the spectrum are chemical lubricants nicknamed "slick 'ems," which are sprayed over pavement, stairs, and other surfaces to make them too slippery for people or vehicles to negotiate.

Policing for the People

Technology will certainly play an important role in the future of criminal investigation and police work generally. However, technology can carry law enforcement only so far. Most authorities believe that the future of effective policing depends on strengthening the ties between the police and the communities they serve. Many see the community policing idea (see "Restorative Justice" in Chapter 6, and Chapter 19) as the way of the future, and all authorities agree that the police must represent the community, must embody its values, and must be perceived as acting on behalf of the community. This requires a commitment on the part of police leaders as well as individual officers, but it also requires the collective will of the community to support the work of the police.

The Least You Need to Know

- Although police work is being revolutionized by technological innovation, the underlying values of protecting and serving the community will remain unchanged.

- The most important technological innovations in police work will be in the area of information gathering, processing, analysis, and sharing.

- The future will see a continuation of the long historical trend toward preventing crime rather than merely reacting to crime; this trend, however, threatens to conflict with the constitutional guarantee of presumption of innocence.

- The field of security—especially identification and surveillance systems—will continue to grow; many basic security functions will probably be assumed by private agencies, freeing the police to devote more resources to investigating crime.

- Police arsenals will likely acquire a new array of non-lethal weapons in the near future.

- The future effectiveness of law enforcement depends on developing strong cooperative and collaborative ties between police agencies and the communities they serve.

Appendix A

Who's Who in Criminology and Criminal Investigation

Abberline, Frederick George (1843–1929). Chief investigator of the Jack the Ripper murders (1888).

Baldwin, Roger Nash (1884–1981). American criminologist who founded the American Civil Liberties Union (ACLU) in 1920.

Balthazard, Victor (1872–1951). French criminologist who pioneered the science of ballistics and the examination of hair evidence.

Barnard, Chester (1886–1961). Brought business management techniques to the modern police department organization with his 1937 *The Functions of the Executive*.

Battle, Samuel J. (1883–1966). First African American policeman on the NYPD; later, New York's parole commissioner.

Bayle, Edmond (1879–1928). French pioneer of the study of fiber evidence and the use of spectrography in criminal investigation.

Beccaria, Cesare (1738–94). Considered by many the father of criminology; founder of the Classical School of criminology, which sought to apply enlightenment social contract theory to issues of crime and punishment.

Bentham, Jeremy (1748–1832) Founder of the school of utilitarianism; like Cesare Beccaria, believed that human nature was hedonistic and that punishments should therefore be based on deterrence.

Bertillon, Alphonse (1853–1914). The "Father of Scientific Detection"; French developer of the Bertillon System of applied anthropometry, the taking of key bodily measurements for positive identification of criminals.

Bonger, Willem Adriaan (1876–1940). Dutch criminologist whose Marxist theories of crime identified economic conditions as the leading cause of criminal behavior.

Bril, Jacques L. (1906–81). American pioneer and innovator in the field of polygraphy (lie detection).

Brussel, James Arnold (1905–82). American forensic psychiatrist who pioneered the methodology of offender profiling; earned national fame in New York's "Mad Bomber Case" of the early 1950s and the "Boston Strangler" case of the 1960s.

Byrnes, Thomas F. (1842–1910). NYPD chief who created the "Rogues' Gallery," photographs of every suspect arrested and booked.

Caldwell, Charles (1771–1853). American physician, advocate of phrenology, and exponent of phrenological explanations of criminal behavior.

Canter, David V. (1944–). British pioneer of criminal profiling, specializing in profiles of serial killers and serial rapists.

Churchill, Robert (1886–1958). Introduced scientific ballistics to Scotland Yard.

Cicourel, Aaron V. (1928–). Pioneering student of juvenile delinquency in the United States; argued that coordination among police and the community could effectively reduce or prevent juvenile delinquency.

Cohen, Louis Harold (1906–55). As co-author of *Murder, Madness, and the Law* (1952), was instrumental in establishing the modern criteria for evaluating criminal insanity.

Colquhoun, Patrick (1745–1820). British police theorist whose *Treatise on the Police of the Metropolis* (1796) is considered one of the founding documents of modern law enforcement.

Curphey, Theodore (1897–1986). First medical examiner of Los Angeles County; gained national celebrity for his controversial direction of the forensic autopsy of Marilyn Monroe (1962).

Dawson, Margaret Damer (1874–1920). Founder of London's Women's Police Volunteers, the first female police presence in the city.

Dew, Walter (1863–1947). Most famous chief inspector of Scotland Yard's CID (Criminal Investigation Division); apprehended the infamous Hawley H. Crippen, who had murdered and dismembered his wife in 1910.

Dondero, John A. (1900–57). American forensics expert who greatly advanced the science of fingerprint identification.

Durkheim, Émile (1858–1917). Founder of modern sociology, who believed that crime was not only normal in society, but actually beneficial to it.

Faulds, Henry (1843–1930). Scottish fingerprinting pioneer who developed techniques to make fingerprinting a practical means of criminal identification.

Faurot, Joseph A. (1872–1942). Called the American "father of fingerprinting"; won national acceptance of fingerprinting early in the twentieth century.

Fedle, Fortunato (1550–1630). First advocate of investigative autopsy in cases of mysterious death.

Ferracuti, Franco (1927–). Advocate of the creation of a medical-legal field of "criminological diagnosis."

Ferri, Enrico (1856–1929). Wrote a pioneering textbook on criminal sociology, which extended the positivism of Lombroso to legal and social issues.

Fielding, Sir Henry (1707–54). Famed English novelist (*Joseph Andrews*, *Tom Jones*) who, as magistrate for the City of Westminster, created the Bow Street Runners, precursor of the modern police force.

Fielding, Sir John (1721–80). Half brother of Henry Fielding and, like him, magistrate of the City of Westminster; led and expanded the Bow Street Runners.

Fodere, Francois-Emmanuel (1764–1835). An early French advocate of investigating the medical basis for crime.

Fosdick, Raymond Blaine (1883–1972). Historian and analyst of police systems in the United States and Europe.

Fuld, Leonhard Felix (1883–1965). New York author of the first comprehensive study of American police administration early in the twentieth century.

Gall, Franz Joseph (1758–1828). Viennese physician who codified phrenology, basis for early medical explanations of criminal behavior.

Galton, Sir Francis (1822–1911). British amateur scientist who improved upon the work of Henry Faulds and William Herschel to revolutionize the classification of fingerprints.

Garofalo, Raffaele (1852–1934). Nineteenth-century writer on the "criminal thought process."

Gates, Daryl (1926–). Outspoken, abrasive, controversial LAPD chief who is credited with developing the SWAT concept.

Gettler, Alexander Oscar (1884–1968). New York City's pioneering chief toxicologist from 1918 to 1959.

Glueck, Eleanor (1898–1972) and **Sol Sheldon Glueck** (1896–1980). Wife-husband team who developed the highly controversial Glueck's Social Prediction Table during the 1950s; the table was intended to enable early recognition of incipient delinquency in children.

Goddard, Calvin Hooker (1891–1955). American ballistics expert who founded the Scientific Crime Detection Laboratory as part of Northwestern University (Evanston, Illinois); also started the *American Journal of Police Science*.

Gravelle, Philip O. (1877–1955). San Francisco–based inventor of the comparison microscope, principal tool of modern ballistics and firearms identification.

Hale, George (1855–?). Author/compiler of the first American encyclopedia of police work (1892).

Hamilton, Mary (active 1917–30s). First female police officer to serve in a supervisory role; first director of the Women's Police Bureau, NYPD.

Hammurabi (ca. 1792–1750 B.C.E.). Ruler of Babylon and creator of the first important body of law in history, the Code of Hammurabi.

Harrington, Penny (1949–). First female police chief of a large American city, Portland, Oregon (1985).

Helpern, Dr. Milton (1902–77). Famed medical examiner for New York City, 1954 to 1973, celebrated as "Sherlock Holmes with a microscope."

Henry, Sir Edward Richard (1850–1931). First fingerprint expert to devise a truly practical method of fingerprint classification and archiving.

Herschel, William James (1883–1917). British fingerprint pioneer, who concluded that fingerprints are unique to the individual.

Hilton, Ordway (1913–). Chicago-based founder of the science of forensic handwriting analysis.

Hindelang, Michael (1946–82). Pioneered the idea of a relationship between low intelligence and delinquency.

Hoover, J. Edgar (1895–1972). Founder and life-long director of the Federal Bureau of Investigation; brought the bureau international acclaim and national controversy.

Inbau, Fred (1909–). American expert on the techniques of interrogating criminal suspects.

Jeffreys, Alec (1950–). British scientist who pioneered "DNA fingerprinting."

Keeler, Leonarde (1903–49). American polygraph pioneer, who founded the first private lie detection agency.

Kefauver, Estes (1903–63). Tennessee senator whose televised congressional hearings in the 1950s exposed organized crime to the American public and helped shape the direction of law enforcement policy for decades to come.

Kersta, Lawrence George (1907–). New Jersey audio engineer who pioneered voiceprinting technology.

Kirk, Paul Leland (1902–70). An American pioneer in standardizing scientific techniques for analyzing physical evidence.

Koehler, Arthur (1885–1967). Famed as America's "wood detective"; an early expert in the analysis of wood evidence.

Kretschmer, Ernst (1888–1964). German psychiatrist who developed the "constitutional theory," arguing that one's physique has a bearing on behavior, including criminal behavior.

Lacassagne, Jean Alexandre (1844–1921). French pioneer in ballistics, who first noted that the unique marks barrel rifling made on bullets could be used to match a bullet to the gun that fired it.

Landesco, John (1890–1954). Pioneering American student of organized crime.

Landsteiner, Karl (1868–1943). Austrian Nobel Prize winner who identified the four major blood groups, providing (among other things) the basis for a new method of forensic investigation.

Lange, Johannes (1891–1938). His *Crime as Destiny* (1931) studied criminal twins to explore the role of heredity in criminal behavior.

Larson, John A. (1892–1965). U.S. police officer, educator, and psychiatrist credited with inventing the polygraph in 1921.

Lavater, Johann Casper (1741–1801). Swiss founder of the pseudoscience of physiognomy, forerunner of phrenology.

Lee, Henry C. (1938–). Chinese-born American forensics expert, specializing in medical forensics at the crime scene; gave high-profile testimony in the O.J. Simpson case.

Leonard, V. A. (1898–1984). American pioneer in police education.

Levine, Lowell J. (1937–). Pioneer of odontology, the forensic identification of tooth imprints and bite marks.

Lohman, Joseph D. (1910–68). American criminologist who advanced progressive programs on community relations and race relations within police departments.

Lombroso, Cesare (1836–1909). Founder of the Positivist School of criminology, which held that criminals were evolutionary throwbacks, atavistic or degenerate.

Malpighi, Marcello (1628–94). Italian physician who first described human fingerprints.

Mannheim, Hermann (1889–1974). A refugee from Nazi Germany, Mannheim settled in England and established the field of criminology as an academic discipline.

Marsh, James (1794–1846). British chemist who developed a laboratory test for arsenic in human tissue; a pioneer in forensic toxicology.

Maudsley, Henry (1835–1918). British author of *Responsibility in Mental Diseases* (1874), which challenged the belief that insane persons act without motive.

May, Luke S. (1886–1955). A private investigative consultant, May combined intuition with science to solve hundreds of cases and earn the nickname "the American Sherlock Holmes."

Mayne, Sir Richard (1796–1868). One of the chief founders of Scotland Yard.

McDonald, Hugh Chisholm (1913–). Associated with the Los Angeles Sheriff's Department, invented the Identi-Kit, an invaluable aid to making criminal identification sketches.

McKay, Henry D. (1899–1980). A Chicago-based pioneer in the field of juvenile delinquency.

Merton, Robert K. (1910–). Major twentieth-century sociologist who developed a model of crime and deviancy based on societal expectations.

Morel, Benedict (1809–73). German-born French psychiatrist who was among the first to advance a legal definition of insanity.

Ness, Eliot (1903–57). Chicago-based federal agent who organized the Prohibition-era "Untouchables," the most effective early force against organized crime.

Norris, Charles (1867–1935). New York City's first medical examiner (appointed 1918), created the model for American forensic pathology.

Orfila, Mathieu Joseph Bonaventure (1787–1853). Spanish chemist deemed the father of modern toxicology.

Osborn, Albert (1858–1946). American author of *Questioned Documents* (1923), the landmark handbook on examining document evidence.

Parker, William Henry (1902–66). LAPD police chief considered by many to be one of the most effective chiefs in American history.

Parkhurst, Charles H. (1842–1933). Effective crusader against police corruption in New York City; raised the ethical standards of police agencies nationwide.

Peel, Sir Robert (1788–1850). British politician who established the London Metropolitan Police and made his "bobbies" (also called "Peelers") international models of professionalism.

Pound, Roscoe (1870–1964). American criminologist who worked to make the legal system socially responsible and responsive.

Quetelet, Lambert Adolphe Jacques (1796–1874). Pioneering Belgian criminologist who attempted to formulate mathematically based norms for social behavior and deviancy.

Ray, Isaac (1807–81). American author of the landmark *Medical Jurisprudence of Insanity* (1838), for many years the standard reference concerning the legal definition of insanity.

Reiser, Martin (1927–). Hired by the Los Angeles Police Department as the first psychologist ever employed full-time by a United States law enforcement agency.

Reiss, Albert John Jr. (1922–). Author of the first definitive study of police brutality in major American police departments (1971).

Sellin, (John) Thorsten (1896–1982). Swedish-born analyst of juvenile delinquency in America (*Culture Conflict and Crime*, 1938).

Simpson, Cedric Keith (1907–85). British pioneer in forensic dentistry and the first forensic pathologist to recognize and define "battered baby syndrome"; one of the world's leading forensic pathologists.

Smith, Sir Sydney Alfred (1883–1969). Author of major pioneering works on firearms and gunshot wounds.

Snyder, LeMoyne (1899–1975). U.S. pioneering advocate of forensic pathology.

Söderman, Harry (1903–56). Swedish police official and principal founder of INTERPOL.

Spitzka, Edward Anthony (1876–1922). American neurologist who refuted the long-cherished belief that criminality resulted from a physical deformity of the brain.

Spurzheim, Johann Christoph (1776–1832). Early and influential advocate of the phrenological basis of criminology.

Stas, Jean-Servais (1813–91). Belgian chemist who refined the science of toxicology by developing a process for detecting vegetable alkaloids in dead tissue.

Stein, Robert J. (1912–94). First medical examiner of Cook County (Chicago), Illinois; introduced many innovations into forensic pathology.

Stringham, James S. (1775–1817). Considered by many to be the founder of medical jurisprudence in the United States.

Sutherland, Edwin Hardin (1883–1950). American criminologist who originated the "white collar crime" concept and term; held that criminal behavior was learned through interaction with others.

Tarde, Gabriel (1843–1904). French criminologist who emphasized the role of environment and peer influence in the creation of criminal behavior.

Thrasher, Frederic Milton (1892–1962). Wrote the first major modern study of gang behavior, *The Gang: A Study of 1,313 Gangs in Chicago* (1963).

Torjanowicz, Robert C. (1941–94). Michigan State University professor who was an instrumental advocate of the community policing concept.

Tyrell, John F. (1861–1955). Wisconsin-born expert on questioned documents.

Uhlenhuth, Paul Theodore (1870–1957). German forensic scientist who discovered a serum that enabled investigators to distinguish between human and animal blood evidence.

Vincent, Howard (1849–1908). First director of the Criminal Investigation Department of the London Metropolitan Police; expanded the detective force of Scotland Yard and built it into the world's premier investigative agency.

Vollmer, August (1876–1955). American "father" of the modern professional police force.

Waite, Charles E. (ca. 1874–1926). Pioneering American ballistics expert.

Wiener, Alexander (1906–76). Codiscoverer of the Rh factor in blood; pioneered the study of blood and other body fluid evidence.

Wigmore, John Henry (1863–1943). Founder of the American Institute of Criminal Law and Criminology and author of the 10-volume *Treatise on the Anglo-American System of Evidence* (1904).

Milestones in Crime and Crime Fighting

Prehistoric: Humans include fingerprints in paintings and rock carvings.

700s: Chinese use fingerprints to authenticate documents.

ca. 1000: Quintilian, a Roman attorney, wins acquittal for his client by proving that bloody palm prints were intended to frame him.

1248: *Hsi Duan Yu* (The Washing Away of Wrongs), a Chinese text, includes a description of how to distinguish a drowning death from death by strangulation—the first recorded application of medical forensics.

1609: François Demelle (France) writes the world's first work on the examination of questioned documents.

1686: Marcello Malpighi (Italy) is the first to describe human fingerprints.

1784: John Toms (Lancaster, England) is convicted of murder because the torn edge of a wad of newspaper in the murder gun matched a piece in his pocket; this is perhaps the first documented instance of the physical matching of evidence.

1813: Mathiew Orfila (Spain) publishes *Treatise on Poisons*, thereby becoming the father of modern toxicology.

1823: John Evangelist Purkinji (Bohemia) publishes a work on the nature of finger-prints and suggests a classification system based on nine major types.

1830s: Adolphe Quetelet (Belgium) provides statistical evidence that no two human bodies are exactly alike, thereby laying the foundation for the later development of the Bertillon system.

1835: Henry Goddard (England) uses a mark (flaw) on a murder bullet to trace it to the mold that formed the bullet, thereby linking a suspect to the murder through ballistics.

1836: James Marsh (Scotland) is the first to present toxicological evidence (detection of arsenic poisoning) in a jury trial.

1851: Jean Servais Stas (Belgium) is the first to identify vegetable poisons in dead body tissue.

1856: Sir William Herschel (England) uses thumbprints to authenticate documents.

1862: J. Van Deen (Netherlands) develops a chemical test for human blood.

1877: Thomas Taylor (United States) proposes markings on palms and fingertips be used for identification in criminal cases.

1879: Rudolph Virchow (Germany) pioneers forensic hair analysis.

1880: Henry Faulds (Scotland) suggests that fingerprints recovered at the scene of a crime could identify the offender.

1883: Alphonse Bertillon (France) demonstrates anthropometry as a method of positive identification.

1887: Arthur Conan Doyle (England) publishes the first Sherlock Holmes story.

1889: Alexandre Lacassagne (France) attempts to match bullets to the gun barrel from which they were fired; founds modern ballistics.

1891: Hans Gross (Austria) publishes *Criminal Investigation*, the first comprehensive description of the use of physical evidence in solving crime.

1892: Sir Francis Galton publishes *Fingerprints*, the first major book on the forensic use of fingerprints.

1892: Juan Vucetich (Argentina) develops the fingerprint classification system widely used in Latin America.

1894: In a sensational case, French army captain Alfred Dreyfus is convicted of treason, in part as a result of a mistaken handwriting identification by Bertillon.

1896: Sir Edward Richard Henry (England) develops the fingerprint classification system widely used in Europe and North America.

1898: Paul Jesrich (Germany) uses comparison photomicrographs in ballistics analysis.

1900: Karl Landsteiner (Germany) discovers human blood groups, which, incidentally, greatly aids the field of forensic medicine.

1901: Paul Uhlenhuth (Germany) develops a test to distinguish human blood from animal blood.

1901: Sir Edward Richard Henry (England) of Scotland Yard replaces Bertillon's anthropometry with fingerprint identification.

1901: Henry P. DeForrest pioneers the first systematic use of fingerprints in the United States.

1902: R. A. Reiss (Switzerland) creates the first academic curriculum in forensic science.

1903: The New York State Prison system begins to use fingerprint identification; first U.S. law enforcement agency to do so.

1905: Theodore Roosevelt establishes the Bureau of Investigation, precursor agency of the Federal Bureau of Investigation.

1910: Victor Balthazard (France) publishes the first comprehensive hair analysis study.

1910: Edmund Locard (France) establishes the world's first police crime laboratory.

1910: Albert S. Osborne (United States) publishes *Questioned Documents*, the first major work on the forensic examination of documents.

1913: Balthazard (France) publishes the first major article on individualizing bullet markings.

1915: Leone Lattes (Italy) develops the first antibody test for ABO blood groups; he soon applies the test to criminal investigation.

1916: Albert Schneider (United States) develops a vacuum apparatus to collect trace evidence.

1918: Edmond Locard (France) suggests 12 key matching points for positive fingerprint identification.

1920: Locard publishes a landmark forensics text, which proclaims the chief principle of forensic science: "Every contact leaves a trace."

1920: Charles E. Waite (United States) catalogs manufacturing data relating to weapons.

1920s: Luke May (United States) develops striation analysis for tool mark comparison.

1920s: The American Calvin Goddard (with Charles Waite, Phillip O. Gravelle, and John H. Fisher) perfects the comparison microscope, the principal tool for bullet comparison.

1921: John Larson and Leonarde Keeler independently design polygraph machines.

1924: August Vollmer (United States) sets up the first U.S. police crime laboratory.

1925: Saburo Sirai (Japan) discovers the secretion of group-specific antigens into body fluids other than blood.

1929: Calvin Goddard is instrumental in founding the Scientific Crime Detection Laboratory at Northwestern University, Evanston, Illinois.

1930: *American Journal of Police Science* is founded.

1932: The FBI crime laboratory is established.

1937: Walter Specht (Germany) develops Luminol, which detects latent blood stains.

1940: Vincent Hnizda (United States) pioneers the forensic analysis of ignitable fluids, laying the foundation for scientific arson investigation.

1941: Bell Labs (United States) builds on the work of L. G. Kersta to develop voiceprint identification.

1945: Frank Lundquist (Denmark) develops the acid phosphatase test for semen evidence.

1950: August Vollmer (United States) establishes the school of criminology at the University of California at Berkeley.

1954: R. F. Borkenstein (United States) invents the Breathalyzer for field sobriety testing.

1971: The U.S. Supreme Court rules that illegally obtained evidence is generally inadmissible at trial.

1974: A group of U.S. scientists use the electron microscope to analyze gunshot residue.

1975: Federal Rules of Evidence, originally promulgated by the U.S. Supreme Court, are enacted into law by Congress.

1977: Fuseo Matsumur (Japan) accidentally discovers the "Superglue fuming" method of latent fingerprint development.

1977: The FBI introduces the Automated Fingerprint Identification System (AFIS), the first fully computerized fingerprinting system.

1984: Sir Alec Jeffreys (England) develops the first DNA profiling test.

1985: The U.S. Supreme Court rules that police cannot use lethal force against an unarmed fleeing suspect who is not deemed dangerous.

1986: DNA evidence is first used to solve a crime; Colin Pitchfork is identified as the murderer of two young girls in the Midlands of England.

1987: DNA profiling is introduced in a U.S. criminal court; Tommy Lee Andrews is convicted of a series of sexual assaults in Orlando, Florida.

1988: American scientists develop a procedure for the analysis of drugs in whole blood by homogeneous enzyme immunoassay.

1991: Walsh Automation Inc. (Canada) begins to develop an automated ballistics imaging system, Integrated Ballistics Identification System (IBIS).

1998: The FBI establishes a DNA database, CODIS (Combined DNA Index System), which enables interstate cooperation in linking crimes.

Appendix C

The "Ten Code"

To facilitate radio communication, police officers use abbreviations and codes to save air time and reduce possible confusion. The so-called "Ten Code" is subject to local variation, but the Association of Police Communications Officers has standardized it and advocates its universal adoption.

Code 1: Your convenience

Code 2: Urgent, no red light and siren

Code 3: Emergency, use red light and siren

Code 4: No further assistance needed

Code 5: Stakeout

Code 6AD: Felony wanted, armed and dangerous

Code 6F: Felony wanted

Code 6M: Misdemeanor wanted

Code 7: Mealtime

Code 8: Box alarm

Code 10: Bomb threat

Code 20: Assist officer, urgent

Code 30: Officer needs help, emergency

Code 33: Emergency in progress, do not transmit

187: Murder

207: Kidnapping

211: Robbery

245: ADW (assault with deadly weapon)

261: Rape

288: L & L (lewd and lascivious) conduct

311: Indecent exposure

415: Disturbance

415F: Family disturbance

460: Burglary

480: Felony hit-and-run

481: Misdemeanor hit-and-run

487: Grand theft

488: Petty theft

502: Drunk driver

503: Stolen vehicle

505: Reckless driving

510: Vehicle speeding

647: Vagrant

647A: Child molestation

10-1: Receiving poorly

10-2: Receiving O.K.

10-4: Message received O.K.

10-5: Relay to

10-7: Out of service at

10-7B: Out of service, personal

10-70D: Off duty

10-8: In service

10-9: Repeat

10-10: Out of service at home

10-12: Visitors or officials present

10-13: Weather and road conditions

10-14: Escort

10-14F: Funeral detail

10-15: Have prisoner in custody

10-16: Pick up

10-19: Return to station

10-20: Location

10-21: Phone your office

10-21A: Phone my home, my ETA is

10-21B: Phone your home

10-21R: Phone radio

10-22: Cancel

10-23: Standby

10-25: Do you have contact with

10-28: Registration

10-29: Check for wanted

10-32: Drowning

10-33: Alarm sounding

10-34: Open door

10-35: Open window

10-39: Status of

10-40: Is available for phone call

10-45: Ambulance, injured

10-46: Ambulance, sick

10-49: Proceed to

10-50: Obtain a report

10-51: Drunk

10-52: Resuscitator

10-53: Man down

10-54: Possible dead body

10-55: Coroner's case

10-56: Suicide

10-56A: Attempted suicide

10-57: Firearms discharged

10-58: Garbage complaint

10-59: Malicious mischief

10-62: Meet the citizen

10-65: Missing person

10-66: Suspicious person

10-67: Person calling for help

10-70: Prowler

10-71: Shooting

10-72: Knifing

10-73: How do you receive?

10-80: Explosion

10-86: Any traffic for

10-87: Meet officer

10-91: Stray animal

10-91A: Vicious animal

10-91B: Noisy animal

10-91C: Injured animal

10-91D: Dead animal

10-91F: Animal bite

10-911H: Stray horse

10-97: Arrived at the scene

10-98: Finished with last assignment

11-24: Abandoned vehicle

11-26: Abandoned bicycle

11-54: Suspicious vehicle

11-79: Accident, ambulance en route

11-80: Accident, major injury

11-81: Accident, minor injury

11-82: Accident, property damage

11-83: Accident, no detail

11-84: Traffic control

11-96: Leaving vehicle to investigate an auto; if not heard from in 10 minutes, dispatch cover

Further Reading and Favorite Websites

Books

Addams, Jane. *Twenty Years at Hull-House*. New York: Macmillan Publishing Company, 1910.

Anderson, Elijah. *Code of the Streets: Decency, Violence, and the Moral Life of the Inner City*. New York: W.W. Norton & Company, 1999.

Axelrod, Alan, and Charles Phillips. *Cops, Crooks, and Criminologists: An International Biographical Dictionary of Law Enforcement*. New York: Facts on File, 1996.

Baron, Larry, and Murray A. Straus. *Four Theories of Rape in American Society: A State-Level Analysis*. New Haven, Conn.: Yale University Press, 1989.

Beccaria, Cesare. *On Crimes and Punishments* [1764]. Translated from Italian by Richard Davies and Virginia Cox. In *On Crimes and Punishments and Other Writings*, edited by Richard Bellamy. Cambridge: Cambridge University Press, 1995.

Becker, Howard S. *Outsiders: Studies in the Sociology of Deviance*. New York: Free Press, 1963.

Beckett, Katherine. *Making Crime Pay: Law and Order in Contemporary American Politics*. London: Oxford University Press, 1997.

Bennett, Wayne W., and Kären M. Hess. *Criminal Investigation*. 5th ed. Belmont, Calif.: Wadsworth, 1998.

Bentham, Jeremy. *An Introduction to the Principles of Morals and Legislation* [1789]. In *A Bentham Reader*, edited by Mary Peter Mack. New York: Pegasus Books, 1969.

Bonger, Willem. *An Introduction to Criminology*. London: Methuen & Co., Ltd., 1936.

Braithwaite, John. *Crime, Shame, and Reintegration*. Cambridge, Mass.: Cambridge University Press, 1989.

Brantingham, Paul J., and Patricia L. Brantingham, eds. *Environmental Criminology*. Beverly Hills, Calif.: Sage Publications, 1981.

Bulmer, Martin. *The Chicago School of Sociology: Institutionalization, Diversity, and the Rise of Sociological Research*. Chicago: University of Chicago Press, 1984.

Clarke, Ronald V., ed. *Situational Crime Prevention: Successful Case Studies*. New York: Harrow and Heston, 1992.

Conklin, J. *Criminology*. Boston: Allyn and Bacon, 1998.

Crutchfield, Robert D., George S. Bridges, and Joseph G. Weis. *Crime and Society*. 3 vols. Thousand Oaks, Calif.: Pine Forge Press, 1996.

Douglass, John E., et al. *Crime Classification Manual*. San Francisco: Jossey-Bass, 1992.

Egger, S. *Serial Murder*. Westport, Conn.: Praeger, 1990.

Ellis, L., and A. Walsh *Criminology*. Boston: Allyn and Bacon, 2000.

Felson, Marcus. *Crime and Everyday Life: Insights and Implications for Society*. Thousand Oaks, Calif.: Pine Forge Press, 1994.

Fox, J. and J. Levin *Overkill*. New York: Plenum, 1994.

Gould, Stephen Jay. *The Mismeasure of Man*. New York: W. W. Norton and Co., 1981.

Greenberg, David. *Crime and Capitalism: Readings in Marxist Criminology*. Philadelphia: Temple University Press, 1993.

———. *Mathematical Criminology*. New Brunswick, N.J.: Rutgers University Press, 1979.

Hagan, F. *Introduction to Criminology*. Chicago: Nelson-Hall, 1996.

Healy, William. *The Individual Delinquent*. Boston: Little, Brown, 1915.

Henry, A. F., and James F. Short. *Suicide and Homicide*. Glencoe, Ill.: Free Press, 1954.

Herbert, David T. *The Geography of Urban Crime*. London: Longman, 1982.

Hickey, E. *Serial Murderers and Their Victims*. Belmont, Calif.: Wadsworth, 2002.

Hochstedler, Ellen, ed. *Corporations as Criminals*, Beverly Hills, Calif.: Sage, 1984.

Hooton, Earnest A. *The American Criminal*. Cambridge, Mass.: Harvard University Press, 1939.

Jacobs, Jane. *The Death and Life of Great American Cities*. New York: Vintage Books, 1961.

Jeffery, C. Ray. *Crime Prevention Through Environmental Design*. Beverly Hills, Calif.: Sage Publications, 1971.

Jenkins, Philip. *Using Murder: The Social Construction of Serial Homicide*. New York: Aldine de Gruyter, 1994.

Kornhauser, Ruth R. *Social Sources of Delinquency*. Chicago: University of Chicago Press, 1978.

LaFree, Gary. *Rape and Criminal Justice: The Social Construction of Sexual Assault*. Belmont, Calif.: Wadsworth, 1989.

Lander, Bernard. *Towards an Understanding of Juvenile Delinquency*. New York: Columbia University Press, 1954.

Liska, Allen E. *Perspectives on Deviance*. Englewood Cliffs, N.J.: Prentice Hall, 1981.

Lombroso, Cesare. *Crime: Its Causes and Remedies*. Boston: Little, Brown, 1911.

Lombroso, Cesare, and William Ferrero. *The Female Offender*. London: Fisher Unwin, 1895.

Mednick, Sarnoff, Terrie Moffitt, and Susan Stack, eds. *The Causes of Crime: New Biological Approaches*. Cambridge, England: Cambridge University Press, 1987.

Nelken, David, ed. *The Futures of Criminology*. London: Sage, 1994.

Nettler, Gwynn. *Killing One Another*. Cincinnati: Anderson, 1982.

Quetelet, Adolphe. *A Treatise on Man and the Development of his Faculties* [1842]. New York: Burt Franklin, 1968.

Rafter, Nicole Hahn. *Creating Born Criminals*. Urbana: University of Illinois Press, 1997.

Reiss, A., and J. Roth, eds. *Understanding and Preventing Violence*. Washington, D.C.: National Academy Press, 1993.

Russell, Diana E. H. *The Politics of Rape: The Victim's Perspective*. New York: Stein and Day, 1975.

Sanday, Peggy R. *Fraternity Gang Rape: Sex, Brotherhood, and Privilege on Campus*. New York: New York University Press, 1990.

Siegel, L. *Criminology*. Belmont, Calif.: Wadsworth, 2000.

Smith, Susan J. *Crime, Space and Society*. Cambridge, England: Cambridge University Press, 1986.

Vold, G., T. Bernard, and J. Snipes. *Theoretical Criminology*. New York: Oxford University Press, 1997.

White, Rob, and Fiona Haines. *Crime and Criminology: An Introduction*. 2nd ed. South Melbourne, Australia: Oxford University Press, 2000.

Websites

Crime and Justice Statistics at www.fedstats.gov/programs/crime.html

Crimelibrary.com at www.crimelibrary.com

Crimetheory.com at www.crimetheory.com

Criminal Profiling Research at www.criminalprofiling.ch/introduction.html

Criminology Mega-Site at http://faculty.ncwc.edu/toconnor/criminology.htm

FBI Laboratory Services at www.fbi.gov/hq/lab/org/labchart.htm

Forensic Science Web Pages at http://home.earthlink.net/~thekeither/Forensic/forsone.htm

Metropolitan Police (London) at www.met.police.uk

New York City Police Department Timeline at www.nyhistory.org/previous/police/ptimeline.html

NYPD Official web page at www.nyc.gov/html/nypd/home.html

Police Chat: Law Enforcement Statistics and Facts at http://home1.gte.net/joking/lefacts.htm

Restorative Justice Online at http://restorativejustice.org

Index

G

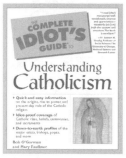

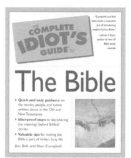

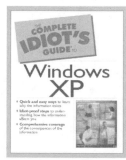